THE
SHORT HISTORY OF
RUSSIA

THE SHORT HISTORY OF
RUSSIA

RETURNING TO ANOTHER
COUNTRY

JEREMY BLACK

For Pete Brown

First published 2026

Amberley Publishing
The Hill, Stroud
Gloucestershire, GL5 4EP

www.amberley-books.com

Copyright © Jeremy Black, 2026

The right of Jeremy Black to be identified as the Author of this work has been asserted in accordance with the Copyright, Designs and Patents Act 1988.

ISBN 978 1 3981 3106 4 (hardback)
ISBN 978 1 3981 3107 1 (ebook)

All rights reserved. No part of this book may be reprinted or reproduced or utilised in any form or by any electronic, mechanical or other means, now known or hereafter invented, including photocopying and recording, or in any information storage or retrieval system, without the permission in writing from the Publishers.

British Library Cataloguing in Publication Data.
A catalogue record for this book is available from the British Library.

1 2 3 4 5 6 7 8 9 10

Typesetting by SJmagic DESIGN SERVICES, India.
Printed in the UK.

Appointed GPSR EU Representative:
Easy Access System Europe Oü, 16879218
Address: Mustamäe tee 50, 10621,
Tallinn, Estonia
Contact Details: gpsr.requests@easproject.com,
+358 40 500 3575

CONTENTS

Preface		7
1	Where is Russia?	9
2	The Long Centuries	25
3	A New Power: The Sixteenth Century	42
4	A Troubled Age: The Seventeenth Century	54
5	Peter the Great to Catherine the Great: The Eighteenth Century	69
6	A Major Power: The Nineteenth Century	104
7	Chaos and Conflict: 1900-23	132
8	The Stalin Years: 1924-53	152
9	From Stalin to the Fall: 1953-91	197
10	A New Russia: 1992-Present	232
11	Conclusions	247

PREFACE

The present always imposes on the past, as Russian history abundantly demonstrates. The Russian invasion of Ukraine in February 2022 and the major war it launched created a major new episode in history and was surrounded by a mélange of historical claims located in rival histories. This book is a guide to the histories on offer about and from Russia; not of course the only guide that is possible but one that seeks to make sense of present issues and future prospects, as well as of the past. There is a heavy emphasis on war and international relations, but that is appropriate not only for the past but also from a present in which both are to the fore.

In 1768, an allegorical ballet entitled *Prejudice Overcome* was staged at the Russian court. Two opposing temples, of Ignorance and of Aesculapius, the God of Medicine, were presented alongside the character Ruthenia, representing the Russian people, worrying about smallpox. Minerva, symbolising the Russian ruler, Catherine II, the Great (r. 1762-96), who had herself been recently inoculated, emerged from the Temple of Aesculapius and agreed to be immunized, whereupon Ruthenia followed and a dance of hope began, celebrating the expulsion of Superstition and Ignorance, two characters in the ballet, from the kingdom.

Reality was otherwise. The trickle-down theory was limited by a lack of interest from many rulers in the plight of the people, including Catherine, who devoted far more attention to international affairs. There was also popular resistance to new ideas. Thus, that Peter the Great (r. 1689-1725), an eager modernizer, was an un-Russian evil substitute was easy to believe, in light of his denial of the divine identity of traditional Russian monarchy, his blasphemy, his theft of time from God when he changed the calendar, and his sacrilegious violation of the image of God in man when he forced men to cut off their beards.

The harshness of the conditions of the majority was highlighted by Alexander Radishchev (1749-1802), a German-educated landowner who became a bureaucrat, in his *Journey from St Petersburg to Moscow* (1790). He denounced the arduous work of the majority, poor living conditions, and the right of lords to sell and to flog serfs. The radicalism of the book led to his arrest and banishment to Siberia until Catherine's death in 1796. Radishchev committed suicide while fearful of another imprisonment.

Aside from major issues of emphasis and interpretation, there is no shortage of disagreement over nomenclature, or even the naming and dating of events, the latter in part reflecting the contentiousness of Western influences. For example, the February Revolution in Russia in 1917 is thus dated because Russia then used the Julian calendar, whereas most of Europe, and indeed the Soviet Union from 1918, employed the Gregorian calendar, such that this became the March Revolution. So also with the October and November revolutions in 1917.

I have benefited greatly from teaching Russia's past at Durham and then Exeter from 1980 to 2020. I would like to thank the stimulus offered by my students. I have profited from the helpful comments of Pete Brown, Alexander Mikaberidze, Patrick O'Meara, Thomas Otte, Matt Rendle and Vladimir Shirorogov on all or part of an earlier draft. They are not responsible for any errors that remain. I do not treat these thanks lightly, as I am well aware of the hard work that is entailed.

It is a great pleasure to dedicate this book to Pete Brown with many thanks for his welcome friendship and scholarly advice over very many years.

{ 1 }

WHERE IS RUSSIA?

Russia, the Russian Federation, independent in December 1991 after the end of the Soviet Union it had formerly dominated, is in 2025 the largest country in the world by area. Yet, as a reminder of the different emphases that can be adopted, Russia is ninth by population, after India, China, America, Indonesia, Pakistan, Brazil, Nigeria and Bangladesh. Population density is very low indeed at 21 per square mile in 2023, and in the same year the population was effectively declining at an annual rate of minus 0.3 per cent, compared to plus 0.5 per cent in America. Extending over eleven time zones, Russia shares land borders with 14 countries, although, unlike America, Britain, France, the Netherlands, Denmark, Portugal and Spain, it does not have farflung island territories. Russia covers 6.6 million square miles (17 million square kilometres), about three-quarters of the former Soviet Union.

A third of Russia is in Europe and two-thirds in Asia, if the contentious but standard boundary between the two, the Ural Mountains, is accepted. European Russia, however, to others is Western Asia – an argument based on the notion that the Westernisation of some Russian cultural élites over the last half-millennium does not make Russia a Western country. There might, indeed, appear to be a comparison with Westernisation in Japan from the late nineteenth century. Yet, this idea of a European identity for Russia appears more pertinent from the perspective of a Christendom that clearly incorporated it, and even more if the Orthodox heritage, Greek and Russian, is seen as European rather than the latter being defined by the Catholic heritage. This is not the case with Japan.

Asian Russia varies greatly, and notably so in environmental and demographic terms, with Siberia in large part 'empty' or, rather, emptier than European Russia, as well as much of what was Soviet Central Asia. Northern Siberia has tundra conditions with permafrost making construction problematic. Further south, there are vast coniferous forests (*taiga*) which support only a sparse population. The poor soil of these lands is significant, not least for grain cultivation, and the mineral exploitation of these lands requires the import into them of grain from elsewhere in Russia.

The Russia of today can be depicted on a map, but not without contention, and if this is also true for China, the situation for Russia has been more violent. This is most obviously due to the conflict in Ukraine that began in 2022, but also a consequence of contention over the Russian annexation of Crimea in 2014, and as a result of the war with Georgia in 2008. The last accentuated the fragmentation of the Caucasus that followed the disintegration of the Soviet Union, notably a longstanding conflict between Armenia and Azerbaijan over the region of Nagorno-Karabakh with particular upsurges in 1992-4, 2020 and 2023. This fragmentation also saw unsuccessful attempts by the Chechens from 1991 to create a republic independent of Russia, leading to war in 1994-6 and 1999-2000.

Discussions in 2025 about peace negotiations made the issue of boundaries central, because those that would be settled for Ukraine of course meant the same for Russia. There was the question whether Ukraine would be left as a result of the consequences of the peace in a vassal status of some form, possibly akin to that of Belarus.

This intractable topic can be discussed, but where, earlier, was Russia, and what should be covered? Finland was part of Russia from 1809 to 1917 and Estonia, Latvia and Lithuania

Where is Russia?

for considerably longer. If we stick with Russia today, we have a history that stretches from Kaliningrad to the Kurils, but the former, known as Königsberg until 1946, was only captured from German forces in 1945, having been a German city from its foundation in 1255, albeit being Polish or a Polish fief from 1454 to 1657. Again thanks to Soviet victory in World War Two, the Kurils have been controlled by Russia since 1945, but the four southern ones are claimed by Japan.

As a different reminder of the problematic nature of definitions, World War Two for Russia was the Great Patriotic War of 1941-5 with Germany, a war followed in 1945 by a short conflict with Japan. In contrast, the invasions of Poland in 1939 and Finland in 1939-40, as well as large-scale clashes with Japan in 1938 and 1939 on the borders of Siberia and Japanese-occupied China, are left out of the definition. However, for Poland and Finland these invasions were and remain important instances of Russian aggression, with major territorial losses to Russia.

Should Russia today be the basis for our discussion, or the Soviet Union, under which Russia gained Kaliningrad and the Kurils? Established in 1922, the Soviet Union eventually had 15 constituent republics: Russia, Ukraine, Belarus, Moldova, Lithuania, Latvia, Estonia, Georgia, Armenia, Azerbaijan, Kazakhstan, Uzbekistan, Kyrgyzstan, Tajikistan, and Turkmenistan. All are now independent, but while in the Soviet Union, Russia was the dominant player. In 1946, the Karelian Union Republic was incorporated into Russia, the land seized from Finland in 1940 and conquered anew in 1944.

The foundation of the Soviet Union was part of the new governmental and political order that followed Communist success in the Russian Civil War that was a consequence of the Bolshevik takeover in 1917. This was a result of the October revolution, itself the unexpected consequence of the overthrow of monarchy in the February Revolution of that year. This civil war saw an unsuccessful challenge to Communist control in Russia, and also the drive for independence by many previous parts of Imperial Russia. At the close of the struggle, as a result of Bolshevik victory, Central Asia, the Caucasus and Ukraine remained under

Communist control and therefore part of the new Soviet Union. However, Finland, Estonia, Latvia, Lithuania and Poland were independent, while Bessarabia (now essentially Moldova) had become part of Romania. There were new frontiers and thus new border regions. There were also new internal frontiers in the shape of the constituent republics.

Instead of modern Russia or the previous Soviet Union being the basis of our discussion, should it be the Romanov empire that came to a bloody end in 1917, in a somewhat different revolutionary period to that of its foundation in 1613? And, if so, at what date, for its borders varied greatly during that period. Between 1850 and 1900, there were major gains in Central Asia and the Far East, and the expansion of Russia's presence in the Caucasus.

Yet, if we start at 1850, or 1800, 1750 or 1700, we can look back in each case over a previous half-century of major territorial gain, each relevant to subsequent history. And also if the years in question are 1650, 1600, 1550 and 1500, with the last three being a Russia before the Romanovs. Thus, there is no stable basis for a territorial 'fixing' of Russia's boundaries after which expansion is the theme, and that is the case whether or not the expansion is regarded as desirable.

Russia arose in response to external challenges and opportunities, with Muscovy the principality based on Moscow, before the core revival after the Mongol invasions in the early thirteenth century. The loss of territories south of the river Oka to the Mongols and west of Mozhaisk to Lithuania help explain southward colonisation and drive by Russia, as well as later westward advance. Ensconced in the forests of the Volga-Oka, and with its back northward to the wastes of the White Sea and the Arctic Ocean, the Muscovite state had a mission defined by the Church as the standard bearer of Eastern Orthodoxy against Latin Christianity and Islam, a mission deployed as the proponent of political, cultural and economic autarky. Russia steadily consolidated its power in the wooded steppe zones until it came up against the outer peripheries of those two civilisations: in the lands east of the Baltic and in the eastern marches of the Polish-Lithuanian Empire in the case of Latin

Christianity, and in the successor states of the Golden Horde in that of Islam.

Over the long term, and from their position of strength, the Russians took advantage of the weakening hold of the Poles, Swedes and Ottomans on their frontier zones in order to manipulate client relationships within those empires, transforming frontier societies into clients of the growing Russian empire. They manipulated these relationships from the outside, not from within, for the Russians were the bearers of an autonomous civilisation engaged in a long-term competition with the civilisations of Latin Christianity and Islam, with which they had (and still have) so little in common.

Separately, it is far from clear why the expansion of Russia and its predecessor, the Principality of Muscovy, should necessarily be seen as the defining point for the history of what is now Russia, however expanded by President Putin, and, earlier, for what was the Soviet Union. To do so, pre-empts other possible definitions and definitions for the history of this area, and risks providing a misleading account of the history itself. It is worth focussing on this idea because it is central to what follows, and what should be the case for every history of Russia. Indeed, the last half-century, and, moreover, the present, fully underlines the point about indeterminacy in developments and contexts. To ignore this point, or even underrate it, pre-empts or lessens other possible definitions and corresponding accounts for the history of this area as a whole; in doing so, it distorts the history of Russia as a whole.

The theme of other possible developments was not simply in the distant past of Mongol invasions or of the repeated struggles with Islamic states, notably the Crimean and Kazan Khanates and the Ottoman Empire, as well as the frequent wars with Poland and Sweden in the period 1540-1790. The theme can also be seen with Napoleon's seizure of Moscow in 1812, or German advances during both world wars.

To treat the more recent of these conflicts as somehow extraneous, as proof of Russian strength in that the challenges were overcome, would be problematic in the extreme, as is underlined by the crisis of 1917-22. Instead, the history of Russia repeatedly is of directions not taken, and, linked to that, of the interplay of contexts, conjunctures and contingencies, the likely outcomes of which were unclear. The contrary view that somehow 'geography is destiny', and history 'dictated' to, or trumped as a consequence, is misleading. This view has proved particularly prominent in the case of Russia due to the difficulties otherwise of shaping and analysing its history, not least access to relevant sources. The idea of a strategic culture and inherent organic identity supposedly defined by geography has proved highly attractive to many commentators. However, that approach downplays the role of politics in the discussion and implementation of policies, and the extent to which strategic culture is dependent on perception and prioritisation.

This discussion does not help us determine when and how to begin our account. It is clearly in part the story of how the Russian state developed from the miscellany of possible options in Eurasia and, more specifically, of what Russia became, and, as a result, what its neighbours became, an approach also worthy of attention for Prussia, one of its neighbours, which like Russia was a state of landowners expected to provide military and governmental service.

It was and is against this background of possible options for Russia, a state created and not drawing on any inherent organic identity however defined, that it is worth discussing what changes were significant. This was recognised by Edward Gibbon when considering in *The History of the Decline and Fall of the Roman Empire* (1776-88) whether 'Barbarian' invasions could recur, first overrunning Russia, and then assaulting Europe as a whole. He concluded that, essentially due to military Westernisation under Peter the Great (r. 1689-1725), this was no longer likely.

The approach taken here is to offer a discussion that is relatively short prior to the reign of Ivan IV, the Terrible (1533-84), and then to proceed with greater detail. The emphasis will be on struggle, notably military struggle, because that was the major theme and means of the history of what became Russia and of how Russia was perceived by others. In doing so, we will include the history of areas that are now Russian but did not become so until over the last two centuries. However, the emphasis will be one that is sensible: thus, what is now the Russian part of former East Prussia can only be meaningfully included in Russian history after it was conquered in 1944-5, annexed, and the German population replaced by ethnic Russians. Nothing is gained by going back to its earlier history.

Turning to the geography of modern Russia is instructive. Alongside the many changes of its frontiers in the last 150 and more particularly 35 years, its diversity is great: from the sub-tropical Black Sea coast at Sochi to the permafrost of Siberia, from rivers, such as the Neva, that flow into the Baltic to those such as the Amur that join the Sea of Japan or the Pacific, from the densely populated heartland round Moscow to the far emptier lands along the Arctic. There was no 'destiny' that dictated a state linking Muscovy, Central Asia and Siberia, each large areas that in themselves had cohesion imposed on them; and it is important to avoid a Russo-centric account of the latter two.

This is particularly so of Siberia for which 'pre-contact' sources are perforce limited. In light of the extent of Siberia, from the plains of its west via the plateau of its centre to the mountains of its east, the history of Siberia can in part be told from both internal perspectives and external, whether from Japan, Korea, China, Manchuria, Mongolia, Central Asia or Turkic peoples and khanates. How far the Russian Far East should be included in the history of Siberia is a matter for debate. The most populous section, in the Amur Valley and near Vladivostok, was only seized in 1858-60 by means of expeditions from 1849 culminating in the treaties of Aigun (1858) and Beijing (1860), which were extorted at a time when China was convulsed by the Taiping Revolution and under pressure from successful British and French attack in the Second Opium War of 1856-60.

Nor was there a 'destiny' by which Muscovy would stretch from the Barents Sea to Ukraine, or the Baltic to the Caspian. The range was formidable, even if subsequently appearing misleadingly modest on maps, showing a state reaching to the

Seas of Okhotsk and Japan. As a consequence, the centres of power of Russia and China were far distant, and it was possible, as well as desirable, for them to co-exist and to pursue other goals, including those on other frontiers, hard as well as soft. This remains the case today, although there is Russian concern about Chinese economic interest in Siberia and with reference to the far greater size of the Chinese population compared to that of Russia east of the Urals.

The extent of Russia brought problems of environment, climate and transport, all of which limited ideas of destiny, as well as moulding human experiences of identity and distance. Ironically, these problems also hindered invaders, for example China in the Amur Valley in 1685-7 and most recently Germany in 1941 and 1942. In contrast, the lifestyle, hardiness and logistical requirements of steppe people were such that they could carry out operations in the winter. The successful Mongol campaign against the northern Russian princes was launched in December 1237 and only stopped with the spring thaw. These principalities, and subsequently Muscovy, were particularly susceptible to attack from this direction, as was China.

Attacking from the north was an axis in which Muscovy was far less vulnerable due to harsh environment and sparse northern demography. Moscow's geographic advantages included the forest zone offering some protection from the Tatars and the city being close to the confluence of the Northern Dvina, Western Dvina, Dnieper and Volga rivers in the Valdai Hills 110 miles to the north-west. The Moscow River connected Moscow to the rivers leading to Novgorod (enabling the Muscovites to block grain shipments to the rival city), and to the Volga.

In contrast to the winter firmness of hard soil, the rainy summer of 1708 made the roads very soft, hindering the Swedish invasion. In part due to the lack of adequate local governmental initiatives but also to the climate and the technology available, improvements to roads were often only of limited value. The most important road, between the new settlement of St Petersburg and Moscow, was laid out by Peter the Great (r. 1682-1725) in the first two decades of the eighteenth century. The roadbed consisted of tree trunks, the usual roadbed, with piles driven into the marshes and low-lying soft spots. Covered with a layer of gravel, sand or soil, such a roadbed was supposed to provide a firm and relatively smooth surface, but the rotting of the wooden base, erosion of the surface and gradual subsidence of long stretches into the soft, marshy soil kept it in a permanent state of disrepair, although there were improvements, notably the building of bridges.

Taking another major route, from St Petersburg to Warsaw in January 1779, Francis Hale, a British visitor soon to be an MP, had a terrible journey: '...losing our way, falling in rivers, breaking an axle-tree, a spring, a wheel etc by which means I was upwards of three weeks upon the road.' Important Russian secondary roads lacked any roadbed and were simply a cleared expanse on which construction and cultivation were forbidden.

Rail subsequently also faced many difficulties, with bold plans, both Imperial and Soviet, repeatedly baulked by the realities of terrain and climate, as well as of the availability of resources. Imperial Russia was joined by rail, with lines to the Pacific and to Central Asia, but the network east of the Urals was sparse. There was a continual battle to overcome the problems of geography, problems that undermined notions of destiny. In 1904, the British geopolitician Halford Mackinder claimed that rail links would make Russia the leading power, as rail superseded the significance of maritime routes and enabled Russia readily to move its forces across Eurasia. Mackinder, however, failed to see the limitations of those links, the resilience of maritime routes, the emergence of systems of asphalt roads and the rise of air power.

The emphasis on rail can lead to a tendency to underplay the major communication method of much of Russian history, water transport, which offered a lot in contrast to the difficulties, cost and delays of road transport. Rivers were not always helpful: many were not navigable, transport was often only easy downstream, and rivers did not always supply necessary links. Thus, the mighty Siberian rivers flowed north to the Arctic, rather than offering east-west links. Furthermore, St Petersburg was separated by the nearby continental divide from the Volga and Dnieper river systems that provided much of the rest of western Russia with a good network of trade routes. Instead, the natural hinterland of the city was confined to a smaller and less developed area based on rivers draining into Lake Ladoga.

Porterage systems, however, could make it possible to deal with the gaps in river systems. In pre-Muscovite centuries the Vikings in the ninth century developed routes from the Baltic to the Black Sea and to the Caspian. Prior to the Vikings, porterages were also employed on long-distance trade routes, notably from the Baltic to the Black Sea and vice versa: Russia was both served by these routes and a conduit for them.

Once the Muscovite state developed into a Russia that controlled an enormous stretch of territory, then there were attempts to improve the transport situation, especially under Peter the Great and his successors, although earlier ideas on improving river transport and projecting national power along rivers to the sea were there during the reign of Ivan III and in the 1550s. Peter was well aware of the importance of water transport between ports and the interior. His original intention was to profit from his conflict with Turkey in the 1690s in order to develop the port of Azov, near the mouth of the Don. Having built up a river fleet he had captured Azov in 1696, largely because he was able to use the Don as a transport route and thus support a siege. In order to increase the commercial potential of his conquest, which offered access to the Black Sea, Peter ordered the construction of canals between the Don and the Volga and Oka. Forced to return Azov in 1711, Peter switched his attentions to the potential presented by his Baltic conquests. In 1709, the passage of a flotilla of boats across the continental divide at Vyshnii Volochek in a canal built by a Dutch expert to link the Neva and Volga systems marked the first successful use of an artificial waterway in Russia. Further improvements led to the amount of freight passing through the waterways at Vyshnii Volochek rising from 2,166 tons annually between 1712 and 1719 to a maximum of 216,000 tons annually in the 1750s.

Improvements to the system later in the century included the extension of the aqueducts supplying additional water for the canals, the rebuilding of the reservoirs and locks in stone, and the construction of sluices and dams on subsidiary waterways. In 1778, permanent staffs of officials were assigned to supervise the movement of boats through each part of the system and to improve navigation by removing rocks and other hazards. The number of boats passing through the canals at Vyshnii Volochek rose from 1,707 in 1769 to 3,958 in 1797. By 1811, Russia had one of the most extensive networks of inland waterways in the world, and it remains important, although the independence of Ukraine has greatly affected the system.

It can be all-too-easy to overlook the hard work entailed by transport systems, their construction, maintenance and operation. This was captured in the depiction of workers straining in the absence of machines in Ilya Repin's painting *Barge Haulers on the Volga* (1870-3), a depiction of hard, mind-numbing labour, and Konstantin Savitsky's *Repairing the Railroad* (1874). These were classics of the Realist school of art in this period. This school was far less propagandist than the Socialist Realism that was to be seen under the Soviet Union.

Neither geographical legacy nor transport improvements prior to rail provided links with Russian Central Asia or Siberia. In each case, there were land systems reliant on pack animals, albeit with rivers used when possible, although most Siberian rivers posed obstacles such as winter ice, and anyway provided unwanted routes essentially to the Arctic Ocean. The Russian embassy that left Beijing on 2 March 1721 reached Moscow on 5 January 1722; its outward journey had taken over a year. It was only really with rail that overland transport could develop a new volume and therefore help travellers – and also ease the process of deportation. Road links never matched this. Distance was also to make internal air travel significant, especially in Siberia.

Ilya Repin's painting *Barge Haulers on the Volga*. Repin (1844-1930) was born on the Volga. Note the youth who fights against his leather bindings amidst the general despair. (Courtesy State Russian Museum, public domain)

The difficulties of travel to and in Russia prior to the impact of steamships, rail and, later, air, helped ensure that most foreigners focused on St Petersburg in the eighteenth century and visited little else, St Petersburg being much easier to visit than Moscow. The route to Russia was far from easy. The overland route was arduous and tourists preferred to travel by sea to St Petersburg, but a Baltic trip was not without its hazards. John, 20th Earl of Crawford, who sailed to St Petersburg in the later 1730s, recorded the dangers of fog, storm, rocks and bad weather, while Reginald Pole Carew wrote of his journey from Stockholm to St Petersburg in March 1781: 'I was a little pinched by the frost, though I put on my whole wardrobe at once ... and yet I sat shivering.' Most who visited St Petersburg, including Sir Francis Dashwood in 1733, Lord Baltimore in 1739, John Jervis, and Lord and Lady Effingham and Lord Howard in 1769, saw nothing else of Russia. This ensured that their grasp of developments there was very limited, not least in their exaggeration of the degree of Westernization: Russia was not an extension of St Petersburg.

More seriously, distance reduced the reality of power and effectiveness of government. This was a problem both in areas where rule was long-established and in newly seized ones. Each could exhibit reluctance, opposition, even rebellion. In practice, alongside the governmental determination to create and direct the élites, there was a tendency to work alongside them, accentuated by the size of the state and the extent to which governmental systems were *ad hoc* in creation and more contingent and episodic in performance than might appear from plans and regulations.

This then created a serious problem when there was a confrontation that made accommodation difficult. The result was often the establishment of a new élite that could prove hard to control, and that lacked the ability to understand the pre-existing situation and to direct local society effectively. This proved a serious problem for Communist rule, but not only then. The co-option of existing local authority was not a solution for the Communists for ideological and political reasons, which meant that they could not cede control of local administration. This problem encouraged a use of exemplary violence, as in 1721 when Prince Gagarin, the former Governor of Siberia, was executed in front of the Senate House in St Petersburg. He had run his province as a private fiefdom, acquiring great wealth, on a pattern that has continued to the present, that of the privatization of authority. Distance was not the sole problem. Jakob Sievers, Governor from 1764 to 1781 of the far from peripheral province of Novgorod, blamed corruption among the police there on the lack of an effective organization and the absence of salaries.

Environmental constraints were important but did not prevent significant change, not only in transport but also, more generally, in settlement, society and the economy. The Central Russian area was largely cleared of forest by the fourteenth century. More generally, the spread of agrarian settlement in North Asia was deliberately pursued as transformative, and state direction remained important, as in the cultivation of the northern Central Asian steppes in the 1950s and 1960s in a much-publicised campaign to raise grain production. The peasant migration that was part of the process could be voluntary, as with movement after the end of serfdom in 1861. However, there was also a strong *dirigiste* element, and notably so during the Soviet era, with large-scale enforced movements of people during the period in which Joseph Stalin was the key figure, 1924 to 1953.

The spread of agrarian settlement all too often meant an imposed transformation of land use. Under Muscovy, Imperial Russia and the Soviet Union, this involved the seizure of land and water resources, and control over labour. These all entailed hardship and aroused opposition, although the power of the state made it ineffectual. The related policies were also often mistaken, due to a failure to understand local ecologies. This was especially, but not only, the case with the complex interplay of irrigation and salination, the impact of over-grazing and more seriously the move from grazing to cultivation, for example of cotton and wheat, that denuded soil nutrients and posed enormous problems for water availability. There were particular difficulties in Central Asia where water resources were notably under pressure, and were part of a bigger disjuncture between colonisers and the majority colonised, one that increased the isolation of the former and the state and therefore it turned to violence to maintain dominance. For each category of resource usage, there was the need to understand and cope with the new realities. In all cases of Russian expansion, especially in Ukraine, the Baltic, Poland, Central Asia and the Caucasus, there were long periods of resistance before Russian control was established and confirmed. If this was less the case across Siberia as a whole, that was in part due to its much lower population density, but did not preclude long conflict, notably in north-east Siberia.

The twin possibilities, and indeed outcomes, of challenge and consolidation were each important to Russia's subsequent history, and they have lasted to the present. This strife reflected other possible narratives for what is now much of Russia, such as the extension of Islamic power from the eighth century and the spread of the Mongol world from the twelfth. Both marked what was subsequently to be called European as well as Asian Russia, and there was no inherent reason why they should not have been the major account, or at least a major theme, in a history of much of what is now modern Russia.

It is unclear how far Russian history should be told as part of Europe's. Vasilii Tatischev (1686-1750), a major administrator, notably of the Urals and as Governor of Astrakhan, whose often unreliable *Russian History* was published posthumously in 1767, was the first to use the expression 'European Russia'. However, that description was aspirational and conflicted with the Russian autocratic system, the bureaucratic system, and social castes, none of which owed anything to the West by way of origin. Eastern European views of Russia tended and still tend to be far less positive than Western European assessments, due to the bitter experience of Russian aggression and rule. It is certainly the case that there is no chance of Russia joining the European Union, an institution and ethos loudly deplored by Putin and his supporters.

A different approach would be to consider the climate zones of pan-Russian territory: tundra, forest, forest-steppe, steppe and desert zones. The last may be dismissed as having little to do with Russian history prior to the mid-nineteenth century expansion into Central Asia. However, that assessment depends on an approach to history in terms of state development. That is important, but insufficient. The individual zones had different agrarian possibilities. Thus, Kiev (Kyiv) lies within the fertile forest-steppe zone (the steppe zone starting about 60 miles south of the city), while Moscow lies within the forest zone and its acidic, podzolic (clayish) soil.

To focus on the period from the sixteenth century represents a choice that precludes other narratives. Much of this earlier history has been elided or destroyed by subsequent developments, notably the role of the Russian and Soviet states. However presented, for example in terms of Russification in the late nineteenth century, or of Soviet campaigns against religion from the 1920s and against particular ethnic groups, as in the northern

Caucasus, there was the diminution or destruction of other consciousnesses. Moreover, to emphasise Islamic or Mongol perspectives and narratives today is politically contentious. That is the background to what follows. There is no sense of an inevitable destiny, and that has not only been the experience of those who live in Russia today but also of their predecessors and neighbours.

{ 2 }

THE LONG CENTURIES

The Kizil-Koba cave, the largest Crimean grotto, is a starting point, as remains of archaic *Homo Sapiens* there provide a link with the evolution of hominids. In Dzhruchula to the north of the Caucasus and at Teshik Tash in Uzbekistan, there are Neanderthal sites. The second, discovered in 1938, is thought to be Middle Palaeolithic and contains the skull of a child, and there is evidence in the findings there of the manufacturing of lithic artifacts, especially side scrapers.

More recently, Neanderthal remains have been discovered in the Altai Mountains and, in 2008, hominid remains in Ust'-Ishim, on the banks of the Irtysh River, western Siberia, the latter about 45,000 years old. This fossil, a left femur, had intact DNA so that its genome could be completely sequenced. Tibetans are the modern population who are closest according to a 2016 study. This is an indication of the importance of new finds, which are suggestive of what may follow. There will be more to come, not least as a consequence of climate change leading to the greater use of the tundra and to more sustained environmental exploitation in general.

Further west, in the Russian heartland, hunter-gatherers of the modern *Homo Sapiens* used Sungir, near Vladimir, as a burial site, probably between 35,000 and 30,000 BCE. Discovered in 1955 as a result of claypit working, this site dates from an interstadial in the

Ice Age, a period in which there was greater warmth and a retreat of the ice. The burials were found with grave goods including ivory-beaded jewellery. A larger concentration of Paleolithic remains was found at Kostenki, close to modern Voronezh. Excavated from 1879, the site was occupied from about 45,000-30,000 BCE. Recent genome study reveals some Neanderthal admixture, and a widespread linkage with European hunter-gatherers.

The last Ice Age saw ice covering what is now northern Russia west of the Urals, with the Moscow area down to about the 55th parallel covered up to about 10,500 BCE. In contrast, it is suggested, to the east only the northern part of the extensive West Siberian Plains was covered by ice. However, very cold conditions restricted vegetation to the south of the ice, and there was polar desert or tundra over much of Russia. This was not the best background for human life, but the situation was transformed with the retreat of the ice and the resulting northwards extension of grassland and woodland. In Russia, this change interacted with human action, the northward movement of deer and bear in particular providing opportunities for humans. They, but more particularly climate change, were also responsible for the extinction of woolly mammoths and other mammals such as sabre-tooth tigers. This process took a long time. Although mammoths disappeared from mainland Siberia in about 8000 BCE, an isolated community on Wrangel Island survived until about 2500-2000 BCE.

As elsewhere, although far more slowly than in warmer climes, hunter-gatherers began other agricultural practices. This was late by the standards of China, India and the Middle East, and unsurprisingly so as the climate was harsh, but in the part of Central Asia that became Russian in the nineteenth century, higher temperatures brought a longer growing season. The length of this season was a key factor in agriculture, and one that was greatly variable, with major consequences for Russian society and history. In Central Asia, there was the cultivation of alfalfa, taro and carrot from about 4500 BCE while agricultural practices spread into European Russia from about 3500 BCE.

The Long Centuries

The Black Sea was a particular source of diffusion northward into steppes where there was already horse-hunting and then the domestication of horses. The Yamnaya/Pit Grave culture on the steppe from the Southern Bug to the Ural rivers saw nomadic chiefdoms reliant on managing large herds. There was some agriculture near rivers, and copperworking reaching Dereivka on the River Dnieper in about 4400 BCE. At Cucuteni-Tripolyne there was a farming village with as many as 150 houses. Copperworking has been traced back to around 1000 BCE in the Moscow area.

The geographical span of modern Russia helps explain the range of peoples within it identified by archaeology, DNA research, and linguistic linkages. Thus, for example, there are Finno-Ugrians and Turks. There is also the influence of changing scholarly engagement. For example, interest in Ancient European civilisations and peoples that were not Mediterranean has lately increased discussion of the Scythians who dominated the Ciscaucasian, Pontic and Crimean steppes from about 900 to about 200 BCE; a nomadic people that used horses in conflict with skill. The term is used to characterise a range of pastoralist nomads in a fashion that reflects the relatively limited nature of the sources, which make it difficult to permit a firm categorisation. The Scythians were one of the civilisations that had ceremonial burial with elaborate grave goods, including horses. There is evidence of human sacrifice on such occasions.

Conversely, what became Russia was not prominent, as far as current evidence suggests, in the evolution of calendrical and numerical systems, or in writing, or in urbanisation. All of this is a major contrast with the civilisations of the Middle East, China, India and the Mediterranean. In addition, most of Russia lacked the later cultural exchange that was to come from the expansion of the Greek world as a result of trade, colonisation and the conquests of Alexander the Great. In the fourth century BCE, Alexander established a Hellenistic presence in northern Afghanistan in what became the kingdom of Bactria.

Yet, a longstanding Greek presence in the Black Sea ensured an important connection, principally through Crimea and the rivers that flowed into the sea. Drawing on Greek colonies settled from about 800 BCE on the north shore of the Black Sea, the Bosporan kingdom was a Hellenistic state that brought together Greek and Scythian society, and from the fifth century BCE had a significant presence centred on the Strait of Kerch. In turn, this kingdom became a Roman client state which lasted until the sixth century CE, notably with 'Barbarian pressure' in the mid-590s; while Byzantine influence in Crimea continued after that. That became a basis for the subsequent Italian presence in Crimea, which linked Europe to the Silk Road and facilitated the spread of the Black Death into Europe, as well as providing a major base for the slave trade to the Mediterranean.

The Roman Empire did not advance territorially beyond the Black Sea as it did past the Alps and even the English Channel, and this lessened the potential interaction between the Mediterranean and Russia. Yet, there was to be significant Roman influence in the shape of the spread of Byzantine Christianity. The degree to which 'Rome' lasted in the shape of Byzantium, the Eastern Roman Empire, was very important to Russian history. In contrast, Lithuania, pagan until the late fourteenth century, lacked these links. Christianisation was not the sole factor in the extent of Roman/Byzantine links. Roman (Arabic) steeds could not paw through the snow to eat the grass underneath during the winter, unlike the hardy, but smaller, Eurasian steppe horse. This was an important ecological barrier to Greek and Roman advance to the north.

With time, the Scythians had also expanded northward into the forest-steppe, a mixture of trees and grass plains (as in southern Iowa). This was a mixed agriculture area, in part woodland, that was in the region where Russia was later to develop. Eventually, invasion and/or assimilation by other peoples, notably Sarmatians and later Germanic tribes, as well as sedentarisation, ended Scythian civilisation. In the meantime, Scythia had been a crossroads of trade, notably between the Black Sea and the forested lands to the north. At the same time, so also had been the Central Asian societies to the south-east.

Population movements that took the form of invasions were to be the history of the steppe for centuries, a process enhanced by improvements in the use of horses. Goths and Huns in succession crossed the south Russian steppe from east to west. There are great problems in knowing whether these incursions were raids, or conquests with large numbers moving in. At any rate, southern Russia proved a transit zone of opportunity in the way that the more wooded lands to the north could not. Some of the nomadic people left only a relatively slight impact on the long march of history, however destructive they might have been in the shorter. Though, as author Jem Duducu points out in his book *The Devil's Horsemen, A Thousand Years of Conquest by Eurasian Steppe Horse Archers*:

> The idea that 'history is written by the victors', is one that annoys me. We have no accounts from Attila the Hun, only the European chronicles describing a very alien culture. Attila won, but the history was recorded by his vanquished foes. The same for the Magyars, early Turkish groups and Genghis Khan, and while we have records from the court of Emir Timur, he attacked so many different places we have more history written by the losers than the winning side.

Polities were formed that created territorial sways very different to modern Russia, for example the Turkic Khaganate of 552-603 that ranged from Crimea to Manchuria, the succeeding western Turkic Khaganate from 581 to 742, and the Khazar Khaganate that replaced it from about 650 to 969. The last had a sway from the Volga and the Don to the Danube, Crimea and the Caucasus. This was a stable state with developed administrative and military systems, and an important commercial position, not least in the slave trade. The Khazar khaganate was a state more powerful than Muscovy was to be prior to the sixteenth century, and yet one that is commonly ignored in the history of Russia, in part due to a lack of information but to the significance there of Jewish influence: the Khazar ruling stratum was formally Judaised.

There is no link between this empire and modern Russia or its geopolitics; but the situation was to be very different with Kievan Rus', a successor state to the west. Its history is obscured by a shortage of sources and by subsequent historical controversy over the degree to which this was a Slavic state, drawing on the Slavic tribes who lived in the area, or one of outsiders in the shape of Vikings (Rus') from the Baltic. The latter initially established themselves through commerce, raiding and the use of mercenaries in lands near the Gulf of Finland, notably in the 850s at Holmgård (Novgorod), and then, in the late ninth century, conquering to the south, seizing Smolensk and Kiev. Small settlements enclosed by a wooden palisade were established on the tops of hillocks near rivers.

The significance of Kievan Rus' history was not only a matter of contention in the nineteenth century. Soviet historical atlases defended the 'anti-Normanist' line on the foundation of the Rus' state, emphasising a largely mythical organic rise in Slav self-awareness and thus statehood in the pre-Kievan era. These tensions continue. In Ukraine in 2008, controversy erupted over the television series *Great Ukrainians*. Victory in the poll of viewers for Yaroslav I 'the Wise' (r. 1019-54) represented a triumph for the pro-Russian east of Ukraine, as Kievan Rus' was presented as the cradle of Russian civilisation and a demonstration of the Russian destiny of Ukrainian history. The West took a nationalist line.

Benefiting from dominance over trade routes, the Rurik dynasty of Kievan Rus' found itself drawn into complex international relations, in particular with the Khazars and the Byzantine (Eastern Roman empire, but also with steppe people, notably the intervening Pechenegs. They, like the Huns, Khazars, Torki and Polovtsy, were all Turkic-speaking peoples, the Mongols had their own language.

The polities played each other off, with Rus' attacks on Constantinople (Istanbul) failing in 860, 907, and 941. In turn, the Byzantines used Christian missionaries to help win over the Rus', who were acculturating to the majority Slavic population. Paganism was replaced by Byzantine (Greek) Christianity. In the mid-tenth century, Kievan Rus' rapidly expanded into the Balkans and at the expense of the Khazars, but divisions within the ruling family provided periodic chaos.

In 1054, in an important development for Russia, Byzantine (Greek) Christianity split with Rome. This was to help in a long-term sense of separateness from the bulk of Europe, one in which Russia was to inherit the Greek Orthodox perception that Catholic Europe was different, flawed and illegitimate in its claims. It did so eventually with greater vigour because Greece and the Byzantine Empire as a whole fell to Islam.

Divisions between the ruling family of Kievan Rus' gathered pace in the late eleventh century. There was fragmentation into separate principalities, based for example on Polotsk and Chernigov. Resulting weakness, including in leadership after the death of Vladimir Monomakh in 1125, led to Kiev being sacked in 1169. Novgorod had become an independent republic in 1136. At the same time, there was an attempt to provide an exemplary history. The first Russian historical text, the *Russian Primary Chronicle* or *Tale of Bygone Years*, set out from the mid-eleventh century to provide an appropriate linkage to the ninth and tenth.

Kiev had precedence among the principalities, but this was challenged by circumstances, not least the ambitions of princes and the vulnerability of Kiev to attacks from Turkic peoples on the steppe to the south. This vulnerability encouraged a shift of energy to the less vulnerable forested zone to the north, where there was competition, but also, in Novgorod's expansion, consolidation. The sacking of Kiev led to a transfer of authority to the ruler of Vladimir-Suzdal, a principality based on the city of Vladimir. Former parts of Kievan Rus' in the south-west and west, notably Galich and Volhynia, were distant and fully autonomous.

In the thirteenth century, there was external pressure from two developments. The most dramatic was the latest instance of pressure from the Mongols. In addition, the 'Northern Crusades' led to the establishment in 1202 of the Knights of the Sword in what is now Latvia and of the Danes in northern Estonia. Both pushed eastward, the Knights occupied Pskov in 1240, but in 1242 they were defeated at Lake Peipus in the 'Battle on the Ice'. This was to be a key episode in a 1938 film by Sergei Eisenstein about the victorious Alexander Nevsky. Prince of Novgorod and Grand Prince of Vladimir, who had already defeated the Swedes in 1240 at the Battle of the Neva.

These battles helped to form what was to be a boundary of considerable cultural consequence, although there were repeated and successful military and governmental efforts to overcome such boundaries. At any rate, the Teutonic Knights, with whom the Knights of the Swords merged in 1237, were able to consolidate their hold on Livonia and to establish a Germanic empire along the eastern Baltic coast. It would have become a territorially contiguous empire had it not been for the rise of Lithuania. Indeed, Russian principalities benefited from the degree of division to their west, and Muscovy inherited this position.

Meanwhile, the Mongols had a dramatic advance in 1223, winning over Kievan and allied forces at the Kalka River in the Donetsk region, with a more major invasion following from 1237. This led to the conquest of the Russian principalities, the northern ones in 1237-9 and Kiev falling in 1240. The last was very important to the political decline of Kiev, indeed its *coup de grâce*. The long-term consequences were affected however by a new political order, with the Mongol world, the inheritance of Jinghis Khan, divided into four khanates. One of these, that of the Golden Horde, with its headquarters at Sarai on the Lower Volga, dominated what is now Ukraine, the southern part of European Russia, and southwestern Siberia. The Chagatai khanate dominated what became Soviet Central Asia. The most powerful khanate was based in China and most famously ruled by Kublai Khan, who was visited by Marco Polo. Kublai Khan's forces overthrew the Southern Song, the rulers of southern China and mounted two unsuccessful attacks on Japan. There was, however, no possibility of using Chinese resources to protect the Mongol presence in European Russia, let alone expand it at the expense of the latter.

The Long Centuries

The destruction, disruption and legacy of the Mongol invasions left earlier principalities in ruin and ensured that those to the north of the Golden Horde had to pay tribute and were exposed to slave raiding. Indeed, that helped define the subsequent memory of the outer world for many families. Meanwhile, because Mongol pressure had weakened the Russian principalities, the Knights of the Sword were able to move eastward to seize Pskov in 1240.

More, lastingly, in the early fourteenth century, again benefiting from the vacuum left by the Mongols, Lithuania expanded eastward, incorporating what is now Belarus and taking Vitebsk in 1320 and later in the century absorbing a number of principalities, notably Kiev, Pereyaslavl and Chernigov. By 1392, the Lithuanians, whose Grand Duchy was in personal union with the Polish throne from 1386, had encroached into the southern steppe, the domain of the nomad, overrun almost the entire valley of the River Dnieper, and reached the Black Sea to the west of the Dnieper. This expansion was similar to that of the House of Wessex in England in the tenth century, as it benefited from the destruction of rivals by the Viking invasions. The Eastern Slavic peoples taken over by Lithuania outnumbered the ethnic Lithuanians.

Not that this was the Lithuanian intention, but in Russia the situation ensured that there were fewer independent principalities, principally Moscovy, Novgorod, Suzda-Nizhegorod, Tver and Ryazan. These were in the shadow of the Golden Horde, and although this relationship was not subsequently to be stressed, Muscovy developed in part as a client state with the rulers both paying tribute to the Golden Horde and gathering tribute for it. Some of the Muscovite élite was to be of Tatar descent. The principality of Moscow developed in the heart of a vast hydrographic network linking it with the Baltic, the Black Sea and the Caspian. Subjugated in 1237, Muscovy became a pliable yet recalcitrant client. The Muscovite Princes rose to power by taking full advantage of a favourable geographical location and from the Golden Horde treating them as a principal vassal, which enabled the Golden Horde to sustain the Mongol achievement of ruling supreme not only in the steppe but even in the forest zone.

The standard account of Muscovite history emphasises gradual consolidation thanks to skilful rulers, but that can underplay the extent to which the history of Russia (as of other countries) depended on developments elsewhere, in this case the fate of the Golden Horde. There was no inherent reason why this should not last nor be succeeded by an equivalent, on the pattern for example of the Ilkhanate, a Mongol khanate in South-West Asia ruled by the Il-Khans, established in the late 1250s. Aside from Persia/Iran, this khanate included much of the Caucasus and part of Central Asia and converted to Islam in 1295. Disintegrating from the late 1310s, this khanate was conquered by the Golden Horde in 1356. However, the Safavid dynasty (1502-1736) was to be a powerful empire there. Further east, the Khanate of the Dzungars was to be a major presence, threatening China, until conquered by it in the 1750s.

To a degree, the rise of Russia was the result of Mongol decline that occurred because of conflict within the ruling élite and their interaction with rebellions and external pressures. The first major threat to the Mongol position occurred not in Russia but in China, where rebellions in 1356-68 led to the establishment of the Ming dynasty in 1356. That did not affect the Golden Horde, but it was hit hard by Timur the Lame (1336-1405; later called Tamerlane). He gained control of the Chagatai Khanate and then attacked the Golden Horde in order to demonstrate his superiority over its Khan, Toqtamysh. Victory in 1395 was followed by the sacking of its capital, New Sarai, north of the Caspian Sea near the lower Volga, and then by the rerouting of trade routes to converge on Timur's capital, Samarkand. However, the Timurid empire collapsed after the death in 1405 of its founder Timur. What became Russia was always tangential to his interests, with the Middle East and India more important; when he died, Timur was preparing to invade China.

The Golden Horde did not recover from Timur's victory and as a result of struggles for leadership that had already been a major problem from 1357, fragmented. There was a continuance in the shape of the Great Horde, but independent khanates developed in Crimea, Kazan, Sibir' and Astrakhan. In addition, the Shaybanid dynasty became powerful east of the Caspian, ruling part of Central Asia, notably Uzbekistan, from the 1420s to the 1520s, family members thereafter ruling Bukhara, Khiva and Sibir. There was also a Turkic loss of other territory to autonomous peoples.

The overall consequence was that there was no dominant Islamic power north of the Black Sea. Fragmentation, which was taken further in the 1450s when the moribund Golden Horde finally split up, was accompanied by serious rivalry. The Crimean Tatars, who had devastated Kiev in 1482, destroyed New Sarai in 1502, bringing the Golden Horde to an end. They indirectly strengthened Muscovy as the Great Horde had been an ally of Lithuania against the alliance of Ivan III and the Crimean khan, a rivalry that had led to conflicts in 1487-94 and 1500-2.

There was no comparison north of the Black Sea to the development in the fifteenth century of the power of the Ottoman Turks. This part of the Islamic world divided unto itself, and, just like rivalry in the Near-East, notably between the Fatimids and the Seljuks, had helped the Crusaders, so similar rivalry assisted the expansion of Lithuania and, separately, Muscovy. Muscovy had faced opposition as it probed new relationships with the Golden Horde, its successor states and Lithuania, and also from the other Rus' rulers. In 1439 and 1445, Kazan forces inflicted serious defeats, while there was division within the Muscovite ruling family from the 1420s to the 1450s and changes in control that included the blinding of rivals. 1425 to 1453 was a period of civil war, one that owed much to the lateral succession practice that helped ensure division in the ruling family. The practice was a continuance of that of Kievan Rus' but was challenged by the idea of vertical succession (between parent and child, not involving brothers), one that ended with the triumph of Vasilii II, who came to the throne as the son of Vasilii I.

Yet, there was a period of rapid Muscovite expansion in the late fifteenth century. In 1456, at Staraia Rusa, Vasilii II (r. 1425-62) defeated an army from Novgorod that was strong in horse archers, in part provided by Tatar auxiliaries. Hitherto, Russian principalities had deployed armoured lancers, maybe as a consequence of the Byzantine example. In their place came cavalry tactics with archers wearing padded heavy coats. This was to help in operations into the steppe, which became more important from the early 1470s as the Crimean Tatars launched raids to acquire slaves to be sold in the Crimean slave markets and shipped to Constantinople.

To oppose this, Muscovy needed to raise cavalry, and these cavalrymen were paid with land inhabited by peasants. The ruler owned the land which was called a *pomest'e* (conditional service land grant). This provided defence against the Crimean Tatars, but by the seventeenth century these cavalrymen proved obsolete in conflict with better-armed and trained Polish and Swedish cavalry. The Russian rulers tended to let the grant pass on to sons, and thus helped develop a servitor military class dependent on the ruler for occupation, status, income and well-being. This was different to the upper service class of senior figures and officials based in Moscow. This service class model has continued to the present and helped ensure that Muscovy was a unitary state. Ivan III continued the practices of his father.

Focusing expansion northwards, Ivan III 'the Great' (r. 1462-1509) conquered Novgorod in 1478, taking advantage of its social and political divisions, and Tver in 1485. Mercantile Novgorod was less militaristic than Moscow. After the incorporation of Novgorod, the Muscovite Church claimed to be the heir to Kievan Rus' while Russia and Poland became rivals for the lands of the Lithuanian principality that had once been part of Kievan Rus'. Ivan also successfully thwarted the attempts of the Great Horde when it sought to intimidate him into resuming the payment of tribute: Khan Ahmed was defeated on the Ugra river about 150 miles south-west of Moscow in 1480. In 1482, the Crimean Tatar attack on Kiev was encouraged by Ivan as he sought to establish dominance over what had been Kievan Rus'. In 1493, Ivan, who supported the emphasis on 'vertical' rulership, took the title 'Sovereign of all Russia'. He had also put pressure on Islamic rulers, in 1467-9 beginning to take the initiative against Kazan to the east, launching a series of campaigns to that end. Ivan subsequently took advantage of dynastic strife within the khanate, and in 1487 his troops helped install a sympathetic claimant.

Yet, it was the Ottomans (Turks) who came to dominate much of the northern shore of the Black Sea, and were thus best placed to recruit local protégés, notably the Crimean Tatars. As a result, the Russians had to protect to/from the south, creating garrison towns and building fortified lines. Moreover, due to the Crimean Tatars, Russian expansion southwards was delayed.

Ivan's successor, Vasilii III (r. 1505-33), continued the consolidation of control in Russia, taking Pskov in 1510 and Ryazan in 1521. He initially maintained good relations with Kazan, but the Crimean Tatars organised a pan-Tatar league which ousted the pro-Muscovite ruler of Kazan in 1521, replacing him with the brother of the Crimean Khan. That year, the Crimean and Kazan Tatars advanced on Moscow from the south and east, and the city was saved only by an attack on Crimea by the Astrakhan Tatars, a dramatic instance of the significance of Islamic disunity. In 1524, as a sign of the growth of rival influence, the Khan of Kazan acknowledged the suzerainty of the Ottoman ruler, Süleyman the Magnificent (r. 1520-66). This was a more extensive projection of Mediterranean/Black Sea authority than the earlier advance of Roman and Byzantine influence.

As a state on Europe's open frontier, Muscovy/Russia faced problems and opportunities, aside from those posed by physical geography, notably a northern location that affected growing seasons; long winters; poor soil with low fertility; long distances which limited economic integration and increased a need for self-sufficiency; low population density and weak urbanisation affecting demand and productive capacity. Had Muscovy succumbed to its Islamic opponents, then Poland-Lithuania would have been the major frontier state and, if successful, the dominant power in Eastern Europe. Such a development might well have affected subsequent views about the relative capability of states and societies, with Polish noble strength and autonomy not treated as a cause of weakness.

However, in 1532, Vasilii III succeeded in installing another pro-Muscovite khan of Kazar, Djan Ali. The Russians benefited from the support of the Nogais ('the Dog Horde'), a Mongol-based tribal confederation that lived north of the Caucasus. In the late 1520s, the centre for the Nogai trade in horses was moved from Constantinople, the Ottoman capital, to Moscow, helping to cement political links and supplying horses that helped the Russians operate outside the forest belt of northern Russia. In turn, the Russians provided goods, including firearms. Meanwhile, there was already a serious and what was to become a longstanding rivalry with Poland-Lithuania. In 1472, Casimir IV had allied with Ahmed Khan against Ivan III. This rivalry continued in the early sixteenth century with conflict over Smolensk, which the Muscovites gained in 1514.

The boundaries of great-power rivalry were being contested at the very time that Muscovy became a major power. It did so as a state with a dynastic monarchy, a clientele of warrior-nobles organised on the basis of military service, and a peasantry that was socially and economically subordinate. Most of the population worked on the land, the major distinction being between those who focused on animal husbandry and the cultivators. There were towns, merchants and artisans, but their economic significance was not matched by political power. More significantly, there were differences to the situation in much of Europe, notably the 'Tatar Yoke', the absence of Catholicism, the autocratic tendencies of the Grand Princes, and the stronger emphasis on noble service.

The fall of Constantinople to the Ottomans in 1453 left Muscovy as effective and thereby independent head of the Orthodox/Eastern Church and greatly enhanced the influence of its rulers. Ivan III married Sophia (Zoe) Paleologue, the daughter of the last Emperor of Byzantium, in 1472, and she introduced elements of the elaborate Byzantine court ritual into Muscovy. The Grand Princes who had derived their legitimacy for so long from the Mongol khans now saw themselves as the heirs to the Byzantine Empire, a claim that would eventually set the stage for the long and bitter

Russo-Ottoman conflict over hegemony in the Black Sea basin. The rulers gained a more pronounced sacral quality that very much differentiated them from the greater aristocrats and led to a monarchy that was different to that in many European Christian states, with the tsar divinely appointed, there not really being a separate political sphere.

Looked at in another light, there was no separate religious sphere, for the authority and power of the tsar were in part ecclesiastical and there was no understanding of individual religious conscience and practice, let alone tolerance for them. The titles of Sovereign and Autocrat made their appearance during Ivan III's reign and signified an increase in the majesty of the Grand Prince, who became a more elevated and distant figure. In the Eastern Orthodox Byzantine and Muscovite tradition, the Patriarch was in practice subordinate to the emperor and tsar. There was no tradition of quarrels with a figure akin to the Pope and, instead, a principle of *harmonia* between ruler and Patriarch, although in practice, that was not always the case.

The fall of Constantinople symbolised the rivalry with Islam and the Ottomans, whose rulers became both Caliphs and Guardians of the Islamic Holy Places. There was also competition with Western Christendom, with Lithuanian expansionism seen as an instance. The 1439 Council of Florence, by which Byzantium made religious concessions in an unsuccessful attempt to gain support, was rejected by the Metropolitan of Muscovy as an attempt to convert the Eastern Orthodox. The fall of Constantinople was seen in Russia as God's punishment against a wicked Byzantium. Ivan III developed a strong bias against Western Christendom. This was sustained as the latter divided in the sixteenth century between Catholicism and Protestantism. The way was open to struggles that were to be of great significance.

Yet, Russia was not the dominant player at the global level, or even the Eurasian one. The fragmentation of the Mongol empire was important to the relative potency of Eurasian nomads, and this was to the great benefit of Russia. Nevertheless, its power was far more modest than that of the Ottomans, let alone the

Chinese. Thanks to European transoceanic exploration, conquest, settlement and trade, it was the Western European states that could benefit from resources elsewhere, pe-eminently Portugal and Spain. The Russian parallel was the conquest of Siberia, but the benefits were less and costs greater.

The development of the Muscovite state was long treated as the destiny of Russia and presented in triumphal terms. This was true both for the Romanovs and later for the Communists. Thus, in the *Atlas Istorii SSSR, 7-oi klass*, 'Atlas of the History of the USSR, seventh class' (Moscow, 1982), this development was depicted in terms of the 'struggle of the Russian people for the overthrow of the Mongol-Tatar yoke'. As with other standard approaches to the history of Russia (and the same for other countries), this approach left no space for any other historical players or accounts, a situation that powerfully contributed to the development and character of Russian nationalism.

When the three-year-old Ivan IV came to the throne in 1533, the situation might have appeared promising for future expansion. However, the divisions that had affected the ruling family the previous century continued. Ivan, the first son of Vasilii III by his second wife, Elena Glinskaya, was proclaimed Grand Prince in accordance with Vasilii's wishes and Elena acted as regent, but they were faced by the claims of Vasilii's surviving brothers, one of whom, Yuri, was executed for treason in 1534, as well as by the boyars of the Shuisky and Belsky families. Linked to Yuri, Prince Semyon Belsky, who had earlier been prominent in conflict with the Kazan Tatars, defected to Lithuania in 1534 and then the Crimean Tatars. His older brother, Ivan, was in effect ruler of Muscovy in 1540-2, only to be overthrown by his rival Ivan Shuisky (acting with the oldest brother Dmitry Belski), and murdered in 1542. Elena had died, probably poisoned, in 1538 when Ivan was eight. (He once complained that Shuiski put his feet upon his bed.) Ivan's only companion for one period was a deaf and dumb relative of his age. By the age of ten, Ivan was a sadist who threw live dogs over the walls of the Kremlin. The Shuiskis were overthrown in 1543.

In one light, the central power was not fragmenting, while the precedence (*mestnichestvo*) system of one's place in the élite being calibrated on the basis of genealogy, service record, and sheer luck had been taking form from the early decades of the sixteenth century. This meant that the members of the upper (Moscow) service class were competing with one another for position and promotion, rather than forming conspiratorial groups against the ruler. Precedence was an important means of keeping the higher ranked servitors (including *boyars*) fragmented, unbalanced and off-guard. Yet, away from the later impression created by maps of expansion, the reality was of division and danger, murder and invasion.

{ 3 }

A NEW POWER
The Sixteenth Century

Brooding and violent (especially in the second part, which was banned until after Stalin's death in 1953), Ivan 'the Terrible' (1530-84, r. 1533-84), played by Nikolay Cherkasov in Sergei Eisentein's four-part film of that name (1945, 1958) was widely seen as a depiction of Stalin. Indeed, the Soviet dictator, who admired Ivan, the defining Tsar of force, regarding him as the founder of the modern Russian state. Ivan, the longest ruling of the Tsars, certainly presides over the historical imagination as none of his dynastic predecessors do, nor any of his successors until Peter the Great, whom Stalin also praised. Based on Eisenstein's study of the sources, the film offered a dialectic of triumph and tragedy.

This parallel was one that was to blacken Ivan's reputation. In part this was due to the reaction against Stalin after his death in 1953. Earlier, there was contemporary uneasiness, the novelist Boris Pasternak observing his surprise in February 1941 at the 'new admiration' for Ivan, which extended to a play by Aleksei Tolstoy and a novel by V.I. Kostylev. The theme of necessary terror was advanced, including by Stalin in a 1947 discussion with Eisenstein. But 'Groznyi' for Ivan in practice is better translated as 'the Awe-Inspiring', an older meaning of the term.

A New Power: The Sixteenth Century

Ivan contributed greatly to the development of a hostile view elsewhere in Europe that characterised Russia as different. It was argued that whereas elsewhere in Europe there was a sense of royal respect for other rights that contributed to an image of government as far from tyrannical, the rulers of Russia and the Ottoman Empire were different, which, indeed, was the case. There was an established vocabulary to describe them: tyranny being the usual term until the close of the seventeenth century, and despotism thereafter. The potent impression of Russian tyranny rested, in part, on an informed assessment of Russian developments. Visitors did their best to amass information, and envoys and merchants argued that monarchical power was much stronger in Russia than in their homelands. Foreigners resident in Russia had a similar view and insisted upon a chasm between the basic patterns of Russian and non-Russian European government.

Preconceptions played a role in shaping the Western experience and presentation of Russia. The most important was tyranny, although several commentators noted that Russian tyranny was at odds with the Aristotelian ideal type. Tyrannies were supposed to be short-lived momentary phenomena created by rogue princes, but Russian tyranny appeared structural. This was depicted by contemporary Western commentators as stemming from the nature of Russian society rather than the character of its rulers.

There were, indeed, important differences with the situation further west. Russian rulers wielded considerable power, in part because of the nature of Russian political practice and thought, specifically the absence of other institutions (bar, to a limited degree, the Church) with independent authority. In practice, however, there were important checks, albeit mostly informal, which limited the freedom of action of Russian and Ottoman rulers. Some recent historians have presented the Tsars as ruling collaboratively with the upper strata of the Muscovite service class. As a separate point, there was a major difference in scale between a tiny, fledging Greek *polis* and sixteenth-century Russia.

This was also the period in which Russia came more to the fore under Western eyes. The foundation in London of the Muscovy

Company and the development of trade links in the 1550s via the White Sea ensured that English interest in Russia increased, as did knowledge about it. Russia was seen as a trade route to Persia via the new conquest of Astrakhan. This interest was encouraged by Ivan's role in Baltic power politics, and Elizabeth I sought good relations with him. Russia appeared a far less dubious ally than the other rising power of the period, the Ottoman empire. Russia appears in William Shakespeare's play *Measure for Measure* when the lengthy case involving Elbow, Froth and Pompey leads Angelo to remark: 'This will last out a night in Russia,/When nights are longest there' (II, i). In *Love's Labour's Lost*, Ferdinand, king of Navarre and his three lords are 'Disguised like Muscovites, in shapeless gear' and described as 'a mess of Russians' (V, ii). In *The Winter's Tale*, Hermione is supposedly the daughter of the Emperor of Russia, who, for Shakespeare's audience, was generally Ivan. He had a reputation for letting bears lose among the people, which is echoed by the bear's murderous entry in the play.

Ivan's long reign was definitely one of an hitherto unprecedented extension of Russian power and of a determination to enforce the will and authority of the ruler. Ivan's father, Vasilii III, had no child for a long time, so Ivan succeeded when he was only three. At the age of 16, in 1547, he was the first Russian monarch or Grand Prince to be crowned the *Tsar* (absolute ruler) of all Russia, a title that reflected the desire to succeed to the prestige of Byzantium and its imperial rulers, and it was also designed to differentiate him from the members of his family as well as the *boyars* (the upper strata of the Muscovite service class grades). These had created many difficulties and much instability in his early years. As with other rulers, Ivan sought to establish control with new governmental initiatives, but in 1553, when very ill, he faced opposition from some *boyars* to swearing an oath of allegiance to his eldest son. This triggered Ivan's divergence from his former close circle, or private council, the *Izbrannaia Rada*, that caused the repression of its former members a decade later, when Ivan faced the opposition of the traditional power structures to his private 'Pretorian Guard' administration, the *oprichniki*. To a degree, Ivan was repurposing, to his advantage, the service classes that had come into existence during the reign of Ivan III and solidified in the reign of Ivan IV. There was an upper (Moscow-raised) service class, with nine ascribed ranks, the upper four of which were a true power elite with immediate proximity to the Grand Prince, later tsar. The top rank of the upper service class was the *boyar*, but it was not the *boyars* alone who had access to the Grand Prince/tsar. The second service class, the middle class, based in the countryside, consisted of cavalry and owed its status to the wishes of the state. If one did not show up for duty, he lost his *pomest'e* (conditional service land grant). This was different to the other European nobilities of the period, more similar to the Ottoman *timars*. The lower service class was also provincial-based and consisted of musketeers and artillerymen.

This was a period of territorial expansion. Ivan brought to fruition past initiatives and took them in a new direction. In 1535, Djan Ali, the pro-Muscovite khan of Kazan, installed with the help of Vasilii III in 1532, had been exiled and replaced by Safa Giray, a relative of the Khan of the Crimean Tatars. Thereafter, relations deteriorated, with frequent raids on Russia by Tatar light cavalry, to whom the Russians were highly vulnerable. In 1545, Ivan took the initiative against Kazan, helped by the divisions among the Tatars that were to be important to eventual Russian success. He attempted two winter campaigns against Kazan in 1547-8 and 1549-50, but these failed because the Russian army had no fortified base in the region, had to leave its artillery behind as a result of heavy rains, and ended up campaigning with an exclusively cavalry army that was of no use in investing the city of Kazan.

For the third campaign, a base was secured. In the winter and spring of 1551-2, the Russians prefabricated fortress towers and wall sections near Uglich, northern Russia, and then floated them down the Volga on barges with artillery and troops to its confluence with the Sviiaga river, 25 kilometres from Kazan; here the Russian fortress of Sviiazhsk was erected in just 28 days. Sviiazhsk not only provided a base of operations against Kazan but also protected the upper Volga towns from raids by the Crimean Tatars. That summer, siege guns and stores were shipped down the Oka, south of Moscow, and Volga to Sviiazhsk and a Crimean invasion of southern Muscovy, with artillery support from the Ottomans, was repulsed near Tula in mid-June. The Russian army then advanced on the city of Kazan, which it reached on 20 August 1552. Including peasants levied as sappers and transport labour, the Russian army was allegedly 150,000 strong. It also had 150 siege guns, ordnance far greater than that earlier in the century, and one on a par with Ottoman and Habsburg forces.

Kazan stood on a high bluff overlooking the Kazanka and Bulak rivers. It had double walls of oak logs covered over with clay and partially plated with stones. There were 14 stone towers with guns and a deep surrounding ditch. The Russians constructed siege lines from which cannon opened fire and also used wooden siege towers carrying cannon and mounted on rollers. The ditch surrounding the city was filled with fascines, and sappers tunnelled beneath the walls. The mines were blown up on 2 October, destroying the walls at two of the gates, upon which the Russian army, drawn up into seven columns, attacked all seven of the town gates simultaneously. They soon broke through and Kazan fell after a 28-day siege.

The campaign witnessed the first large-scale use of artillery and mining by Russians, and in part they owed their success to more advanced weaponry. The war demonstrated the effectiveness of Ivan's new infantry and artillery units; but there were other important factors. Over the long term, the demographic balance favoured Russia and over time there was a clear difference in consistency and quality of leadership, with repeated changes in leadership in Kazan providing numerous opportunities for Russian intervention. Furthermore, Kazan was the closest Islamic state and the one most exposed to Russian intervention. As so often, a multiplicity of factors should induce caution in arguing that one was clearly the most significant.

Once the city of Kazan had fallen, there were several serious rebellions in the khanate – in 1553, 1554 and 1556. They were repressed with great brutality: towns were destroyed, men slaughtered, women and children taken prisoner, and the countryside devastated. Only in 1556 did organised resistance cease. A similar pattern of violence and cruelty was to be seen with Russian expansion elsewhere, notably in Siberia with the *iasak* (fur tribute-taking system), but more generally at the cost of those of different religions, especially Islam. Cruelty was not absent elsewhere, for example the depredations of the English in Ireland.

After conquering Kazan, Russia was able to expand rapidly across the Urals into western Siberia, as well as down the Volga to Astrakhan, swiftly conquered in 1556, and towards the Caucasus. This expansion owed much to non-state military entrepreneurs, largely Cossacks. Their motivation and success were strikingly similar to those of the Spanish *conquistadores* in the Americas. Russian success was highly significant for the reconfiguration of the geopolitics of Eurasia, both in the short and the long term, with the Urals and Siberia providing opportunities for mineral and fur exploitation, and the advance to Astrakhan severing the steppe and nomadic movement across it. On the global scale, there was a similar impact from Portuguese and Spanish expansion.

Although the Russians suffered setbacks, this expansion was never reversed. There was a bold attempt to do so in 1568-9 with the plan for the advance of an Ottoman-Tatar force from the Ottoman base at Azov in order to besiege Astrakhan and co-operate with the Uzbeks. However, food, water and artillery shortages all wrecked the expedition, which had an inherent lack of viability in terms of the idea for building a canal between the Don and Volga Rivers. A lack of support from the Tatars also hit plans for a joint Uzbek-Ottoman attack on Astrakhan in 1587-8.

Within Russia, the 1560s and 1570s were a far less easy period for Russia than the 1550s, due to famine, disease and the strains of war. Increasingly paranoid, Ivan, in the context of a form of government with weak checks and balances, became even more arbitrary, notably toward some of the *boyars* and other high-ranking members of the service élite but also toward a large number of rank-and-file service cavalrymen. Commander of the army that conquered Kazan in 1552, Prince Alexander Gorbatyi-Shuisky, a member of Ivan's earlier circle and head of the formal estate power structures as the leading aristocrat, was executed in

1565. Instead of *boyars*, Ivan relied increasingly on the *oprichniki*, a personal guard that he turned into a new landowning élite, especially in the *Oprichnina* (the 'stand-apart realm'), the part of Russia where Ivan took total power.

The *oprichniki* was used in particular to massacre in 1570 much of the population of the city of Novgorod, whose leaders Ivan, unreasonably, suspected of planning to help Poland. Although paranoia played a role, this was a major instance of the sense of precariousness that characterised the expansion, and indeed position, of Muscovy. The episode also reflected the interaction of foreign and domestic policies.

Meanwhile, conflict continued elsewhere. From the south, the Crimean Tatars mounted powerful attacks, advancing into Moscow's suburbs in 1571 and starting a fire that the wind blew on to destroy the city. As an instance of the selective nature of history and of the weight of the more recent, this destruction is far less known and commemorated than that of 1812. Similarly, the revolutions of 1917 had far more impact on the collective memory than those of the early seventeenth century.

The *Oprichnina* severely weakened the frontier defences, the lines of field fortification about 250 kilometres south of Moscow, which helped the Crimean Tatars to break through in 1571. The next year, Ivan dismantled the *Oprichnina* and returned to Moscow. He broke up the *Oprichnina* parallel government with its own officialdom and offices. A Tatar attack in 1572 was defeated at Molodi by Prince Mikhail Vorotynsky in close-quarter fighting that lessened the Tatar use of mounted archers, only for the general to be executed by the jealous Ivan in 1573. This prefigured similar conduct by Stalin.

The vulnerability of Moscow led to its further fortification. The royal, religious and governmental heart of the city was the inner walled Kremlin (from *kreml'* or 'citadel', a term that dates from the fourteenth century when the Kremlin was enclosed by a white stone wall in 1367) and its later connecting *Kitai-gorod*, meaning 'the city enclosed by an earthen-basket wall', the walls of which were built in 1535-38. To the east, north and

A New Power: The Sixteenth Century

west was the 'white town' (*belyi gorod*) stone wall, so called because either the stone was white or the enclosed part contained tax-exempt settlements. Earthen reinforcement was an important component. Five miles long and with 28 towers, these walls were built in 1583-93. Surrounding that was a wooden palisaded area and beyond an outermost earthworks and wooden wall with 12 major gates, constructed in 1591-92 and known as *zemlianoi gorod* ('earthen city'). Stone, wood and earth was an established hierarchy of permanence and significance.

To the west of Russia, Ivan sought to exploit the possibilities created by the Reformation which brought the end to the crusading orders, the Teutonic Knights and the Livonian Knights. In particular, Ivan sought to gain a position on the Baltic. However, as for Tsar Alexis in the 1650s against Poland, initial successes could not be sustained, in large part because other powers also sought to exploit the situation. Having conquered most of Livonia in 1577, Ivan met firm resistance from Stephan Báthory, king of Poland (r. 1576-86). Joined with the Swedes, he drove the Russians from Livonia, while the Swedes took Estonia, which was valuable as a source of naval stores that were exported to Western Europe and which also consolidated Sweden's control of Finland. Ivan was forced to make peace with both Poland and Sweden. The former, the Truce of Yam-Zapolsky (1582), saw Ivan renounce his claims to Livonia and Báthory abandon the siege of Pskov. Over-extension in a lengthy war had turned into a disaster and brought Russia nothing.

Indeed, Russia was so weakened that it was left in a vulnerable position during the reign of Feodor I (r. 1584-98), Ivan's third and surviving son, the oldest, Ivan Ivanovich, dying in 1581, probably killed by his father in a jealous rage. Power was wielded by Boris Godunov, Feodor's brother-in-law, who had served Ivan as an *oprichnik* and been promoted to the rank of *boyar*. Unsuited to be Tsar as a result of personal weaknesses and his strong focus on religious acts, Feodor had been left by Ivan a regency council, which Godunov came to dominate. Ivan's remaining son, Dmitri, was possibly killed on Godunov's instructions in 1591, or he stabbed himself during an epileptic seizure while playing a knife game. At any rate, the death was convenient for Godunov.

Feodor's reign saw the defeat of a raid by the Crimean Tatars in 1591. In considering such episodes, there is the question of whether to emphasise the threat or its failure, and, in either case, how best to compare Russian defensive practice with that of the Chinese who had a wall system. The Russians used field fortifications, field artillery and musketeers, but also developed fortified lines.

After conquering Kazan and after the end of the Livonian War, Ivan launched the colonisation of the Wild Fields, the contemporary Russian name for the Pontic steppes, which at the time was more important than the advance into Siberia. The new territories that Ivan and Feodor colonised increased the size of Muscovy and advanced it toward the Black Sea by 300-400 kilometres, about a third of the distance. This advance was to produce most of the explosive elements of the 'Time of Troubles', especially the Cossack bands and dissatisfied petty gentry. The expansion southward did not lead to any recentring of the Russian state, comparable for example to the medieval *Reconquista* in Spain and Portugal. There was no return to a centring of rule at Kiev. Nor was there a new capital, as in Savoy-Piedmont (Turin) and Spain (Madrid) in the sixteenth century.

As a reminder of the wider geopolitics, war with Sweden had resumed in 1590. The Russians regained the fortress of Ivangorod (lost in 1581) but then found it prudent to accept a peace treaty in 1595 that left Sweden with Estonia, Narva and Kexholm (eastern Karelia); so that Russia's presence on the Gulf of Finland was only a foothold. In negotiating a settlement with the Swedes, the Russians were concerned by the possible implications of the 1590 peace between the Ottomans and the Safavids of Persia, the danger that the Ottomans, once free of the major war in which they had been engaged, would now support an attack on Muscovy by the Crimean Tatars. This was a new variable from Russia earlier benefiting from bitter divisions to its south. Feodor's death in 1598 brought the Rurik dynasty to an end. At once ambitious and vulnerable, Godunov, backed by the Patriarch of Moscow, declared himself Tsar with the support of the *Zemsky Sobor* (Assembly of the Land), a body that had come into being in 1549 and was to last until the 1650s. Godunov's reign was to see the launching of the Time of Troubles.

Ivan the Terrible's reign was successful compared to the Time of Troubles, but the triumphs of expansion in the 1550s, Kazan and Astrakhan, were not matched in other aspects. While the administrative, military and village reforms of the 1550s were really devised by others, that was commonplace for rulers. More

Tsar Ivan the Terrible by Victor Vasnetsov (1848-1926). (Courtesy Tretyakov Gallery, Moscow, public domain)

significantly, the Livonian War and the *Oprichnina* dragged the country down. These helped explain why Ivan III was more innovative.

Ivan IV was to be treated subsequently as an important figure in the development of Russian power, notably through expansion, consolidation and modernisation. All three factors were then seen as characteristics of the reign of Peter the Great (r. 1682-1725), and the two were praised accordingly by Soviet historians.

Stalin's stance can be deduced from a textbook, the 1937 *Short Course in the History of the USSR for 3rd and 4th levels of the Middle School* (children of 10-11 years old). Stalin made his comments on the textbook's typeset version and compiled a letter to its author. The textbook mentioned the 'progressive importance' of Ivan's activity and Peter's reforms in general, although Stalin always emphasised that Peter was 'a tsar of landlords and merchants' and an oppressor of the people. Stalin divided Ivan and Peter's activities into three areas. First, they had progressive importance in terms of the transition from feudalism to capitalism. Secondly, they were patriotic in an exemplary fashion in their struggle against international enemies and in achieving important geopolitical gains such as access to the Baltic. However, thirdly, they belonged to and served oppressive social classes.

Although Ivan's reign led to closer geopolitical and commercial relations with European powers, especially Sweden and England, his expansionism accentuated a hostile perception. In particular, Poles put the Russians alongside the Ottomans, with Poland therefore a barrier protecting Catholic Europe. The Poles wrongly presented the Russians as heirs to the Mongols. The anxieties arising from Russian expansionism explain why Poland in particular, but also Sweden increasingly, put energy in the early seventeenth century into restraining Russia, and intervened in its politics accordingly. This intervention was to be perceived in Russia in terms of lasting antipathy, but in practice, there were choices in prioritisation. The Poles faced Ottoman and Swedish expansionism, while the Swedes confronted Danish enmity and Polish interventionism. That Russia came to the fore for both Sweden and Poland as a

A New Power: The Sixteenth Century

threat, albeit not always so, was a product of Ivan's expansionism. That was far from inevitable in its direction. Indeed, Russia, out of pragmatism and necessity, had long focused on Islamic opponents in a way that was explicable in terms of Russia's Christian ideology and of the challenge posed by nearby Islamic powers.

The European focus of scholarship is such that expansion to the Baltic and against Poland has attracted attention at the expense of this Islamic expansion. Always misleading, this interpretation rests on reading the situation in the twentieth century back into earlier periods. That, however, is a flawed way to approach the sixteenth century: it was the slave-raiding Crimean Tatars who attacked Moscow then. In the Time of Troubles, however, the situation changed, and it was to be the Poles who seized the city.

Muscovy had benefited from the reign of Vasilii II (1425-62) onwards from a series of rulers who were conscious of power, determined, not frivolous, and in particular sought to avoid splitting their authority amongst heirs, as with the division of the Habsburg inheritance by Charles V. Muscovite government demanded much from itself and the people, and mobilised the latter as well as natural resources, successfully creating a service state that was maintained in the face of other influences and pressures, including Westernisation through increasing contact.

{ 4 }

A TROUBLED AGE
The Seventeenth Century

Boris Godunov, Tsar from 1598, was initially successful but then faced growing problems, largely as a result of poor weather and the resulting crop failures from 1601. He suffered from the 'Little Ice Age' of the period. In the 1604 Bolotnikov Uprising, Godonuv was challenged by a man claiming to be Dmitri, the youngest son of Ivan the Terrible, who had died aged eight in 1591. Rumour repeatedly had great political consequence. The False Dmitri's claims provided the cover for opposition to Godonuv and to reject him as a usurper, and in that year, supported by some Polish nobles, the False Dmitri invaded Russia and raised support among the Cossacks, an essentially autonomous social group living in the southern regions of Russia and Poland. The success of the False Dmitri's cavalry thwarted the initial attempt to defeat him that December. However, as a reminder of the need to advance hierarchies of relative military success with care, the second battle at Dobrynichi in January 1605 had a different outcome. The success of the False Dmitri's cavalry on the right flank was followed this time by an unsuccessful attack on the centre, which was repelled by Russian infantry protected by mobile fortifications. Designed to diminish vulnerability to steppe cavalry, such fortifications were a characteristic of Russian campaigning.

A Troubled Age: The Seventeenth Century

Although a serious defeat followed by the mass execution of prisoners, as was the norm with rebellions, Dobrynichi, like many battles in civil wars, did not mean the end of the conflict because it did not lead the False Dmitri and his supporters to surrender, which was the only way to end the war. The rebellion continued, Godunov died in April 1605 aged 52, and his weak 16-year-old son, Feodor II, deserted by many of the *boyars*, was overthrown and murdered in Moscow that June in a coup by the supporters of the False Dmitri, who was then proclaimed Tsar. However, his Polish and Catholic connections helped make him unpopular and he, in turn, was overthrown and killed in May 1606 by a mob as part of a conspiracy organised by Prince Vasilii Shuiskii, who was proclaimed Tsar. Rivalries between the *boyars* were an important part of the instability of these years, or, looked at differently, this instability was the politics of the period. Thus, *boyar* opponents of Godunov, notably the Romanovs and Shuiskys (Feodor Romanov being released from monastic imprisonment and made Metropolitan of Rostov), were restored to favour when the Godunovs fell in 1605 and the first False Dmitri came to power.

Rebellion persisted in southern Muscovy, without any particular battles of note, until in December 1606 rebel forces under Ivan Bolotnikov, who claimed to be acting for Dmitri (although he could no longer produce him), were defeated at Kolomenskoe as a result of the defection of their second-in-command and his men. Defection was important again in May 1607, when Shuiskii's forces were defeated on the Pchelnia River by those of the False Peter, another claimant to the throne. Betrayal as the battle-winner reflected the porous nature of allegiance in a complex civil conflict. It was also commonplace in much civil (and not only civil) conflict elsewhere, notably in India.

In June 1607, the army of Bolotnikov en route to join that of the False Peter was heavily defeated at Vosma by Shuiskii. He thereafter besieged and captured Tula as a result of the damming up of the River Upa which flooded the city. Bolotnikov was then executed. In July 1611, the city of Novgorod fell to the Swedes when a gate in the walls was opened by a traitor.

The second False Dmitri invaded, with Polish support, in September 1607, but he could not capture Moscow, although Shuiskii could not defeat him. The war became a matter of trying to win noble support, of raids designed to hit opponents' supplies and force them to retreat, and of a quest for foreign intervention. Swedish support for Shuiskii outweighed Polish backing for the False Dmitri in 1609, although the weaknesses of the latter's support base were as significant, as was the skill of Mikhail Skopin-Shuiskii, the Tsar's nephew and general: in civil wars, such personal links are crucial in the choice of commanders. Full-scale Polish intervention in 1610 combined with a collapse of support for the Tsar. He was suspected of murdering his allegedly ambitious nephew, and the Tsar was abandoned by his Swedish mercenaries. This crisis culminated in the overthrow of Shuiskii in July 1610, again in a conspiracy involving noble leadership and mob action. Shuiskii was forcibly made a monk.

At Klushino, the Poles defeated a much larger Russian army (including a Swedish auxiliary corps), the Polish cavalry relying on shock charges. Polish troops entered Moscow in September 1610, and its *boyars* swore allegiance to Władysław, the eldest son of Sigismund III of Poland, who was acclaimed as Tsar. Shuiskii was taken to Warsaw. The major fortress of Smolensk was stormed by the Poles in 1611 after its walls had been breached.

Polish intervention came about because of opportunity, in the shape of the disunity of Russia and the collapse of its central government, and the apparent possibility of forging a dynastic union and perhaps bringing Russia into the Catholic fold. Polish leaders also saw an opportunity to send rebellious noblemen to Muscovy so that they did not cause problems at home.

Opposition in Russia to the prospect of Polish control and Catholicism, however, resulted in rising opposition and the besieged Polish garrison in Moscow surrendered in October 1612. The only way the Russians would have accepted Władysław in the longer term would have been if he had converted to Orthodoxy and 'gone native'. Stalin was convinced both from his experience of conflict with Poland during the Russian Civil War and from his reading of the Time of Troubles that the Poles were a threat to Russia and had to be weakened and brought under control.

The hostile reaction to Władysław led in 1613 to the election of a new tsar, Mikhail Romanov, whose family was to reign until 1917. Mikhail was the son of the Patriarch of Moscow, Feodor Romanov. His choice by the *Zemsky Sobor* (Assembly of the Land) apparently owed much to the fact he was not a foreigner, and some of the *boyars* may have believed that he was malleable. At the same time, the explanations offered were later rationalisations, and the particular politics of the moment were also significant in the selection of a family that was not the most exalted in dynastic terms. The *Zemsky Sobor* consisted of members of the upper and middle service classes, townsmen, and some clergy. Peasants were excluded.

Mikhail restored order. The Cossacks were brought under restraint, the second False Dmitri had already been murdered in December 1610, and the return of stability within Russia was followed by a stabilisation of the international system. Władysław and a Polish army was able to advance as far as Moscow in September 1618, but he failed to take the city, and that year Poland and Russia agreed a truce at Deulino that left Smolensk in Polish hands. Inconclusive fighting between Sweden and Russia from 1613 resulted in the Treaty of Stolbovo in 1617, a compromise peace under which Russia was able to regain Novgorod.

Tsar from 1613 until his death aged 49 in 1645, Mikhail was a consolidator, with his father a key figure in his early years. Somewhat weak, Mikhail was manipulated by the Cherkaskii faction until 1633, when the senior Cherkaskii died, and then by the Sheremetev faction. Consolidation principally involved dealing with external challenges and thus sustaining the overcoming of the Time of Troubles. As so often, the interaction of wider international geopolitics was crucial, not least the benefit for Russia brought by conflict between Poland and Sweden in the 1620s. However, peace between the two in 1629, one that served French interests by allowing Swedish intervention in Germany against the Habsburgs, was followed by a recurrence of crisis between Poland and Russia.

Yet, the latter benefited greatly from Gustavus Adolphus of Sweden intervening in the Thirty Years' War from 1630, which lasted until 1648, rather than attacking Russia.

Mikhail, conscious of Swedish military developments and dissatisfied with the *streltsy*, the permanent infantry units equipped with arquebuses founded in 1550, decided in 1630 to form 'new order' military units, officered mainly by foreigners and trained in Western European methods. Eight such regiments, totalling about 17,000 men, amounted to half the Russian army in the War of Smolensk with Poland (1632-4). This conflict met Swedish hopes for a second front against the Poles.

As with Kazan in 1552, a siege was a key determinant of success and indicator both of long-term developments and of the short-term factors that affected campaigning. The Russian siege of Smolensk, fortified even more strongly by the Poles using Italian-style bastions, was unsuccessful, and the Polish relief army under Władysław IV (r. 1632-48) inflicted a heavy defeat on the Russians. The siege was broken in September 1633, and, in October, the Poles fought their way round the Russians, so that their position was enveloped. Without relief, the Russian army surrendered on 1 March 1634. The 'new order' troops proved less experienced that Poland's mercenaries, although the principal reasons for the failure to capture Smolensk was the delayed arrival of Russian artillery due to poor weather and primitive roads, and the operational flexibility the Poles enjoyed thanks to their superiority in cavalry. This superiority enabled them to win the struggle for territory and supplies once the siege was raised. The Russian infantry lost its ability to operate offensively.

A Crimean Tatar invasion of central Muscovy during the Smolensk campaign in 1633 that led to the enslavement of large numbers of captives helped force Mikhail's government to negotiate peace with the Poles at Polyanovka in 1634, paying a large war indemnity in return for Władysław surrendering his claims to the Russian throne. Mikhail then turned his attention to the securing of Muscovy's southern steppe frontier. As with the Crimean Tatar advance to Moscow in 1571, this was a reminder of the significance of the southern frontier, a continuing factor that long helped determine the strategic geography of Russia.

Mikhail was not a victorious expansionist, but set the scene for his son and successor, Alexis (1629-76; r. 1645-76). Again, foreign policy and war dominated his reign, but there was also the recurrence of domestic tension, although not at all with the intensity and length of the Time of Troubles. In 1648, as in many other European countries in the 1640s, there was a rising in Moscow, in part in opposition to Boris Morozov, a *boyar* who had acted as Alexis' tutor, and who had just married the sister of the Tsar's new wife. High taxes, notably on salt, and suspicion of Morozov, provoked the murderous Salt Riot, with Alexis obliged to dismiss Morozov, just as Mazarin in France, Olivares in Spain, and Stafford in England also had to go. With his personal ability and drive ensuring that he gained the initiative, Alexis was able to turn from concessions to reprisals, with Morozov returning to power. His son, Peter the Great, showed the same characteristics. Alexis was well aware of the international context. Anger with the execution of Charles I of England in 1649 led the Tsar to expel the (English) Muscovy Company, though it swiftly regained its position.

The violence in Russia in 1648 was a clear sign of social tension, in part concerning and then leading to the accentuation of serfdom, a prevalent social practice that was closely linked to the character of power, including its extension through Muscovite and then Russian imperialism. Serfdom was a system of forced labour based on hereditary bondage to the land. Its purpose was to provide a fixed labour supply, particularly a mass agricultural labour force, and the legal essence of it was a form of personal service to a lord in exchange for the right to cultivate the soil. It was distinct from slavery, both legally and linguistically. But the word *rab* or slave was sometimes used when referring to serfs. With severe restrictions on personal freedom, serfs could be bought and sold, and families could be split up or moved against their will.

Russian slaves comprised as much as 10-15 per cent of the seventeenth-century population, for the most part consisting of limited contract slavery, wherein one sold himself/herself into slavery and remained the owner's slave until either the owner or the slave died. In large part, this was a 'welfare measure' in a society that provided no state support. Muscovite slavery, which enjoyed a major upsurge from the 1560s when serfdom also developed, was a 'moderate' strain, not the chattel slavery type of the Roman Empire and the Americas.

Townsmen were part of the serfdom world in the sense that they (artisans, draftsmen and others) were bonded labour and tied in place, but towns in their entirety were not part of the serfdom world if the town lacked an owner. Although they differed greatly in age, size and other factors, such places were subject to the same regulations and contrasted legally with settlements that were the property of an individual or an institution.

Labour shortages, not least as a result of the population stagnation of the seventeenth century, meant that landlords sought to prevent the flight of their serfs, a flight made more possible by the major expansion of Russia in the period, notably eastward into Siberia and southward into the Ukrainian borderlands. Strengthening controls over the peasantry was an aspect of a wider attempt to impose control, grasp the future and protect the present, an attempt that brought that brought tsar, service classes and the central administration together

The rights of the serfs were even more circumscribed in the *Sobornoe Ulozhenie*, the legal code of 1649 promulgated by the *Zemsky Sobor*. Surviving until 1832, this code replaced that of 1550 introduced by Ivan the Terrible, and it brought slaves and free peasants together as serfs. The code satisfied the upper service and middle service classes, some urban interests, and the Church. The code firmly immobilised the peasantry and townsmen and eliminated tax-exempt areas and households in towns. Earlier, the Muscovites adopted the Mongol system of tax assessment wherein fields and towns were judged on the basis of the money they could generate. If peasants and townsmen departed, fewer people had to pay the same overall tax amount, so that per person the amount of taxation rose. That changed in 1678 with the adoption of the household tax.

Furthermore, rulers made few efforts to see that surviving rights were observed. Serfs were subject to their landlords and outside the normal legal system for all but the most serious criminal offences until the 1860s. Landlords had a powerful incentive to protect serfs from the demands of the state, and from adverse economic and environmental circumstances that could affect their labour force. However, the succession of a new landlord could transform the tolerable into the merely survivable. At any rate, the profit of the agricultural economy did not reach the serfs to any worthwhile extent.

The situation was inherently unstable, with periodic violence against conditions. There was a more general failure to perform obligations adequately, and a reluctance to consider new demands. 'To work as you work on the demesne' (the landlord's land) described indolence. Demands considered excessive were commonly not fulfilled, and outright malingering was widespread. Flight was another response to adverse circumstances, and the attempt to prevent it by harsh laws was weakened by the willingness of many landlords to receive runaways.

Most violence was small-scale and directed against property, whether theft, the killing or maiming of the landlord's animals, or the destruction of his property. Yet, insurrection could become an element as in the Time of Troubles. In addition, Alexis faced a major rebellion under the leadership of Stenka Razin. It was mounted along the Volga Valley in 1670 by disaffected Cossacks, serfs, townsmen, priests and members of the middle service class (service cavalry). Some of the serfs had run away from conscription. In the rebellion, landlords were slaughtered alongside officials, but the army was deployed to overcome it in 1671.

Meanwhile, although of limited immediate significance, Siberia had been overrun from the 1580s, ensuring that for the first time China acquired a land frontier with a European state. Siberia was a vast area inhabited by small numbers of nomadic and semi-nomadic peoples who were well attuned to the hunting, fishing and pastoral possibilities of their environment. Siberia was also the world's leading source of fur, a vital form of wealth and prestige. Russian access had long been blocked by the Khanate of Kazan, but its capture by Ivan IV in 1552 made possible an advance to the Urals and then across the accessible southern Urals, through which there were a number of low passes.

In 1581, an 800-strong Cossack force under Yermak Timofeyevich, in the service of the Stroganov merchant family, conquered the Tatar Khanate of Sibir' in 1582 after several battles. Their firearms gave them a major advantage over their opponent's bows and arrows, but the Tatars were superior in numbers and mobility and in 1585 wiped out most of Yermak's force. The Siberian Tatars were not overcome until 1598. As a result, Ottoman links with Sunni co-religionists in Central Asia were cut.

With serious logistical problems, it was difficult to replace stores of powder and shot and they had to be used with care, but the Cossacks in Russian service employed firearms effectively in their subsequent advance across Siberia. This advance was anchored by the construction of towns including those at Samara and Ufa, both of which are to the west of the Urals and not in Siberia, and at Tyumen (1586), Tobolsk, near the site of Sibir' (1587), Yeniseysk (1619), Yakutsk (1632) and Okhotsk (1647). By 1650, Russia's borders were essentially the same as those today, although conspicuously not in the Russian Far East. The Pacific had been first reached by 1633, and a post was then established at the mouth of the Ulya river. Russian towns were typically stockaded, and each contained buildings of control and power: a fort, a barracks, a prison, a church and the governor's residence. Forts maximised the defensive potential of firearms, although Okhotsk was stormed by the Tungus in 1654.

As with the earlier Russian conquest of Kazan, and the more general processes of imperial expansion, resistance was weakened by local divisions. Several of the mutually hostile Siberian tribes provided the Russians with support. The Russians exploited conflicts on the Yenisey between Kets and Tungus, gaining the support of some of the former against the latter. Prominent Tatars and others who agreed to become vassals of the Tsar were allowed to retain their position in return for military service.

A Troubled Age: The Seventeenth Century

Those who resisted were treated barbarously. A combination of the cruel way in which the Russians extorted *yasak* – forced-tribute in furs – the seizure of local women, and the spread of new diseases, particularly from the 1630s smallpox, led to a dramatic fall in the population. This fall hit native capacity for resistance. Eighty per cent of Yakuts perished due to smallpox. However, successful resistance to Russian expansion continued in north-east Siberia and Kamchatka. Again, there was a clear parallel with Spanish expansion in the Americas.

In south-west Siberia, where the Russian frontier of settlement advanced southwards, the Russians had to fight warlike horsemen who were able to acquire firearms technology by capturing Russian guns or by illegal trade. Yenisey Kirghiz were using guns against the Russians as early as the 1640s. The Russians found it necessary to construct fortified lines in south Siberia, such as the Ishim Line, just as they did in European Russia with the Tula, Belgorod and Izium Lines.

They also reached the limit of their effectiveness further east where, in 1683-9, larger Chinese forces drove the Russians from both the Amur basin and from lands to the north, sustaining sieges of the Russian fortress at Albazin. In this period, the Chinese also proved more successful in the forest zone than the Russians. Thereafter, Russia did not expand in the Amur basin until the late 1850s. However, Russian achievements (and failures) in Siberia were peripheral to those of rulers focused on west of the Urals. In part, this was a matter of the practicalities of distance and environment, but goals and priorities were more significant factors.

Further west, in Ukraine, there was a use of defensive positions in support of cavalry patrols to move Russian power southwards, with the construction in the 1580s and 1590s of garrison towns such as Belgorod and Voronezh. This process continued in the seventeenth century, with successive southward advances. The Russian policy of exploiting local divisions had only limited success in the northern Caucasus, where Russian attempts to create anti-Ottoman coalitions failed in the 1580s and 1590s, and

Russian expeditions were totally routed in 1594 and 1605. Persia, not the Ottoman Empire or Russia, became the dominant power in the region.

Far more significant, and not only in the short term, was the revival of conflict from 1648 when the Cossacks rebelled against Polish control. Alexis saw both opportunity and the need to intervene, not least to protect Russia against Poland: there was no sense of clearly opposed identities or obvious boundaries. In 1654, at Pereiaslav, a small town south-east of Kiev, Alexis took the Dnieper Cossacks under his protection, with the Cossack leaders swearing loyalty. Alexis then moved his troops into Ukraine. The agreement in 1654 was subsequently to prove a matter of contention, with Russian commentators emphasising a juncture that Ukrainians were to see as more conditional. This has lasted to the present, with the current modern Russian government very much influenced by the Soviet-era presentation of 1654 as a union of two fraternal peoples, a precursor to the Soviet Union, with the Russians senior in both. The events of 1654 launched the Thirteen Years War of 1654-67 with Poland in which Alexis also set out to conquer modern Belarus. He wanted to recover Smolensk, which he did in 1654, Chernigov and Seversk, but victory that year led him to expand his objectives, overrunning much of Lithuania in 1655 and offering protection to Gdańsk, a major Baltic port. Further south, another Russian army invaded Galicia and threatened Lwów.

There was a strong religious element, with Russian troops sprinkled with Holy Water and fighting under holy banners, officers ordered to take communion, and Orthodox churches built in captured towns. A similar religious complexion was in evidence in Russia's struggle with Germany in the world wars and with Ukraine from 2022, especially once serious difficulties were encountered. Thus in 2025, Patriarch Kirill, the head of the Russian Orthodox Church, sent crosses and religious icons bearing President Putin's initials to Russian commanders for the Orthodox Christmas. Some Russian troops in Ukraine received icons featuring images of Putin for Orthodox Easter in 2023.

A Troubled Age: The Seventeenth Century

In 1655, as a reminder that a number of powers were involved, Charles X of Sweden also attacked Poland. In turn, attempting to stop Swedish expansion, Alexis in 1656 attacked Charles, following up by allying with Poland in return for the promise of the succession to the Crown, a promise that was readily made as Poland did not have a hereditary monarchy, the situation in Russia in the Time of Troubles. The Russians overran most of (Swedish-ruled) Livonia, but well-fortified Riga successfully resisted Russian siege. There was a clear economic dimension to this as Riga was one of the major ports for exports to Western Europe, and therefore for the profits to be had, in particular the trade in naval stores, including tar and hemp, that had secure markets in Britain, the Netherlands and elsewhere.

As so often, the emphasis should be on difficulties as well as expansion. Alexis was exhausted by several years campaigning and could not sustain a war on so many fronts. In 1658, he found himself faced with Polish and Crimean Tatar attacks and with trouble in Ukraine, where the Cossack élite was increasingly concerned about Russian intentions and therefore turned to Poland. In response, Alexis sought to limit Ukrainian autonomy and abandoned his hopes of a Baltic seaport, signing a truce with Sweden.

Once Sweden settled with Poland, Russia, fighting alone, was left exposed to Polish pressure. The conscription of serfs and slaves which started in 1655, a form of Muscovite *levée-en-masse* replacing an earlier emphasis on a specialised military, did not yield well-trained or well-motivated troops for Alexis and led to a major rebellion under Stenka Razin (see above). The conscripted recruits were put into the 'new order' military units established in the 1630s, which were greatly expanded. The end of the Thirty Years' War and the British civil wars meant that many mercenaries could be hired from elsewhere in Europe. Overall, they offered decent training, although there were considerable variations. The major problem was sub-standard leadership at the top.

Exhausted by the length of the conflict, by stalemate, and by economic strains including coinage debasement, Alexis in 1667 accepted the Truce of Andrusovo, a 13-year truce tthat left him with eastern Belarus, Smolensk, eastern Ukraine and Kiev, while the Poles retained western Ukraine. This offered Russia a new steppe frontier designed to offer protection against the Crimean Tatars. The Belgorod and Simbirsk Lines built between 1635 and 1654 had provided defences, but were joined in 1679-80 by the Izium Line further south, which protected the region today of Kharkiv in Ukraine and a part of Donetsk. The context and compromise were very different in the politics, international and domestic, of the late 2020s.

As a reminder of the very different narratives that could be offered, these years also saw an attempt to settle Church differences. The Tsar convened a synod in Moscow in order to depose Patriarch Nikon of Moscow, who had pushed through reforms designed to bring the Church more into line with Greek practice, not least in revising service-books and in regulating Church construction and the form of icons. Nikon was a particularly dominant figure in 1652-8, close to Alexis, only to lose power in 1658 when he was seen as encroaching on the position of the Tsar. When he was deposed, however, his reforms were endorsed. The opponents of this, notably Avvakum Petrov, were known as the Old Believers.

It is possible to present Russian expansion under Alexis as the key theme, but in the 1670s and early 1680s it was rather the Ottomans who appeared to be the key players, pressing both Poland and Russia hard. In 1676, Podolia, part of western Ukraine, was ceded by Poland to the Ottomans. That year, Alexis was succeeded by his eldest son, Feodor III (1661-82, r. 1676-82), and, after defeat in 1678, the Russians agreed by the 1681 Treaty of Bakhchisarai to a 20-year truce, to the Dnieper River as a border line, and that the Russians would pay an annual tribute to the Crimean Tatars as the cost of retaining eastern Ukraine and Kiev. Luckily for Feodor, the Ottomans turned to exploit Hungarian opposition to the Habsburgs, encouraging them to make peace with Russia.

Ill, possibly due to scurvy, Feodor had progressive views that prefigured those of Peter the Great, not least considering merit rather than pedigree in appointments, but he died young and childless. Competition over the succession led to rioting in 1682, with the Moscow regiments of the *streltsy* killing prominent opponents. Stability of a type was provided by Feodor's brother, Ivan V (1666-96, r. 1682-96), youngest son of Alexis by his first wife, becoming co-ruler, as senior Tsar, with his half-brother, Peter I (1672-1725, r. 1682-1725) as junior. Ivan's older sister, Sophia (1657-1704; Regent 1682-9), an opponent of Peter's claims, was made Regent. The first woman to rule Russia, her regency saw the development of female accounts of traditional conventions of rule, which prepared for the four sovereign Tsarinas of the following century: Catherine I (r. 1725-7), Anna (r. 1730-40), Elizabeth (r. 1741-62), and Catherine II, the Great, (r. 1762-96).

Sophia relied on Prince Vasilii Golitsyn as the head of the government. He backed a more assertive stance in foreign policy. The Treaty of Perpetual Peace with Poland of 1686 confirmed the 1667 Truce of Andrusovo and committed Russia to the anti-Ottoman coalition. Russia fought until 1700. The focus on Ottomans and Tatars from 1677 differed from the general emphasis from the 1560s on Western opponents, but it reflected contextual circumstances and opportunities. The permanent cession of Kiev by Poland in 1686 was significant for the focus on the Ottomans and the Tatars. Peter was to establish a major fortress there. The possibility of defeating the Ottomans was offered by their isolation in the face of the coalition created as a result of the total Ottoman failure at the siege of Vienna in 1683. Subsequently, there was a major Austrian advance into central Hungary.

Initially, however, this war did not go well for Russia. While Austria, Poland and Venice all made significant gains from the Ottomans, Russian advances on Crimea in 1687 and 1689 failed with heavy losses, in part due to severe logistical problems, which were accentuated by the Tatars setting the steppe alight. By advancing as a single force, which provided a margin of safety, the Russians increased their already serious logistical problems arising from the limited amount of food and water available on the steppe and the need for large supply trains. Defences across the Isthmus of Perekop at the northern approach to Crimea helped thwart the 1689 offensive. These failures contributed to a political crisis in Russia in 1689. Golitsyn's return was greeted with a 'cover-up' campaign of receptions, prayers, rewards and eulogies, but the court factions opposed to Sophia were encouraged by the failure. Sophia was pushed aside by Peter, who benefited from Ivan's weakness. Sophia was sent to a convent for the rest of her life, while Golitsyn was banished to internal exile. Paradoxically, Peter was to do far worse against the Ottomans in 1711, but without these consequences.

Very different in character, context and consequences to the contemporaneous 'Glorious Revolution' in Britain in 1688-9, though similarly linked to a division within a royal family, the crisis left Peter committed to the war with the Ottomans while uncertain of his control over the army. Luckily, the Ottomans focused their efforts on Austria, which fought on until 1699. In the event, and in contradiction to an Austrian promise in 1697 to fight on so that Peter could obtain Kerch, he only gained Azov, which he had captured in 1696, in the peace treaty. This was a more peripheral target than Crimea.

Peter was a junior partner in the conflict with Charles XII of Sweden that began in 1700, a project developed by Frederick IV of Denmark and Augustus II of Saxony and Poland. The scheme offered Peter a limited role and few conquests, whereas Augustus was allocated Livonia and was hopeful that he would be able to increase his power in Poland. Neither was welcome to Peter, who was heavily defeated by Charles XII at Narva in 1700. The new century appeared to be beginning very badly, with isolation in his peace settlement with the Ottomans, and a minor and unsuccessful role against the Swedes, mutually reinforcing suggestions that Russia was far from a great power and that Peter would achieve less than his father, Alexis.

{ 5 }

PETER THE GREAT TO CATHERINE THE GREAT
The Eighteenth Century

In 1776, Adam Smith observed:

> Whoever examines, with attention, the improvements which Peter the Great [r. 1689-1725] introduced into the Russian empire, will find that they almost all resolve themselves into the establishment of a well-regulated standing army. It is the instrument which executes and maintains all his other regulations. That degree of order and internal peace, which that empire has ever since enjoyed, is altogether owing to the influence of that army.

In 1755, Frederick II, 'the Great' of Prussia replied to a suggestion from his then ally France that Augustus III of Saxony-Poland be encouraged to prevent the possible movement of Russian troops through Poland in order to attack Prussia, by arguing that the Poles would be able to resist for a fortnight only, that they would fail, and that the consequence would be the ruin of the state. Like his father, Frederick William I in 1725-6, Frederick II was prepared to defy Russia, but in general Prussia's concern about Russian strength encouraged caution. In 1726 a fearful Frederick William had switched sides, taking care not to defy Russia for the rest of his reign, including when the Russians invaded and occupied Poland in 1733-5. This was an aspect of the hegemony that Russia managed to create over much of Eastern Europe. Achieved in 1708-74, although stemming from longer-term international and domestic developments, this hegemony lasted until 1989, albeit with very serious interruptions in 1917-20 and 1941-4.

There were complex interrelationships in Russian geopolitics. Most notably, between 1697 and 1763 successive opportunities for conflict with the Ottomans were not pursued because of Russian concerns about European (excluding the Ottomans) power politics; although the extent to which there was a consistent Russian strategic culture is unclear, because such an argument underrates the central role of politics, both domestic (at Court and within the tsar's advisory council) and international, in Russian policy. This is a point that is still relevant today.

Russia's success in defeating Sweden in 1709-10, and again in 1742, and in overawing Poland in 1710, 1733-5 and 1768-72, was the precondition for the campaigning against the Ottomans in 1711, 1735-9, 1768-74 and 1787-92. In 1739, when the Russians were making major advances at the expense of the Ottomans, the French encouraged the Swedes to threaten Russia in order to distract them. In the event, Russia made peace with the Ottomans that year because its defeated ally, Austria, had already done so, but Russian gains in the treaty were far less than in the war.

In contrast to the Ottomans, the frontier with China, fixed in 1689 and 1728 by the Treaties of Nerchinsk and Kyakhta, which respectively excluded Russia from the Amur Valley and settled the border, was seen as acceptable. This was an acknowledgement that Russia could not advance south into what became the Vladivostok region, let alone Manchuria. Aspirations that were viable in the late nineteenth century were not feasible two centuries earlier, or at least not pursued. The Manchu had conquered Ming China in the 1640s and 1650s. The Russians were not to seek to do the same.

Peter the Great to Catherine the Great: The Eighteenth Century

Ambitions, however, were pursued in the case of Persia, where the now weak Safavid dynasty was badly affected by a victorious Afghan invasion in 1721-2 and, partly in order to thwart possible developments, Ottoman intervention followed. Yet again, Russia sought to benefit from the rivalries of others. Peter's presence with the invading troops in 1722 on what was a distant front was an indication of the significance of the campaign. In 1723, Baku and Rasht were occupied, and Shah Tahmasp II of Persia was persuaded to yield by the Treaty of St Petersburg the provinces along the southern and western shores of the Caspian. This was marginal in impact and extent compared to the Afghan and Ottoman interventions. The Treaty of Constantinople of 1724 between Russia and the Ottomans divided much of Persia, but the Ottomans made more consequential gains.

At war for most of his reign, Peter necessarily had a somewhat *ad hoc* or expedient response to the implementation of his often bold domestic reform policies. Yet, however much a response to problems, notably the political instability of the 1680s and 1690s and to the need to support military efforts, the ambition was impressive. Although his authority looked back to Muscovite influences, Peter sought to modernize his country to a degree that was alien to his royal predecessors and to his counterparts, although there were reform aspirations and attempts elsewhere in Europe, notably in Prussia, Britain and France. Drawing heavily on current Western models – Swedish and Prussian in government, British and Dutch in technology and trade – Peter helped to give Russian government and élite society a Western orientation, widening the gulf between them and the bulk of the population, among whom he was widely perceived as a diabolical changeling and an Antichrist.

There was a cultural dimension to this Westernisation. Under Peter, there was a great increase in the number of book titles and quantity of copies published, a move to secular topics, and an insistence on the use of secular language more in them; these developments were designed to increase the tempo of modernity, aof modernity, although in the seventeenth century about 95 per cent of the population was fully illiterate, and the use of Swedish and German administrative and military terminology was conceptually beyond the understanding of most people. Under Peter and his successors, Russian leaders and commentators came to regard themselves as the bearers of reforming, indeed Enlightenment, values and to see their neighbours, both Islamic and Polish, in the light of a civilizational hierarchy. This approach encouraged imperial expansion and interacted with the increasingly insistent tendency of Western European intellectuals to present Eastern Europe as unimportant, if not primitive, in comparison.

Peter had a complex personality, which probably derived from the uncertainties of his upbringing, notably his witnessing of the murder of relatives and others in the *streltsy* (musketeers) revolt of 1682, and from the failure of his first marriage. Peter's treatment of his son Alexis was a consequence. Rejecting a sacral image for monarchy, Peter's energetic determination nevertheless retained an autocratic reality. Peter, however, faced aristocratic factionalism at Court that he could not control but had to accommodate and seek to lead. This ensured an essential continuity between his reign and those of his predecessors and successors.

As a boy, Peter had displayed curiosity and an engagement with Western mechanical objects and with military affairs. Subsequently, his travels were very important, especially for exposing Peter far more to Western influences, notably in 1697-8 when he visited London and Holland and was particularly interested in shipbuilding, although this was brought to an end by the *streltsy* rising of 1698 that was intended to restore Sophia. In the winter of 1716-17, Peter revisited the Netherlands, spending most of his time in Amsterdam. He was only too happy to revert to his Dutch shipwright's identity as 'Pieter Baas', worked with bellows and hammer in a blacksmith's shop at Zaandam and is reported to have objected when some Dutch merchants addressed him as 'Your Majesty', replying 'Come brothers, let us converse like plain and honest ships carpenters.' Going on to Paris in 1717, Peter drank much and, allegedly, had sex with a prostitute in the bed of the recently dead 'Sun King', Louis XIV. Whether true or not, the contemporary account captured a sense of Peter as assertive and disruptive, no respecter of status or norms.

The new capital Peter founded at St Petersburg on the River Neva symbolized the new Westward-looking attitude and was far closer than Moscow to the rest of Europe, in distance, travel time, and accessibility. The city was founded in 1703 and the court and government transferred in stages from 1709. Moscow, the epitome of old Russia, was no longer acceptable to Peter as the capital. With its determined emphasis on novelty, and a breach with the past that may have owed much to his drive to protect himself from the uncertainties of his youth, Peter's reign marked a potentially radical departure in the use of state power, as well as in Russian history. The 'Europeanisation of Russian culture' he encouraged, whatever the myth, did not start, but was important at the governmental and élite levels.

In practice, change, novelty and radicalism at the level of the state, for example the reform of town administration in 1699, provincial administration in 1708, and of central government in 1717, were tempered by the nature of administration, especially the difficulties of ensuring effectiveness for new bureaucratic mechanisms such as the Colleges created in 1717, and by the apathy, if not resistance, of the bulk of the population towards Peter's policies. To an extent, the myth of Peter's reign was in some ways more important than the reality. His legacy was a troublesome one, both with respect to the long-term development of Russia and, in the short term, as far as his successors were concerned. This was especially so for his son Alexis, who was killed in 1718 as a consequence of his opposition to his father. This was more extreme than the response to the opposition of other heirs, including the future George II of Britain, Frederick the Great, Charles Emmanuel III of Sardinia, and Paul I of Russia.

As with much else, Peter's military reforms were prefigured by his predecessors, notably Alexis and Golitsyn. That there were failures in the 1680s and 1690s did not mean that Peter had to start afresh. However, a large standing army maintained out of tax revenues did not become a reality until Peter's reign. A major reorganisation of the army was carried out in 1699-1700. Regulations drawn up in 1698, and possibly written in part by Peter, emphasised the importance of regular armies, organised in a hierarchical fashion and maintained by training. In November 1699, Peter ordered the creation of 29 'new' (Western) regiments. They were designed to be both permanent and regularly trained, and their novelty was expressed in part by their German-style uniforms.

Peter therefore continued his father's rejection of dependence upon the noble cavalry of the feudal host, whose defects were castigated in *On the Conduct of the Army*, an essay in 1701 by Ivan Pososhkov, an advocate of reform, notably in economic matters, who came from an artisan background. As an instance of the problems of debating policy, the publication of his *The Book of Poverty and Wealth* (1724), which argued that the prosperity of Russia depended on that of the population, sought to reduce poverty and criticized corruption, led to his arrest in 1725. He died in prison the following year.

The crushing defeat at Narva led Peter to press ahead with his policy based on the 1655-6 practice of one recruit for twenty households. They were made responsible for his replacement if killed or incapacitated. New regiments were created by Peter, twelve in 1705-7 alone, and by 1707 the army was perhaps about 200,000 strong. The well-established practice of recruiting foreign officers continued and indeed was expanded as a consequence of the need to provide skills for the new Baltic navy. More generally, Peter was governing in the Muscovite mould.

This, however, was not true of the navy. A fleet was constructed for the Azov campaign in 1696, foreign experts were imported, and Russians sent abroad to learn shipbuilding. The subsequent development of the fleet reflected both Peter's personal enthusiasm for it, which led him to devote a lot of time to its details, and the need to challenge Sweden for control of the Baltic if Russia was to succeed in dislocating the structure of the Swedish empire and preventing a Swedish reconquest of her eastern Baltic provinces, lost to Russia in 1710. A naval academy and a large admiralty yard were constructed at St Petersburg and a school of navigation at Moscow, although Pososhkov criticised the wasteful means of selecting and delivering timbers for the navy. By Peter's death (1725) Russia had a fleet of 34 ships of the line and numerous galleys, and these played a major role in forcing Sweden to make peace in 1721 and in threatening Sweden with attack in 1723 and 1726-7.

Military education was an important theme in Peter's reforms. He founded artillery and engineering schools, while officers were trained by service as ordinary soldiers in the guards regiments. Peter insisted on progressing through the ranks himself and tried to ensure that no noble received a commission without some form of training. Peter's attempt to make state service (whether in the military or in government) a central focus for the aspiration of many, led to the proliferation of uniforms, a mark both of service and of the state's role in allocating rank. Peter was the first monarch to require all Russian soldiers to wear specified uniforms. For the nobility, military uniforms replaced gold-threaded robes as their principal dress, and beards were shorn.

Under Peter, the armed forces, particularly the army, replaced the Church, with which his relations were poor, as the lodestar of monarchical action and, to an extent, of national unity. Instead of a semi-sacral figure, Peter made the monarch a military leader. The nature of his successors from 1725 to 1796 – four women, one youth and only one adult male, Peter III, whose reign was very short – prevented the consolidation of this image. Nevertheless, there was no return to the earlier presentation of monarchy. In particular, there was less emphasis on sacral monarchy, while Peter differentiated the person of the monarch from the state and in so doing in theory undid the Muscovite patrimonial concept of the Grand Prince/Tsar owning all of Muscovy and his subjects as his own personal property.

Peter transformed relations with the Church by enacting general religious toleration, which was effectively limited to Christians, in 1702. The Patriarchate was left vacant in 1700 and abolished in 1721, giving Peter more authority, power and influence in the Church, notably in the appointment of bishops. In 1701, the running of Church lands was brought under greater state direction to help in the mobilisation of resources for war with Sweden. The Spiritual Regulation, published in 1721, made the role of state-directed change apparent, and thus made all ecclesiastical arrangements appear tentative. The Church was put under the authority of a College, or ministry, although this body rapidly altered its title to 'Most Holy Governing Synod', which was under lay control. The Spiritual Regulation emphasised the Tsar's authority over the Synod, and so that the new bureaucratisation was still ultimately personal in character. In 1720, parish priests were ordered to announce in Church all decrees about new taxes, while Peter's principal clerical agent, Feofan Prokopovich, who became Bishop of Pskov in 1718, Vice-President of the Most Holy Governing Synod in 1721, and Archbishop of Novgorod in 1725, asked in his *Russian Primer*: 'What doth God require in the fifth commandment? He commands us to honour and obey our parents, a name which includes our sovereign, our spiritual pastors and civil governors, our teachers, benefactors and elders.'

There was also change in society, at least in so far as the regularisation of an existing emphasis on service to the ruler was concerned. As more recently with Sweden, Denmark and Prussia, in 1722 Peter issued a Table of Ranks. This provided a set of regulations by which those who already had nobility could be ranked on criteria favourable to the ruler by reference to this service, while noble status could be awarded to those who achieved high rank in his, or her, service. All officials who reached at least rank 8 received hereditary noble status and thus at least legal equality with the hereditary nobility.

Nobility of birth was also recognised in the Russian Table of Ranks, which stipulated the grant of a coat of arms to those who could demonstrate at least 100 years of noble status, despite their failure to serve. However, Peter also decreed that a born nobleman who did not serve and therefore had not achieved rank in the Table was to be regarded as inferior to a ranked commoner.

The potential radicalism of this should not be exaggerated. The Table addressed tension between 'old' and 'new' nobles, but

Peter the Great to Catherine the Great: The Eighteenth Century

Peter had to strive hard over the issue of merit, and to inculcate the nobles into the norms and expectations of state service. Indeed, the landed estates of the monarchy were nearly halved by his grants to the service nobility. Again, far from Russia being different, there were similarities to the situation elsewhere in Europe in the rewarding of noble backing.

There was no radicalism in the case of the serfs. Peter's unpopularity with them was indicated by their tendency to imagine him as an Antichrist or a changeling, rather than as a peasant Tsar, and by the failure of later pretenders to claim his name. If he allowed the peasantry to retain their traditional customs and beards, it was because he was fundamentally only interested in the élite that he wished to mould. The peasantry was designated for the service of monarch and nobility. Peter turned down suggestions that the nobility should not be rewarded with land, and that, instead, the state should retain this land and be financed by peasant taxes, because he felt that officials should own land as a matter of course. Furthermore, during the reign of Elizabeth (1741–62), the Senate consistently supported landowning nobles in their disputes with the peasantry, while the granting to the Ukrainian Cossack nobles of equality of status with the Russian nobility extended their rights over the peasantry. The process continued under Catherine II (r. 1762-96).

In the 'Summary Account of Russia as it was in the Spring of 1710', Charles Whitworth, the British envoy from 1707 to 1712, noted the process of rapid change including the introduction of Western dress and Peter's unpopular attempt to make Russians shave off their beards. Whitworth argued that the brutal forms of public punishments demonstrated the essential barbarity and backwardness of Russia. He suggested that Peter had deliberately set out to weaken the power of the old nobility, and that there was much public discontent, not least over increased taxation. Whitworth was in no doubt that the Westernisation policies were poorly handled as well as unpopular. There was a parallel in his account with Pososhkov's later critique of government practice.

Peter more generally sought to control the situation and end problems. He settled Ukraine and Baltic questions that had defied his predecessors, both crushing the rebellious Ivan Mazepa, the Hetman of the Zaporizhian Host of Cossacks who dominated eastern Ukraine in 1708, and heavily defeating Charles XII of Sweden in Poltava in Ukraine in 1709. Peter then overran Swedish-ruled Livonia (northern Latvia and southern Estonia) and Estonia in 1710, following with Finland in 1713-14. The fertile diplomatic imaginations of Russia's rivals led to many plans to reverse Peter's success, notably in a European league in 1719-21 and in a Russo-Swedish war of 1741-3, but they were all unsuccessful.

Compared to this, Russian failures, such as defeat at Narva by Charles XII in 1700 and at the hands of the Ottomans at the River Pruth in 1711, proved of limited consequence. Indeed, in 1719-74, Russia won far more success against the Ottomans than Austria, which in 1737-9, in its sole war of that period, lost territory after a costly struggle that encouraged a half-century of cessation in its Balkan expansion. When war between Austria and the Ottomans resumed in 1788-91, the Austrians were less successful than the Russians in 1787-92.

Peter guaranteed the political and religious privileges of the local German Protestant nobility when he overran Estonia and Livonia. Securing their support grounded his conquest and aided his wider modernisation programme; although he adopted a harsher position in Ukraine. In contrast, this approach to Estonia and Livonia was to be compromised by the Russification policies of the last of the Romanovs and the brutality of the Soviet Union, which helped ensure that their position, notably that of the second, was far weaker.

Success against the Ottomans, however, was territorially most significant only from victory in the war of 1768-74. Indeed, in place of a picture of inevitable triumph, it is possible to note the far more contingent character of Russian success. The conflicts of the period saw serious challenges to Russia's achievements. From 1701, Polish 'patriots' pressed for cooperation with Charles XII in order to regain the lands lost to Russia in 1667, lands which succeeding Kings of Poland on their election had sworn to reconquer. In the Polish-Swedish treaty of 1705, Charles promised to help in their reconquest, challenging the fragile territorial stability of Russia's western and southern border. In addition, this promise opened up the possibility of an alliance between Sweden, Poland and the Ottomans. In 1699, Charles had encouraged the Ottomans to continue their war with Russia.

It was fortunate for Peter that in the 1700s the Ottomans, exhausted by recent warfare, sought to avoid conflict with him, ignoring pleas for assistance from the Crimean Tatars and the opportunity for intervention in Ukraine. Furthermore, Charles, busy dealing with the issues of Polish politics, was not free to attack Russia until 1708. In practice, the conflicting interests of Russia and Sweden in Poland made peace between them impossible. Peter was fighting not only for his 'window on the west' but also to prevent Poland from becoming a Swedish client state. Peter sent money and troops to the aid of Polish nobles opposed to Charles. Through victory at Poltava, Peter surmounted that crisis in 1709.

When Peter visited England in the 1690s, he was a curiosity. By the 1710s, he was a dramatic conqueror. In the mid-1710s, Russian forces moved into northern Germany (to use the modern term) and Denmark, with Peter spending several months in Copenhagen in late 1716. He planned a joint Danish-Russian conquest of southern Sweden that was not brought to fruition, but he overwintered his army in Mecklenburg. The British government, under the influence of George I (r. 1714-27) and his Hanoverian concerns, became conspicuously hostile to the possibility of a remodelling of the international system by Peter, and notably so after George and those Hanoverian worries were crucial to ministerial changes in 1717 and to the linked Whig Split. Mecklenburg bordered Hanover.

There was no suggestion that there was any natural boundary that could, or would, block Russia's advance. In that respect, international politics and physical geography appeared as one. A political barrier to Russian expansionism had to be established. More particularly, in order to ensure that such a geographical boundary to Russian expansion did in fact pertain, it was clearly necessary for Britain to act: by diplomatic or military means, or both. *The Political State of Great Britain* for September 1719 argued that 'the interest of our British trade does demand the Czar's being again shut out of the Baltic.' However, prefiguring a similar attempt in 1790-1, the British attempt to organise a coalition to restrict Russian gains failed totally, in part due to its contradictions and in part to the impact of fiscal crisis in Britain – the South Sea Bubble. Instead, in 1721 by the Treaty of Nystad Russia's acquisition of Ingria, Estonia, and Livonia was confirmed. Finland was returned to Sweden.

Thereafter, Russian expansion continued to be regarded as a threat until Russia more commonly became an ally of Britain, its power thereby employed against other threats. International relations proved the key focus for British dealings with Russia, and that focus was very much reflected in the press. Governmental changes, religious disputes and metallurgical discoveries in Russia all received coverage. Nevertheless, it was foreign policy and related military steps that attracted most attention. This attention was a reflection of anxiety about the emergence of an apparently new power, at least to the extent of the unprecedented success it enjoyed. There was no awareness of any comparison in terms of the Russian advance across the Urals and Siberia and to the Pacific from the 1580s to the 1630s, nor of the Russian advance southwards in the late seventeenth century toward the Black Sea. Peter's expansionism was seen as new.

The capacity of political geography to deal with disconcerting novelty was the issue. Whatever George I and his ministerial supporters might suggest, it was widely believed that British interests from 1714 were being sacrificed for the sake of Hanover. This argument was not without foundation. The handling of political geography, its content, context, language and tone, by contemporary commentators had to address the specific politics as well as the more general, and that need greatly complicated the discussion of causation and consequences. As an instance of the range of media in which Russia was mentioned, ballads offered a platform independent of literacy. 'Safety and Tranquillity – An excellent new Ballad' of 1722 ably expressed the British sense of unprecedented Russian strength and the belief that Peter could take revenge on any hostile British use of naval power:

> Well, well, sail off, Replied the Czar
> Tho digne de Chatiment;
> But when you want your naval stores
> You'll not ride top Gallant.
> Full of it the Russian monarch wish'd
> To have him in his Paw;
> And swore he instantly would Roast,
> A Minister so Raw.

Tensions in Anglo-Russian relations continued in Peter's last years, with particular fear of a Russian attack on Sweden in 1723.

Peter miscalculated badly with the Ottomans. His determination to treat Ukraine as Russian, rather than as the buffer territory that the Ottomans wanted it to be, was exploited by the anti-Russian party in Constantinople. In 1710, the Ottomans declared war. Although Peter had not ended his war with Sweden, he focused on the new opponent. His ambition was now very different to that of the 1690s, with its focus on Azov. The Balkans now beckoned. This looked toward Constantinople, which was a theme in Russian foreign policy, one that owed much to a semi-mystical vision of Russia's role, a vision that drew both on the theme of the Third Rome and the idea of Russia as a crusading power that would free the Balkans. Constantinople also offered a way to break into the Mediterranean.

Peter's enforced redirection of Russian ambitions towards the Baltic in 1700 had served a more secular goal, the modernisation of Russia, as well as reflecting Peter's need to exploit the opportunities presented by alliance politics. In 1711, however, Peter followed a different path. Proclamations were issued urging the Balkan Christians to revolt, and agents were dispatched accordingly, while Peter had the Cross inscribed on his standards, with the motto 'In this sign we conquer.' In 1711, the *Hospodar* of Moldavia, Demetrius Cantemir, signed a treaty with Peter through which he was to become hereditary Prince with Russian protection; only for Peter to fail at the Pruth. To a degree, Russian history was affected in the long term by his success in the Baltic and failure in the eastern Balkans. Polish weakness had made possible Peter's conquest of Sweden's eastern Baltic and domination of Ukraine but could not ensure success at the expense of the Ottomans.

Under Peter, Russia was integrated into European diplomatic practice, with the establishment of regular relations, with foreign envoys in St Petersburg and with Russian envoys across Europe. This reduced the extent to which Russia was a potentially dangerous outside force to the European international system. Peter sent Russian nobles abroad to increase their knowledge, especially of foreign languages, but the composition of the Russian diplomatic service was eclectic and included a number of foreigners, which was also true of the military. This was a more general European pattern.

Russia's rise was very much an aspect of a new geography of awareness and concern. Russia itself was scarcely an unknown country for the English, better known than the Balkans. Elizabeth I of England had pursued links with Ivan the Terrible in the late sixteenth century. Moreover, Russian expansionism had already been an issue for the European powers in the late sixteenth and late seventeenth centuries, both under Ivan and under Alexis. But the situation was transformed under Peter the Great.

Tensions in Anglo-Russian relations continued under Peter's successors: in accordance with the destabilising 1722 Law of Succession permitting the ruler to choose his successor his widow Catherine I (r. 1725-7), his grandson, Peter II (r. 1727-30), and, initially, under his niece, Anna (r. 1730-40). These tensions interacted with political differences within the London press, helping ensure that the accuracy of news from Russia became an issue. For example, the *Weekly Journal, or British Gazetteer* of 25 January 1718 attacked an opposition paper of a week earlier:

Peter the Great to Catherine the Great: The Eighteenth Century

'See how his scribbling blockheads are stumbling in profound ignorance, saying the Czar is going to Muscovy with 50,000 men, when he is at home already; but they meant Moscow, the chief city of his country.'

The British newspaper-reading public was kept informed. For example, the *Flying Post* of 1 September 1726, a pro-government London newspaper, printed the memorial presented by the Danish envoy in St Petersburg complaining of Russian naval preparations and of the threat to peace they represented. Such a war would probably have involved Anglo-Russian hostilities, as Britain was then committed to the support of Denmark and Sweden. From 1726, Russia was allied to Austria and aligned with Prussia, both of which were then opposed to Britain and Hanover. Relations with Russia remained poor until the negotiation of a commercial treaty in 1734, and this opening had been made possible by Britain's alliance with Russia's ally Austria in 1731 and by the easing of Hanoverian disputes with Russia in 1731-2.

Despite the atmosphere of diplomatic tension, by the mid-1720s reports in the British press were reasonably free of prejudice, possibly because by then Russia was seen as already an established part of the European system. Moreover, there was not the ideological threat to Britain posed by France, Spain and the Papacy. Russian expansion *per se* did not appear to challenge the nature of British society and culture, in large part because Russia was not Catholic. Russia was distant. There were reports about Russian support for Jacobitism, but nothing to compare with anxieties about such backing from France, Spain, Austria and Sweden, each of which provided assistance to the Jacobites, or the prospect of assistance, between 1700 and 1730. Indeed, the rapidly discovered willingness of the Protestant Charles XII of Sweden to discuss such help in 1717 helped make his opponent Peter appear less menacing.

Rather than hostility toward Russia, although that was expressed, there was increasingly, as immediate political crises ebbed from 1727, the uncertainty and rumour that characterized territories on the margins of established political geography. For example, the

Flying-Post of 4 July 1727 printed a report from The Hague, the centre of European news:

> The accounts that have been published as from Petersburg of the indisposition of the young Emperor [Peter II], of the assassination of the Duke of Holstein [son-in-law of Peter the Great], and of the mobbing and insurrections there, prove all of a piece, and to have been without foundation; all things have been very quiet, his Imperial Majesty has been, and is, very well; they are quiet and easy at home.

These rumours of instability, and other reports of hostile Russian intentions, owed more to confusion as to Russian developments than to any campaign of defamation. The *St James' Evening Post* of 13 July 1727 reported Russian intentions of supporting Austria, then adopting a hostile stance toward Britain, whilst other papers flatly contradicted these reports, which captured the instability of international relations at this juncture. More helpfully, Russian policy was not presented as a single entity but as a product of complex factional feuds. The interests of major aristocratic families and the rifts between the 'Old Rus' nobility and the westernizing foreign advisers were all described, which was a reasonable approach. So also were the probable consequences in terms of foreign policy.

Peter the Great's policies and attitudes were rejected by some at the élite level. His grandson, Peter II, sought to reverse both, moving the capital back to Moscow. He died young of smallpox; whereas, as a reminder of chance, Louis XV of France survived his attack in 1728 and reigned until 1774.

1730 saw an attempt to restrict royal authority, but things were resolved in favour of the new ruler, Peter the Great's niece, Tsarina Anna. While she was only accepted upon conditions, these were swiftly reversed. At stake was less the nature of the Russian constitution than the identity of those who would wield power. The Supreme Privy Council created under Catherine I demanded that Anna should rule with the advice of the Council and not make war or peace, marry, name a successor, grant titles or estates, make use of state revenues and make senior appointments without their consent. These demands have been seen by some as designed to create a noble oligarchy, or as a precursor to establishing a legislative body that might have become a Parliament, but the opposition to them was led by prominent aristocrats excluded from power, as well as by lower-ranking members of the service nobility who threw in their lot with the monarchy.

There was no tradition of common action, and neither a leadership nor an institutional framework that could provide noble cohesion. If the power of the Russian nobility was effectively represented throughout the century by individual families linked by kinship and patronage, these families sought imperial favour and had to operate in a political world destabilised by the mortality of monarchs, uncertainty over the succession, and the role of favourites. In response to the crisis, Anna over time purged a quarter of the upper four ranks of the Table of Ranks. Chronic uncertainty and unease characterized the upper reaches of the Imperial Russian service nobility, as members never knew when they might be cast out and lose estate, title and other assets.

In the British press there was an attempt, as also for other powers, to assimilate Russian developments to British patterns and examples, and thus make them more explicable. The accessions of Peter II in 1727 and of Anna in 1730, led to reports of intended constitutional changes in Russia and to the possibilities of an Anglo-Russian rapprochement. At times, though very briefly in each case, these two monarchs appeared as model, even Whiggish, sovereigns, rather than as some cross with an Oriental despot, as Russian rulers had generally earlier appeared. *Applebee's Original Weekly Journal*, a Whig London newspaper, reported on 5 August 1727 that Peter II 'hath openly declared in Council, that the end of government is chiefly designed to redress grievances, and to contribute as much happiness as possible to the people, because in their prosperity consists that of his own.' This paralleled reaction to the recent accession of George II.

In 1730, much attention was paid to the attempt by the aristocrat-dominated Council to limit Anna's powers as part of the conditions for her accession to the throne. The *Daily Post Boy* of 28 March devoted two and a half columns to these changes. Anna's apparent support for constitutional reform was presented as an example of a 'moral' quality in the *British Journal* of 30 May, as was the fall in 1727 of Prince Alexander Menshikov, then the sole Russian to bear the title of Prince, who had run the country under Catherine I in 1725-7.

In general, however, such Whiggish episodes appeared as brief moments and Russia was seen as a despotic autocracy. This situation was not usually criticized on the grounds of difference to British arrangements. Instead, on a pattern adopted throughout the earlier period, it was regarded as endemic to the country and to its inhabitants: 'the savage Muscovites,' as the *Flying Post* described them in its issue of 5 September 1727. This approach contrasted with the attitude to Western European states that were regarded as ruled autocratically. The view that autocracy was a natural response to the supposed innate national characters of the French, Spaniards and Italians did exist, but it was contradicted by a strong 'historical' approach to the problem. In the latter case, autocracy was presented as the result of evil misgovernment at a certain period, for example of France by Cardinal Richelieu. In British accounts, the destruction of representative institutions commonly provided a key historical cause. Russia was not treated in the same fashion, a point relevant for more recent history.

Prior to the eighteenth century, Russia was seen as a different kind of state to the rest of Europe, having elements in common with the Ottoman and Persian empires. In the case of all three, the relative ignorance of their histories of Western Europeans helped to confirm their alien nature. In the eighteenth century – and today – Russian news tended to be presented without as much explanation or background information as offered in the case of Western European news. Coupled with the natural tendency of Russian news to be confined to events in St Petersburg and Moscow, this ensured coverage covered little more than territorial expansion or factional strife. This was a failing, and one shared by the despatches of foreign diplomats, partly a consequence of the size of the country, the largest with which Western commentators came in regular contact, and of the parlous nature of Russia's internal communications. The policies of the Russian government did not appear to be dependent on the wishes of any section of the people. Thus, the political factions could be seen as ones that only needed to be understood in terms of the Russian Court.

On a longstanding basis, opinions about the stability and effectiveness of the Russian government were of importance because of Russian military power. The information available as to the scale of this power made it likely that Russia could confront and defeat its various bordering countries, and that, indeed, repeatedly proved the case. It was apparent that Russia could project its power even further.

British attitudes to Russia were reshaped because of greater concern about France and better relations between Britain and Russia's ally Austria from 1731, and the Anglo-Russian trade treaty of 1734, a treaty that was much welcomed in Britain. The fate of the Poles at the hands of Russia in the War of the Polish Succession of 1733-5 aroused very little sympathy in Britain because they were notorious for for the persecution of Protestants, with the Thorn massacre of 1724 receiving particular attention. Comment on the fall of Danzig (Gdańsk) to a Russian siege army in 1734 was not marked by any extravagant trumpeting of a danger to European civilization. The *Daily Post Boy* of 8 July 1734 was particularly phlegmatic: 'The Dantzickers, like other people, must suit their spirits to their circumstances, must cut their coat according to their cloth.'

In contrast, the French consistently regarded Russian successes as an appalling triumph of barbarism. There was much support in Paris for the Polish cause, notably in 1733-5 and 1768-72,whereas Britain was delighted by the humiliation of France's Baltic policy. This contrast was born of Catholic internationalism and the longstanding French idea of Poland as an ally against hostile powers, variously Austria, Prussia, Russia and Sweden. Differences over Poland between Britain and France remained later in the century, and notably at the time of the First Partition of Poland at the hands of Austria, Prussia and Russia in 1772. Britain proved less critical of the partition than France. The geopolitics of neighbourly antagonism in part dictated the response to more distant geopolitics. This helped explain why, in 1791, there was only limited support in Britain for war with Russia, in the Ochakov Crisis over the fate of what is now part of Ukraine. The French notion of a *barrière de l'est* against Russia lacked traction in Britain. Broader geopolitical considerations encouraged an inclusion of Russia in Europe by British commentators. The balance of power, the measure by which international relations were best explained, could be variously defined and had a dynamic quality in response to new threats and possibilities. Russia was both as far as British commentators were concerned.

Russian success in Poland in 1733-4 led to the possibility in 1735 that their forces would be employed further west against the French army, and thus prevent the French exploiting successes in campaigning in Germany. This was a policy repeatedly pursued, as in 1748, 1799 and 1805, one that culminated in 1815 with the westward move of a large Russian army, the ultimate guarantor of Napoleon's failure whatever happened at Waterloo. That autumn, 150,000 Russian troops were reviewed at Chalons-sur-Marne, near the modern Euro Disney. This westward power projection was very much one sought by Britain between 1734 and 1755 and from the 1790s to 1815. The immediacy of this advantage took precedence in Britain over questions about the nature of Russia as a political system. On 28 October 1734, the *Daily Post Boy* asked: 'Must Christendom always owe its safety to the North? And must Russia come now, and save it from slavery, as the Polanders once did under the brave Sobieski?' This was a politically charged comparison with the relief of Vienna from Ottoman siege in 1683, one that readers were expected to understand. Anti-Western international policies were associated with the attempts by the 'Old Russ' to turn Russia away from Europe and to reverse the policies of Peter the Great.

Peter the Great to Catherine the Great: The Eighteenth Century

And so to the present. In 1997, a fringe body looking back to the Communists, the Revolutionary Military Council of the Russian Soviet Federative Socialist Republic, claimed responsibility for an attempt to blow up a statue of Peter. His reputation, however, now appears secure within Russia due to Vladimir Putin's support for his example of territorial expansion.

In the late 1720s, both for the foreign press and for Western diplomats, the drive to turn Russia away from Europe was encapsulated by the attempt to return the capital to Moscow. The *British Journal* of 21 March 1730 claimed that the state of Anglo-Russian commerce depended on the policy of the new Tsarina (Anna), and on whether the capital was in Moscow. The writer argued that if so, Russia would lose control of its Baltic provinces, which had only been recently taken from Sweden:

> Was the city of Petersburg swallowed up in the sea, as is not unlikely to be its fate in a few years; and were the ports of Riga, Narva, Tallinn and Viborg lost to the Russians and become Swedish again, as they were before, yet we should never want for hemp, potash, Russian leather, and other valuable imports from thence, as we had them before, when those towns were in the hands of the Swedes. But the inland trade of Russia for the consumption of British manufactures, that will never be restored, unless the Empire of Russia rouses itself from under the lethargic slumber, which it is now fallen into; their furred gowns and long petticoats will return upon them, and all the sordid affectation of a singularity from all the world, which made them so truly contemptible before, will do the like again, and where shall our trade be carried on?

The capital remained in St Petersburg and this helped guarantee the Western focus of Russian politics and élite culture. The relationship between the location of the capital and general Russian Westernisation was a given, as far as Western commentators were concerned.

Nevertheless, in part in response to already-established views of Muscovy, the theme of a possible Russian return to barbarism was a common one. Each change of monarch led to such comments, they reflected a genuine belief in the mutability of Russian power and of the achievements of Peter the Great, and the more general conviction that power was not fixed and that empires in particular rose and fell. This attitude towards Russia was especially pronounced up to and including the early 1740s. Earlier in the century, the rise of Russia and the consequent reshaping of Europe had not been accepted as permanent. Russia, indeed, tended to be viewed as an especially unstable part of a dangerously unstable system.

The sense of stability was one that was essentially addressed in the early 1740s, when Russia faced and overcame a serious crisis of domestic problems and attack by Sweden. There was a greater awareness and recognition of Russian attainments and importance. Travel accounts were written by merchants and a diplomat, James Spilman's *Journey through Russia into Persia* (1742), Jonas Hanway's *Historical Account of the British Trade over the Caspian Sea* (1753), and Charles Whitworth's *Account of Russia, as it Was in the Year 1710* (1758).

The childless Anna was succeeded by Ivan VI (1740-64, r. 1740-1), great-grandson of Ivan V, but Ivan VI and his mother, the Regent Anna Leopoldovna, were overthrown in a coup in 1741 by Peter the Great's daughter Elizabeth (r. 1741-62), whose reign was dominated by international relations and conflict, firstly war with Sweden. The focus was on Europe rather than any continuance of earlier conflict with China, Persia and, in particular, the Ottomans. The Russians had failed in Persia, as a result of disease and resistance, and abandoned their earlier gains there in 1729, 1732 and 1735. In contrast, Russia had become more assertive in Europe, most dramatically so when Russian troops moved into Germany in 1716, 1735, 1748 and during the Seven Years' War (1756-63). Russia's determination to retain influence in Poland was central to her diplomatic and military strategies until the late twentieth century. With her dominant international position in Eastern Europe, Russia was able to integrate her Baltic and Ukrainian acquisitions.

Tsarina Elizabeth provided a welcome note of domestic political continuity for allies until her death in 1762, but relations with Britain deteriorated because in the Seven Years' War Russia was an inexorable opponent of Prussia, then allied with Britain. As a result, Elizabeth's replacement in 1762 by the Prussophile Peter III (r. 1762) provided Frederick the Great of Prussia with an opportunity to escape destruction that appeared almost miraculous.

Peter also made an important domestic innovation in ending compulsory nobleman service, the character of a service nobility and a garrison state was now gone. As a result, many former service noblemen retired to their country estates, but the great majority still had to support themselves in state administrative or military service and spent most of their time away from home. The creation of the state-backed Noblemen's Bank in 1754 allowed the nobles to borrow money at will without being forced to repay their debts. These typically arose from gambling losses and poor land-deals. By the 1830s, the nobility's indebtedness exceeded the value of its estates.

Catherine II, the Great (r. 1762-96) came to the throne as the result of the assassination of her husband, probably by her lover or his brothers, and her position was strengthened in 1764 when the imprisoned Ivan VI was murdered, thwarting an attempt to release him. She wished to reform Russia after the Seven Years' War and to protect Russian hegemony in Eastern Europe. As so often, Polish developments provided the element of unpredictability for Russia, though Sweden and the Ottoman empire were also to play a similar role by 1772.

The first Polish crisis had been anticipated. Augustus III died in 1763, and, in the following year Catherine was able to secure the election of a former Polish lover, Stanislaus Poniatowski, as King. Active Russian military intervention and the alliance of Prussia produced a speedy success for Stanislaus, which contrasted markedly with the more protracted Russian intervention of 1733-5 that had been produced by the previous election.

Having reinforced the protectorate nature of Poland, it did not seem probable that Russia would play a major role in partitioning the country within a decade. However, Polish politics, ever volatile, became more so as Stanislaus Poniatowski's attempts at reform increased tension. His proposal in 1766 to strengthen the royal position, and his refusal to support Catherine's policies of extending the rights of Poland's Protestant and Orthodox religious dissenters, led to Russian military intervention. Catherine saw no reason why her policies of religious reform should not extend to her Polish protectorate.

Russian action provoked resistance among the Polish nobility, the Confederation of Bar being formed in 1768. Combined with its activities in Crimea, an Ottoman vassal state, the intervention of Russia in Poland seemed to threaten the destruction of the buffer zone between Russia and the Ottoman Empire, a danger made more apparent when Russian troops pursuing Polish confederates violated Ottoman territory. In 1768 the Ottomans declared war.

The war went very badly for the Ottomans, the Russians destroying their fleet in 1770 at Cesme off Chios in the Aegean Sea, and overrunning Crimea, Moldavia and Wallachia. By the 1770s, Russian armies were able to operate hundreds of miles further from Moscow than they had done in the seventeenth century. This enabled commanders such as Rumiantsev and Suvorov to make their own decisions in the field without being hobbled by constricting orders issued from a distant capital. Russian success led to the prospect of major territorial changes from the Ottomans and aroused the fears and ambitions of other powers, particularly Austria and Prussia. Keen to gain territory, Frederick the Great in 1771 promoted the idea of a partition of Poland, a scheme agreed to by Catherine and Austria. In August 1772, the three powers settled their shares, while Russian military pressure led the Polish Diet to accept the partition the following year. The First Partition deprived Poland of almost 30 per cent of her territory and 35 per cent of her population. The Habsburgs gained the most populous share, Galicia, while Russia gained the largest, significant advances in Polish Livonia and Belarus, and Frederick gained Polish Prussia, and so joined his dominions of Brandenburg and East Prussia. Seven years later, under the Peace of Teschen, Russia, in a major sign of international prestige, was to be co-guarantor with France of the peace settlement between Austria and Prussia.

Meanwhile, though the Pugachev revolt (a peasant-Cossack rising of 1773-4) and continued Ottoman resistance forced Catherine to moderate her demands, the Treaty of Kutchuk-Kainardji (1774) rewarded her with gains from the Ottomans in the Caucasus and along the northern littoral of the Black Sea, on which freedom of navigation was guaranteed, and with a measure of protection for the Orthodox in the Ottoman Empire. The treaty marked a major turning point in relations, and Russia was able to use it to make further gains that reinforced her new position of superiority over the Ottomans. In 1783, Russia overran Crimea. Russo-Ottoman treaties in the period 1774–1804 awarded the former considerable advantages in Moldavia and Wallachia, including significant commercial and consular concessions, land grants and an effective veto over the Sultan's choice of *hospodars*. The effect of these changes was further to destroy Ottoman buffer zones, to carry Russia nearer the heartlands of Ottoman power and, by altering the balance of power in Eastern Europe, to influence the attitudes of all other Eastern European powers, particularly Austria.

Under the influence of her favourite and one-time lover, Grigory Potemkin, who was interested in expansion to the south and had been appointed Governor General of the new southern provinces in 1775, Catherine was keen to gain further advantages from the Ottomans, and according to the Emperor Joseph II, who visited her in the Crimea in 1787, she was eager to fight them again. The visit offered an impressive display of the benefits that could flow from acquisitions and the potential wealth of the region. Joseph was very impressed by his visit to the Russian Black Sea fleet base at Sevastopol, noting that the success of her schemes had excited Catherine's imagination. In the event, the Ottomans attacked that year in an unsuccessful attempt to recapture Crimea. This became a conflict lasting until 1792, in which Russia made major gains.

Gustavus III of Sweden's attack on Russia in 1788 threatened St Petersburg, as Russia's northern provinces were only lightly defended, while Russia's attempt to thwart Gustavus by supporting the anti-royalist noble opposition in the Estates failed. Russia had long interfered in the domestic policies of opponents and potential opponents. Gustavus's military successes led Catherine to conclude peace in 1790. Russia recognized the constitution of 1772 and promised not to interfere in Swedish politics, a promise fulfilled in the instructions to the new Russian mission to Stockholm.

The Swedo-Russian conflict played a part in schemes for a more extended confrontation with Russia. Repeating elements of the policy of Charles XII, Gustavus himself had recognised the wider importance of the struggle, negotiating a subsidy treaty with the Ottomans (1789) and attempting an entente with Poland, a country whose crown he considered seeking in the winter of 1790-1. However, the strength of the developing anti-Russian coalition depended on the plans of Britain and Prussia. The Triple Alliance of Britain, Prussia and the United Provinces (1788) had become by 1790 an anti-Russian league. In 1791 during the Ochakov Crisis, Russian determination and British hesitation led to a climbdown that destroyed the Anglo-Prussian alliance. Russia was left to fight the Ottoman Empire without Swedish, Polish, Prussian or British intervention.

The crises of 1788-91 had been surmounted and in the Peace of Jassy (1792) Russia acquired the territory between the Dniester and Bug, an area that consolidated her position on the northern shores of the Black Sea and made the prospect of a Polish-Ottoman alliance less credible. This prospect was to be extinguished by the Second and Third Partitions of Poland (1793, 1795), which destroyed the country and reflected Russia's dominance of North-Eastern Europe after 1791, a dominance also seen in the Swedo-Russian alliance of that year. Gustavus III's eagerness to ally with Russia and Catherine's determination to regain control of Poland and destroy the Polish reform programme both arose from a common fear, that of the revolutionary hydra in France. The destruction of Poland by partition in 1795 increased Russia's ability to intervene effectively in Western Europe, which it did in 1799 with the beginning of the War of the Second Coalition.

Territorial gains, especially from Poland in 1772-95, helped to push Russia's population from 15 million in 1719 to 35 million in 1800, a figure that put her ahead of France. Thanks in part to the greater availability of food, the population rose, although not really the ethnic Russian population. This increase brought many difficulties, notably epidemics, which included the bubonic plague in the late 1730s, 1740s, and early 1770s. In the last, over 100,000 people died in Moscow, where there were rumours that doctors in alliance with the nobility were spreading the disease instead of fighting it. In Kiev, where 18 per cent of the population died, the obscurantist clergy refused to approve the burning of the clothes of the dead. The spread of agriculture southwards led to increased settlement of lands occupied by plague-bearing rodents: rats loved to live in thatched roofs.

Territorial expansion, notably in the black-soil region of Ukraine, brought tremendous opportunities for an increase in food production, not least as areas that had been hitherto zones of animal husbandry had not yet had their fertility denuded by cereal cultivation. In a situation that has lasted to the present, Ukraine and the Don Valley became significant grain-exporting areas. This helped increase interest in trade through the Black Sea. The Volga area possessed enormous economic possibilities. As a result, there was internal migration from areas of high population density and limited economic opportunity to lands that were essentially open, in part due to the subjugation of the indigenous population. There were also migrants from Central or Western Europe. The second Russian census, begun in 1744, showed that over the previous quarter-century the steepest percentage increases in population had occurred in settled frontier or peripheral areas such as the lower Volga, the northern Urals and Ukraine. Catherine II's proclamations of 1762 and 1763 offered significant privileges to immigrants, most of whom were German. This was an aspect of cosmopolitanism in her views and assumptions that was not welcome to critics of Westernisation.

Large Russian landowners were particularly interested in expanding their estates into the more fertile territories of southern Russia and there producing grain, flax and hemp for the European market. They were aided by the pacification of what is now Ukraine, improvements in communications, and *barshchina*, a harsh labour regime in which peasants worked the lord's lands. In the mid-1730s the completion of the transport system linking the new market of St Petersburg with the river Volga led to a fall in transport costs and a decline in grain prices in the capital, as supplies increased from the new producing areas of the northern steppe and along the Volga.

In spite of the rapid growth of St Petersburg during the 1740s and 1750s, the high productivity levels of the new lands provided an abundant supply of grain at low prices for its population. In the 1760s rising international grain prices, caused by the growth in the European population, led to a geographical extension of Russian production. In the early 1760s, Catherine, a keen supporter of agricultural development, backed the policy of her adviser Gerhard Linke to relieve the grain trade from restrictions and allowed the free export of grain from several Baltic ports. Agricultural improvement contributed to Russian strength as resources came closer to the zone of military operations. This was a product of success in transforming what is now Ukraine geographically, politically, socially and with Russian settlement, ethnically.

Aristocratic enterprise was also important in Russian rural industry. Most Russian manufacturing was dispersed and domestic. Industries apparently characterized by large concerns such as the Tula metalworking area, a centre of weapons production, often consisted of dozens of separate units of production. Coarse woollen cloth was produced on aristocratic estates or in villages of state peasants that had been acquired by merchant entrepreneurs early in the century. Peter I allowed merchants to purchase serfs for industrial labour, and a law was passed in 1721 permitting merchants to buy entire villages for their enterprises. This practice was prohibited in 1762 as part of a reaction against merchants and in favour of nobles.

As a result, the second half of the century witnessed significant production of a number of goods, including paper and woollen and linen textiles by serf labour on manorial estates, but productivity was often poor. In parts of central Russia, the shift after about 1760 from labour services to payment in cash or kind was associated with a sharp rise in domestic (household) industrial production.

The factory serfs of the Urals were brutally treated by the manufacturers, who forced them to neglect their agricultural pursuits and to purchase provisions from factory stores at high prices. The tension in the Urals, which was to lead to violence in the early 1760s and during the Pugachev Rising of 1773-5, was but one instance of the stress caused by such industrial activity, an important indication of widespread tension. Launched by Cossacks under Yemelyan Pugachev, who claimed to be the dead Peter III, numbers in the Rising were swelled with peasant runaways, especially from the harsh working conditions of the mines and metallurgical plants of the Ural Mountains region. Regular farming serfs also played a major role. Some disgruntled priests, townspeople, and some unhappy members of the lower service echelons of the nobility joined in. Cossacks and Bashkirs (Turkic-speaking Muslims to the west of the southern Urals) were promised their traditional way of life, including the freedom of land and water. Under the Communists, the rebellion was presented as by peasants; rather than with the emphasis more accurately being on non-Russian participation, especially by Cossacks.

The fortress of Orenburg on the River Ural was besieged, Russian relief forces beaten off and the insurgency spread, especially into the Urals. However, despite Pugachev establishing a College of War that was modelled on the Russian War Ministry and dividing his troops into regiments, there was no real coordination of the insurgent bands, and also a shortage of cannon and ammunition. The important Urals armaments industry was not organized to the benefit of the insurgents, many of whom were armed only with spears, axes, and sticks. While Pugachev remained unable to take Orenburg and Yaitsk, whose fortifications defied attack, Russian troops advanced from a number of directions in the winter of

1773-74, and in March Pugachev was defeated at Tatishchevo. A separate insurgent force was defeated near Ufa. Insurgent morale collapsed and the garrisons of Orenburg and Yaitsk were relieved.

Nevertheless, Pugachev raised another army and captured the fort of Osa in June and Kazan in July. Those in Western dress were killed. Pugachev won fresh support by promising freedom to the serfs of the Volga valley, which demonstrated the social radicalism he represented, although the rebels were primarily interested in the diminution of serfdom's abuses and not in the elimination of the institution itself. The response was a widespread slaughter of the nobility in the Volga region. There was also a religious element in the rising, support for the Old Believers, who kept to traditional forms of religious behaviour, as well as a strong antipathy to the Westernization of Russia.

A mutiny by the garrison of Saratov, a major city on the Volga, led to its fall to Pugachev, but the insurgent movement still lacked effective organizational structure. Moreover, Pugachev's appeals were increasingly unsuccessful as his arrival brought unwelcome chaos and fighting, and the resilience of the government was becoming more apparent. Meanwhile, underlining the ever-crucial international element, Russian troops were withdrawn from the Balkans from the war with the Ottomans, with whom peace terms were finally agreed in July 1774. This withdrawal ensured that the insurgents' military position deteriorated and afforded the Russians a new operational axis from which to assault the rebels. Defeated in late August, Pugachev was betrayed by disillusioned supporters in September and executed the following January. Residual disturbances set in motion through his uprising, albeit of lesser magnitude, continued after his death, but were suppressed in 1775.

The Pugachev Rising did not lead to any improvements for the peasantry. The domestic Russian market for goods was greatly limited by their poverty and heavy tax burden. In contrast, the state provided a significant market for several industrial sectors, particularly metallurgy. The copper and iron deposits of the Urals were the basis for a major growth in regional industry, particularly of iron foundries, and the region became the principal foreign supplier of iron to western Europe, supplanting Sweden. There was a great expansion of silver production.

In other respects, Russian industrial developments were not impressive. Russian goods were frequently poorer in quality and higher in price than imports, and Russian merchants often found it hard to sell them. The coal and iron of Ukraine were not worked on a scale comparable to the Ural metal deposits. The value of the unskilled compulsory labour that was widely used was limited. Many industrial establishments, such as those that produced cloth for the army, did not become foci for urbanisation or further industrialisation. However, compared with her principal political rivals, Sweden, Poland and the Ottoman Empire, Russia achieved significant industrial growth. If it was regionally specific, that was little different from the situation elsewhere in Europe. Most Russian enterprises, such as the hat, stocking and rope factories at Saratov in the 1770s, did not produce goods for export, but that also was unexceptional.

The emphasis on Russian expansion, growth and development has to be balanced by an awareness of serious limitations, and not only in peripheral regions. St Petersburg was not the only town unable to cover the expenditure that a discharge of its legal commitments would have entailed. In 1724-7, the first four years of the collection of the poll tax in Russia, arrears in the towns amounted to 64 per cent of assessment, although by the 1730s the collection of the poll tax was increasingly effective. However, at the accession of Catherine II in 1762, the annual revenue of the imperial government was unknown, and in a pre-statistical period, there was no list of towns. The College of Landed Estates was supposed to record all transfers of landed property in a land register, but as transactions could be registered only in St Petersburg or Moscow, many were not recorded, and the register suffered from poor record-keeping. The imposition of the death penalty in 1766 for interference with the activities of land surveyors was a poor substitute for the necessary administrative structure and for general political support. This was a situation that looked towards that under the Soviet Union, when the force wielded by the regime did not ensure effectiveness; in both cases there was a lack of intermediate institutions in which consent was present. The Soviet situation was more dire due to hostility to its policies, which were antisocial in terms of existing practices.

Russian options in taxation and local government were limited by the absence of an accurate land survey. In the Baltic provinces conquered from Sweden in 1710, the nobility, who remained powerful, refused to accept a new survey by the Russian government.

Russia was at the fore when Edward Gibbon, in his *The History of the Decline and Fall of the Roman Empire* (1776-88), addressed the question of whether Europe could fall anew to the attacks of 'barbarians' from Central Asia, as Classical Rome had done. In Gibbon's view, civilization had led to science and a process of invention, application and diffusion, such that 'cannon and fortification now form an impregnable barrier against the Tatar horse.' In short, the political geography of Eurasia had fundamentally changed, and very much for the better. There was a link with progress in his account, and with British views on the need to avoid a French-dominated Europe, views that left much space for co-operation with Russia. As a result, despite some ministerial interest, the British government did not respond positively to French approaches in 1772-3 to co-operate in opposing the First Partition of Poland and/or Russian pressure on Sweden.

Nikolai Ge's striking painting *Peter I interrogates Tsarevich Aleksei Petrovich at Peterhof* (1871) related to the wider tension between Westernisers (Peter) and Slavophiles, a dispute that had erupted in the 1830s, although the tensions were always there going back to the late 1400s. Hero to the former and villain to the latter, Peter's reputation became a way to advance the debate over Russia's culture and future, because the imprisoned Aleksei (Alexis) was an opponent of Peter's Westernising policies.

This tension was far from new and was central to the relations between the Orthodox Church and Catholicism. But the tension became more significant in the eighteenth century due to Peter's conscious modernisation. Moreover, Catherine the Great, who had only a precarious link with the dynasty, proved willing to deploy the Petrine legacy, not least by living in St Petersburg. She saw herself as Peter the Great's successor. Born in Stettin as Princess Sophie of Anhalt-Zerbst and fluent in German, Catherine presented herself as a central patron of European culture, commissioning the Hermitage Palace in St Petersburg for her art and books, and was a fan of French culture, German science and British gardens. The cosmopolitanism of her reign was referred to at the very start of Tolstoy's novel *War and Peace* (1865), when the statesman Prince Vasili in 1805 is described as speaking 'in the elegant French in which our forefathers not only spoke but also thought.' An active moderniser, Catherine sought to standardise a range of activity from education to urban government, although she did not implement her policies except in a few channelled instances. But during her reign oppression in the countryside increased and she did not permit the emancipation of the serfs.

Russia was now acting as a great power. The development and success of Russia's military rested on broader currents of economic growth. Despite major costs, financial and social, and an inability to meet the expenses of war that led to a reliance on foreign subsidies, Russia had attained an international position very different from that in the mid-seventeenth century. This, however, was to be put to the test in a bitter struggle with Napoleonic France.

As a reminder that differing narratives are possible, it is instructive to consider the perspective of the indigenous peoples of eastern Siberia. Relying on bone or stone-tipped arrows and on slings, the poorly armed Itelmen were brutalised in the Russian search for furs. They rose in 1706 but were suppressed. When they resisted in 1731, the Itelmen had some firearms obtained from the Russians and were able to inflict many casualties as a result, but they were eventually crushed, while their numbers were further hit by the diseases that accompanied their adversaries. Isolated communities proved especially vulnerable to disease as their immunity was low due to limited earlier exposure. Another rising in 1741 was defeated. However, the Koraks of Kamchatka proved more formidable than the Itelmen, and were effective with bows and captured firearms. The Russians responded brutally and were willing to kill as many Koraks as possible, not least in the war of 1745-56. The Koraks then submitted.

The Chukchi of north-east Siberia posed greater problems, defeating a Cossack expedition in Russian service in 1729 and resisting genocidal attacks in 1730-1 and 1744-7. The Russians eventually stopped the war, abandoning their fort at Anadyrsk in 1764: established in 1649, it had been a key base in operations in Kamchatka from the late 1690s and it had successfully resisted siege as recently as 1762. Trade links developed and the Russians finally recognised Chukchi rights to their territories. Though there was no risk that the Chukchi would advance to sweep the Russians from eastern Siberia.

The Russians also made a significant inroad on steppe independence, building on the seizure of Astrakhan in 1556. In the late 1730s, the Bashkirs to the northeast of the Caspian were suppressed with great brutality, including the killing of many women and children. Many others were seized as serfs and moved elsewhere in Russia. Many men were seized as conscripts. Possibly about half the Bashkir population was killed or moved, and Russian control over them was anchored by a new line of forts from the Volga to Orenburg, built in 1743. The southward advance of fortification projects further east closed the way for nomadic invasions, sealed off regions from hostile reinforcement, and prepared for subsequent Russian advances into Central Asia. Fortresses included Omsk in 1716, established to protect trade routes to China and Central Asia, and Troitsk, a key fortress in the Orenburg line of forts, in 1743. By the second half of the century, a chain of Russian forts stretched from the Caspian to Kuznetsk in the foothills of the Altai Mountains on the border with China. In 1783, the Nogais in the Kuban, to the east of the Black Sea, were defeated at Urai-Ilgasi and the River Laba.

The Aleutians initially posed few problems for the Russians in their quest for furs, but in 1761 effective resistance began on the Fox Islands, the easternmost archipelago in the Aleutians. This was overcome in 1766 by an amphibious force deploying cannon organised by Ivan Soloviev, a merchant from Okhotsk on the north shore of the Sea of Okhotsk. Massacre and disease secured the Russian 'achievement'. In 1784, the Russians established a permanent base on Kodiak Island in the Aleutian Islands and thereafter started to expand their activities along the Alaskan coast, helped by the impact of European diseases, which, alongside Russian massacres, led to a dramatic fall in population of the eastern Aleutians.

Distance and climate put this expansion at the limits of the Russian world. Russian Alaska could not grow the grain to sustain its small colony and could not import a labour supply due to distance and serfdom. Nevertheless, a Russian North Pacific was being established. By the 1790s the southward extension of Russia along North America's Pacific coast was a matter of concern to Britain and Spain, both of whom it was indeed designed to pre-empt. The solution to Alaska's issues was to go south to northern California, where Fort Ross was established in 1812. However, this did not work out as the shoreline was too humid and too cool, even for rye.

News of developments in the Pacific took a long while to reach St Petersburg; with trial and use, the flow of information improved and increased, and this enhanced the possibilities for government, not least for the information-based policymaking the Russians sought. The Russian-America company was founded in 1799. More generally, the development of the postal system in Russia also provided greater economic and social opportunities.

However impressive, the development of a Russian North Pacific scarcely matched the overseas colonisation of the Atlantic-facing Western European societies. Yet, in terms of Eurasia, Russia was an empire of unprecedented scale, even if it lacked a transoceanic dimension of any significance. At the end of the century, Russia's rulers were able to consider fresh territorial expansion and distant power-projection. The leading Russian role in the Partitions of Poland (1772-95) also demonstrated a power in Eastern Europe that would have seemed extraordinary in 1700.

{ 6 }

A MAJOR POWER
The Nineteenth Century

In September 1815, on the third anniversary of the battle of Borodino (in which the French had pushed back the Russians before Moscow), Alexander I of Russia reviewed a parade of 150,000 Russian troops east of Paris, alongside the rulers of Austria and Prussia, both of whom were also dressed in Russian uniforms. This was the highpoint of Russian power, greater in relative terms even than that in 1945. And the Russians, while distrusted and even loathed by many, notably Poles, were seen in a better light than was to be the case in 1945. Then, there was a wider sense of Russia as a conqueror, rather than as an ally or liberator.

The impact of the crushing of the French invasion in 1812 was a lasting one. It affected Russian views of Providential Destiny but also foreign views of Russian power. This power, however, is difficult to evaluate. In the 1830s and 1840s, Russia had the largest gross national product (GNP) in Continental Europe, but, as it had the largest population, it had a low per-capita GNP, and its major agricultural role in production and exports was not matched by a comparable industrial strength. In 1750 Russia produced more iron than Britain, by 1850 Britain far outproduced it.

As Tolstoy and Tschaikovsky (most famously with his 1812 Overture) demonstrated so well, the nineteenth century

A Major Power: The Nineteenth Century

was always in the shadow of war. This might appear somewhat surprising given the subsequent stress on the world wars, as well as the lack of much popular awareness of Russia being at war between 1815 and 1914, the exception being British and French memories of the Crimean War (1854-6). The general impression is of a period that was largely peaceful, one dominated by domestic matters, notably the emancipation of the serfs, industrialisation, the growth both of a middle class and of a proletariat, and the novelists.

Contemporaries, however, were more aware of Russia as imperial state and militaristic society. The nineteenth century affirmed Russia's dominance of Eastern Europe and much of Central Asia came under Russian control. War was central to both. Tolstoy's novel *War and Peace* (1865-9), with its epic account of Napoleon's invasion in 1812, drew on the author's military experience in the Crimean War.

The significance of Russian power was fully demonstrated during the French Revolutionary Wars, which began in 1792. In particular, the absence of Russian participation in the First Coalition against France weakened it and was seen in that light. There was no reason for Russia to participate and this was the period in which Russia made further gains from Poland, which was partitioned out of existence in 1795. In contrast, the Second Coalition saw Russian forces demonstrate unprecedented range in 1799, Suvorov advancing into northern Italy and Switzerland while a Russian force also joined the British in an unsuccessful attack on Holland, which was then a French-client state, and a Russo-Ottoman expeditionary force captured Corfu, the Russian force moving on to invade southern Italy. Russia was very important to the coalition strategy of cumulative pressure. This was asymmetrical warfare: France could bring no comparable pressure on Russia. That August, Lord Grenville, the British Foreign Secretary, wrote to the envoy in St Petersburg about the need for Anglo-Russian cooperation 'for the cause of religion and morality, and for the maintenance of civilized society'. Russia was seen as within this matrix and important to it. However, a lack

Suvorov crossing the Alps in 1799 by Vasily Surikov (1848-1916). (Public domain)

of Austrian support helped lead to Russian defeat by the French in Switzerland and encouraged the unpredictable Tsar Paul I (r. 1796-1801) to withdraw Russia from the war. This seriously undermined the Second Coalition in both military and political terms.

As a further instance of the fluidity of international relations, Paul, even more of a maverick than Peter III (r. 1762), fell out with Britain in 1800. He joined in creating a League of Armed Neutrality that opposed the British searching of neutral shipping, a method earlier followed by Catherine II and one that showed how Russia was very much part of the diplomatic world. In 1801, Paul advanced the idea of Franco-Russian cooperation against British India, but a crisis for Britain was avoided, in part because Napoleon was unwilling to heed Paul's views on Italy, Malta and the Ottoman Empire. Paul sought to limit French expansion. Furthermore, the strategy, to which Napoleon returned in 1808 was not credible: Russia could deploy force into the eastern Mediterranean if Britain was supportive, as in 1769-70, but lacked the naval strength to make a significant impact on British India. Overland, the distances, logistics and likely opposition were too great. Paul's 'difference' was also seen in 1797 when he sought to limit the amount of work landlords could demand from peasants.

The overthrow and assassination of Paul, suffocated in his bedroom (although apoplexy was the official cause of death) in March 1801, and his succession by his son, the reactionary but less quixotic Alexander I (r. 1801-25), ensured a dramatic break with the already problematic agreement with France. Relations were swiftly mended with Britain. Alexander was concerned about Napoleon's forward policy, not least the threat in the Mediterranean to Russia's interests in the Balkans. Napoleon curtly rejected his 1803 peace plan and in 1804 relations were broken off. This was important to the the War of the Third Coalition, which saw Russia mount a firmer resistance to France than Austria and Prussia did. Advancing in person into Europe as no Tsar had done since Peter the Great, Alexander I and his Austro-Russian army was defeated by Napoleon at Austerlitz (modern Czech Republic) in 1805. This led to Austria leaving the war and in 1806 was the background for a further marked deterioration in the Russian position. Russian troops were withdrawn from southern Italy while Sultan Selim III moved to Napoleon's side, agreeing to close the Bosporus and the Dardanelles to Russian warships and replacing pro-Russian *hospodars* (governors) in Moldavia and Wallachia. Russia occupied Moldavia in a failed attempt at intimidation, and Selim declared war. The extensive fortifications in the Ottoman defensive system on the Danube were to delay the Russians, but in 1809-10 they captured them and in 1811 inflicted a major defeat at Ruschuk. The Russians had been able to start their advances further south due to past territorial gains from the Ottomans and Poland.

Meanwhile, in 1807, the French had pushed eastwards into East Prussia, with the Russians inflicting heavy casualties at Eylau but being defeated at Friedland. This led to the Treaty of Tilsit of 7 July 1807 under which Alexander left Napoleon dominant in Western and Central Europe, an acceptance that previous Tsars had refused to France. Handing over the Ionian Islands (its Mediterranean base from 1798) to France, Russia itself lost little territory (and gained some in Prussian Poland), but its policy was now intertwined with that of Napoleon. More positively, Alexander gained from Tilsit a free hand in Finland, the Danubian Principalities and the Caucasus. He was able to take over Finland and make major gains in the Caucasus, but Napoleon, belatedly, tried to constrain Russia's ambitions in the Danubian Principalities, which was one of the core factors in the growing disagreement between the empires.

Most dangerously, Napoleon carved a Duchy of Warsaw out of Prussian Poland, giving it to the ruler of Saxony in a way that overthrew the Russian view on Poland and a longstanding and important Russian achievement. The Franco-Russian entente also isolated Britain, and Alexander refused to back Austria against Napoleon in a new war in 1809, but the entente proved difficult to sustain due in large part to Napoleon's apparently inexorable ambition. The Russians themselves were scarcely free from ambition. Aside from expansion in the Balkans, Swedish-ruled Finland fell to Russian attack in 1808-9 in a conflict that was kept separate from the main war, like the Winter War between Russia and Finland in 1939-40.

Napoleon's refusal to accept a draft convention negotiated in January 1810 by his ambassador to Russia guaranteeing, as Alexander demanded, that the kingdom of Poland would not be revived, greatly increased Russian distrust of Napoleon about Poland and much else, and ensured that French actions were viewed through this prism. Napoleon was unable to sustain an alliance in which compromise played a role. Perfunctory alliances and limited compromise were his norm. Alexander's respect for Napoleon had encouraged him to try to build on their Tilsit agreement, but Napoleon's failure to reciprocate wrecked such hopes.

There was no true peace, and the French were very unenthusiastic about supporting Russian ambitions in the Balkans at the expense of the Ottomans, a position that continued that under the *ancien régime*. Matters were made worse in December 1810 by the French annexation of the north-west German Duchy of Oldenburg, which had dynastic links with the Romanovs and had been guaranteed at Tilsit. Meanwhile, the strategy of the Continental System, the economic warfare aimed at Britain, was made tougher for others in 1810 when in the face of large-scale evasion by means of smuggling, exports from Europe to Britain were only permitted if they passed through French ports or were carried on French shipping. The economic disruption that followed helped cause serious economic difficulties. In December, Russia left the French economic camp. It abandoned the Continental System which was proving ruinous to the economy. Such a unilateral step threatened the cohesion of the French economic and political systems and challenged Napoleon's insistence on obedience and his treatment of allies as servants.

Napoleon responded to Russian independence, first with bluster, but also by greatly stepping up the military preparations for war. He went east in part in an attempt to bring down Britain, in the same way as Hitler, in a different context, was to do in 1941. At the same time, both men were also motivated by a determination to control Eastern Europe. French military preparations against Russia had already begun in October 1810, but at that stage they were designed for intimidation, not conflict. Napoleon, however, did not respond positively to Russian diplomatic approaches the following spring, approaches designed to make possible an armed neutrality and the avoidance of another war to add to that with the Ottomans.

Napoleon was clearly thinking of war from the late summer of 1811 on, which meant war in the 1812 campaign season. From October, French military preparations were accelerated and in January 1812 France's position in the Baltic improved with the occupation of Swedish Pomerania. More significantly, Napoleon forced an isolated Prussia to accept an offensive alliance treaty against Russia in February.

However, the French were operating in a doubly precarious position. Any resort to war both risked provoking problems in their alliance system and also did not address the potential erosion of France's relative advantages. On land, the French lacked a lead comparable to that enjoyed at sea by Britain after its victory at Trafalgar in 1805. Moreover, the extent to which the difficult warfare in 1807-9 had failed to shake Napoleon's confidence arising from his victories in 1805-6 was serious. The degree to which there was a capability gap between France and Russia is debateable anyway, but, at any rate, the advantages of France's warmaking strength was certainly under challenge. The Russian army had been significantly improved under Michael Andreas Barclay de Tolly.

Having assembled a powerful coalition against Russia, Napoleon invaded on 24-25 June 1812 with over half a million men, many of whom were allied troops, principally German, Italian and Polish. Napoleon's closest advisers opposed the invasion, on the grounds that it was as unnecessary diplomatically as it was foolish militarily. As with his earlier attacks on Austria, Prussia and Spain, and his planned invasion of Britain in 1805, Napoleon resolved to strike at the centre of his opponent's power, thus gaining the initiative and transferring much of the logistical burden of the war to his enemy. In geographical terms, the centre meant an advance to Moscow, thereby cutting links between northern and southern Russia and establishing control over the symbolic seat of power. The actual capital was St Petersburg, which was a difficult target overland. Indeed, on that axis, Étienne Macdonald was only able to advance as far as Jekabpils on the Western Dvina, and this brought no benefit. Riga, at the mouth of the river, was not captured, and this meant that there was no port as a base for operations and a possible negotiating chip. Further upriver, Nicolas Oudinot reached Daugavpils, but did not exploit this advance. The northern axes of advance did not take the pressure off Napoleon's central axis. Instead, some of the Russian forces in the region moved to play a role in the resistance on the central axis.

Russia was a major naval power and, although he had ports in the Baltic, Napoleon lacked a navy able to launch an effective amphibious attack on the capital. The fleet of his Danish ally had been lost due to British naval action in 1801 and 1807, while Sweden was neutral. There was to be no equivalent to the Anglo-French fleet sent into the Baltic during the Crimean War, let alone that sent to the Black Sea. This meant that Napoleon could not draw on naval support for land forces.

The Russians fell back, denying Napoleon a decisive battle. Undoing the results of the partitions of 1792-5, a Commission for the Provisional Government of Lithuania was formed, and there was interest among some of the nobility in a restored independent Grand Duchy of Lithuania, free from Poland as well as Russia. Nevertheless, Napoleon, whose strategy lacked a political dimension, found little local support. He considered proclaiming the freedom of the serfs, a measure the French Revolutionaries in their radical stage of 1793-4 would have pursued, but did not do so: such a move did not accord with his limited goal of forcing Alexander to re-enter the Continental System.

Like the Germans in 1941, the French were totally unprepared for the nature of their task. Russian scorched-earth and guerrilla activity limited supplies in the area of operations and the French lost heavily, both men and horses, through hunger, disease and fatigue. In 1812, despite the scale of the logistical preparations, notably ammunition depots and supply trains with 40 days' supply for the invasion, there were grave deficiencies including a lack of the smaller carts necessary for the inadequate roads. Logistics became a matter of eating the horses; and retreating from Moscow along the way they had advanced was to make the situation even more serious for the French.

The Russians withdrew successfully, their divided and confusing command structure not preventing their army from operating with some effectiveness. Finally, at Borodino, 75 miles west of Moscow, on 7 September, the Russians sought to stop the advance in prepared positions. In a battle of attrition that involved 233,000 men and 1,227 cannon, the indecisive Napoleon, who had far fewer troops at his disposal than in June, in part due to leaving them in garrisons, did not try to turn his opponent's flanks. Instead, he focused on breaking into and through their position, the method he was also to pursue at Waterloo in 1815. The Russians resisted successive attacks and when finally driven back, did so without breaking. Saving the army exposed Moscow but left it able to continue operations. Russian casualties were heavier, but Napoleon lost a quarter of his army without inflicting a serious defeat. There was no damaging pursuit.

Napoleon entered an undefended Moscow on 14 September, but instead of any negotiating with those he might intimidate and coerce, the largely deserted city was set ablaze that night, probably by the Russians. The enormity of the task, logistical problems and the endurance of the Russian foes had defeated Napoleon militarily before the difficulty of securing any settlement politically even arose. He had no terms to propose, faced an opponent who would not negotiate, and could not translate his seizure of Moscow into negotiations.

Some advised Napoleon to winter in Moscow, taking advantage of the shelter and food available. During the Russian Time of Troubles, the Poles had maintained a garrison in the Kremlin from 1610 to 1612, although, this was with support from some of the

Russian *boyars*. Napoleon lacked that degree of support and there was no equivalent to the Russian divisions of the Time of Troubles. The Poles had anyway been starved into surrendering in 1612.

Napoleon's army was not intended as the basis for a garrison but as a key field force, and that role would not be served if it remained in Russia. By withdrawing his army, Napoleon would be able to shorten his lines of communication and supply, to fall back on and collect garrison forces, and to remain in touch with Paris, from which news of an attempted conspiracy on 23 October arrived on 6 November. Although weak and unsuccessful, it underlined the political cost of Napoleon's military failure in Russia.

Due to disease, heavy snowfalls, supply breakdowns, and repeated Russian attacks, the retreat, which began on 19 October, rapidly turned into a nightmare. The Russian attempt to cut Napoleon off at the Beresina River on 26-28 November failed, but the French rearguard suffered heavily there, and the army that left Russia had had over 500,000 casualties, with astounding losses also of horses. In Soviet era accounts, the peasantry were presented as taking a major role and heroically contributing to the invasion's failure, which was an exaggeration.

There was no real attempt then or later on the part of Napoleon to accept the military verdict and offer Russia terms that would assuage its hostility. Napoleon could neither conceive of a new ethos in French foreign policy nor of a new system in Eastern Europe. Both would have required compromise. This situation greatly contributed to Russia's determination to implement the decision in December 1812 to press on against France, and thereby put Prussia, which Napoleon had instructed to raise another 30,000 men, in the front line. Russia overrunning the Duchy of Warsaw ensured that France would not be able to raise troops there. An offensive Russian strategy appeared necessary to gain security.

Russia's position had been greatly strengthened in May 1812 by the Peace of Bucharest with the Ottomans, a peace that did not serve French interests. Although Russia did not obtain Moldavia, Wallachia or an alliance with the Ottomans, as had been hoped, previous wars had also ended in compromise, as was the norm, and Russia still gained Bessarabia (modern Moldova) and peace. However, there was still interest among Russian policymakers in stirring up the Balkan Slavs against both the Ottomans and Austria.

Russia's advance played the key role in bringing Prussia and Austria into the war with Napoleon in 1813, and the Russians played a major part in his defeat then and his overthrow in 1814. This was celebrated in monuments such as that to the Russians in the battle of Kulm in 1813. In 1815, the advance of Russian forces helped ensure that even had the returning Napoleon been victorious at Waterloo, he would have been unlikely to succeed.

The new international system established by the Congress of Vienna in 1814-15, in which Alexander played a major role, left Russia dominant on land in Europe, with most of former Poland under Russian rule, technically as a separate kingdom. The new system was to be guarded by Alexander's Holy Alliance of Christian monarchs, or at least those of Russia, Austria and Prussia. By the Protocol of Troppau of 1820, Austria, Prussia and Russia agreed on intervening in order to reverse the overthrow of a government by revolution, and this was followed by the Austro-Russian Treaty of Münchengrätz of 1833. Security was bound up with a desire for stability and a fear of ideological radicalism.

To that end, Russia, at least on paper, continued to maintain a large army. In 1816, Alexander noted: 'Russia is in such a position that it must maintain an army the same size as the combined forces of Prussia and Austria.' This led to serious financial problems, which were exacerbated by poor financial control as well as by serious corruption. The German-born Egor, Count Kankrin, the former Quartermaster General who was a fiscally conservative Minister of Finance from 1823 to 1844, was highly sceptical about the efficiency of the War Ministry.

Although early on interested in aspects of liberalism, Alexander became increasingly reactionary in his later years, evident in his political and religious attitudes and policies, including a degree of millenarianism, and in his appointments. He died of typhus aged 47 while touring southern Russia, and left no legitimate children.

A Major Power: The Nineteenth Century

The elder of Alexander's brothers, Konstantin, had no interest in the succession, and the younger, Nicholas, was the heir presumptive. Marked confusion in the royal family led to a challenge at the centre of Russian power. In 1825, the Decembrists, army officers, some radicals but many liberals, sought to seize power but without seeking civilian support. Officers had been radicalised by the experience of serving in Western Europe and in reaction to the conservatism of Alexander's later years, though the liberals accepted many elements of conservative society. These factors separated them from the later members of Russian revolutionary movements, while, unlike in the very different Pugachev and earlier risings, there was no reference to the idea of a true tsar being found.

In any event, the new Tsar, Nicholas I, was able to call on larger numbers of loyal troops and overcame the rising on the day it began, at the cost of over 1,000 deaths. There was an unsuccessful supporting rebellion by troops in Ukraine. Whereas the suppression of risings in 1905 contributed to a sense of crisis that, in the context of failure in war, helped engender revolution in 1917, there was no such aftermath in 1825. Nicholas's response to the Decembrists, having executed five convicted ringleaders in July 1826, was to develop domestic policing. Moreover, the longstanding interpenetration of Russian military and civil government was taken further with the even more extensive employment of military officers as ministers and provincial governors in what was an increasingly autocratic government. This was an aspect of Nicholas's commitment to autocracy, Orthodoxy and nationality, a reactionary and Slavophile combination proposed in 1833 and referred to as Official Nationalism. There have been suggestions that Vladimir Putin has a similar approach.

In place of his predecessors', notably Alexander's, emphasis on allowing existing non-Russian élites to play a key role in the administration of areas that had been conquered, particularly the Baltic Provinces but also the Polish lands, western Ukraine, Belarus and Lithuania, there was now an emphasis, notably after the repression of the Polish rising on 1830-1, on integration within the empire. This rising led to a declaration of independence, to which Nicholas responded with the deployment of over 100,000 troops and a demand for unconditional surrender. The rebellion was crushed, with the Poles suffering (as in 1794-5 and 1863) from the absence of any significant diversionary threat to the overwhelming Russian strength.

Understandably, this integration was focused on the Polish lands, with the nobility losing many of their distinctive rights and authority. In 1840, the Lithuanian legal code was replaced by Russian law. In turn, the regulation of serfdom in the Polish lands in 1844-8 weakened the landowners, as did its abolition in 1861. Authoritarianism was a key element in Nicholas's reign, and also a hostility to cosmopolitanism that led him, like other conservatives, to reject the legacy and example of Catherine the Great. Nicholas had a phobia about the French Revolution and concerning anything that smacked of European new thinking.

Religion remained a driver of Russian policy, with the Orthodox religious sympathies of Alexander I leading him to favour the Greeks in their rising against Ottoman rule. This was an aspect of a Russian self-appointment in the role of protector of the Orthodox and, more generally, of Balkan Christians, and as opponents of Islam. This joined national interest in expansionism to a sense of national mission, a combination seen today with Putin's assumptions. As now, there was also both long-term intentions and short-term opportunism, and violence and other means of influence. Nationalism and empire building were combined, with both helping mould political, social and cultural developments within Russia. In 1827, the Russian navy joined with the British and French in destroying the Ottoman-Egyptian fleet in the battle of Navarino Bay, which helped sway the struggle in Greece in favour of independence.

Russia's desire to quash rebellion in its empire meant she was against rebellion challenging her allies, such as Greece in 1831. In 1849, with the Hungarian republican uprising of 1848 against Habsburg rule still resilient, the Russians, keen to stop the spread of nationalism and to deliver a lesson to their own subjects, intervened with 170,000 troops, mostly moved from Poland. This intervention helped the Austrians crush the rebellion.

There was also a more general Russian expansion against the Islamic world. Victory over the Persians in 1804-13 and 1825-8 resulted in the Russian takeover of the entire south Caucasus. At war with the Ottomans in 1828-9, a larger-scale struggle, the Russians advanced into the Balkans as they had done in the war of 1806-12, and Nicholas I personally directed the successful siege of Varna in 1828. In 1829, the advance was as far as Adrianople (Edirne), the treaty of which forced the Ottomans to abandon their position on the Circassian coast on the north-eastern shore of the Black Sea where gains had been made by Russia in that war. Also in the 1820s, the Russians operated against the Chechens, harrying them into the Caucasus mountains in order to starve them into submission. This was to be a long and intractable struggle which continued into the 2000s, when it was settled only by means of an alliance with a local warlord.

Beginning in the 1730s, Russian pressure on Central Asia greatly increased after the Napoleonic Wars ended. In 1822, Russia annexed the lands of the Middle Kazakh Horde, introducing authority based on forts and using fortified lines to bring much of the best pastureland under their control. Kazakh opposition in the 1830s and 1840s was weakened by divisions, while the advance of settlers continued and more forts built. The weakness of other imperial systems played a role, Chinese influence among the Kazakhs being in marked decline. The Russians also advanced in Turkestan; General Perovskii's 1839 campaign against the Khanate of Khiva, in retaliation for the robbing of Russian traders, was unsuccessful, but afterwards fortresses were constructed to anchor the Russian presence. From the later 1850s, pressure increased.

Russia's potential role was certainly apparent in the threat she was seen to pose to the British position in South Asia. Alarmist concern about growing Russian influence in Central Asia led the British to intervene in Afghanistan. In fact, Nicholas I paid more attention to continuing earlier Russian expansion at the expense of the Ottomans. This triggered the Crimean War. The crushing Russian naval victory off Sinope in 1853 provoked concerns about the weakness of the Ottoman Empire and about possible Russian domination of the Black Sea and the Balkans. Echoing the geopolitical ideas of the day, British commentators saw this as a threat to the overland route to India, although they considerably exaggerated this threat. Prime Minister Viscount Palmerston declared in 1855: 'The real object of the war is to curb the aggressive ambition of Russia.' Other powers now also began to be concerned about Russian designs. In 1854, Napoleon III saw the situation as both crisis and opportunity. By intervening, he could achieve prestige to strengthen his domestic position and to enhance France's diplomatic position.

This was to be no 1812. Austrian pressure helped to force the Russians to withdraw from the Danubian principalities (in modern Romania) that they had occupied. The Allies were far more powerful at sea: the Russian navy was capable of beating the Ottomans, but not the British. The war focused on naval and amphibious action against the Russians. Such operations in the Baltic threatened St Petersburg, as did the (unrealised) idea of persuading Sweden into the war by agreeing to back a reconquest of Finland. There were also Allied naval and amphibious operations elsewhere on Russia's Pacific coast.

A full-scale Anglo-French amphibious expedition to the Crimea in order to capture the naval base of Sevastopol seemed an appropriate response to the Russian naval victory at Sinope. However, the Allies began the campaign late in the season (landing in Crimea on 14 September 1854), had not properly assessed the difficulty of the task, and lacked the necessary manpower. In the first battle, the 55,000-strong Anglo-French force attempted a contested passage of the River Alma on 20 September. In the end, more effective firepower broke down the strong defence and ensured that the frontal attack was successful. The poorly trained Russians did not have enough rifles and rifled artillery. Had this not been the case, the frontal attack would certainly have led to very heavy casualties on the Allied side.

A Major Power: The Nineteenth Century

The Allies then surrendered mobility and besieged Sevastopol, although the siege was not fully effective as road links to the north of the port remained open, a consequence of the lack of sufficient Allied troops to mount a comprehensive blockade. The Allies also had to face both particularly bad weather, which hit supply links across the Black Sea, and attempts by the Russian army in Crimea to disrupt the siege. These attempts became more serious as the Russians were reinforced from the Danube theatre. The Russians mounted unsuccessful attacks on the ports through which the Allies were landing all their supplies, and this was the cause of the battles of Balaclava and Inkerman.

At Inkerman, on 5 November, attacking Russian columns seeking to close to bayonet point took heavy losses from the Enfield rifles of the British, but firepower was compromised because the Russians, advancing in darkness and mist, had the advantage of surprise, and because the British experienced overnight rain as well as ammunition shortages. As a result, the British relied heavily on bayonet charges. In the later stages of the battle, the heavily outnumbered British (7,500 men to 35,000) were helped by the bringing up of heavier siege guns to counter the Russian artillery, as well as by the arrival of French reinforcements. This was a 'soldiers' battle', with the fighting resilience of the British troops in defence compensating for the more mixed quality of the British command. Russian casualties were far higher (about 5,000 killed to about 800 British and French killed), but the shock suffered by the Allies discouraged them from trying to storm Sevastopol that year.

The Russian failure to breach the supply lines was an Allied defensive success, but it was matched by the more significant Russian defensive success at Sevastopol. Despite heavy artillery support, Anglo-French land assaults in 1855 initially failed (as had a naval attack by Admiral James Dundas the previous year), for Sevastopol was well defended. The Russian army was strongly entrenched outside the town, making able use of earth defences, and was supported by over 1,000 cannon. In the end, Sevastopol fell after a successful French surprise attack on the Malakov redoubt, a key position in the defences.

In Britain, the Crimean War is generally seen in terms of folly, futility and horror, with attention focused on the incompetent command, mismanaged heroism, the heavy casualties of the charge of the British Light Brigade at Balaclava on 25 October 1854, and the horrific conditions in the winter siege of Sevastopol, with a lack of adequate food, clean water, shelter and clothing. This led to very heavy losses from disease. During the war as a whole, about 3,000 British troops were killed in action; 19,000 died of disease, exposure or infected wounds. If the British army was unprepared for the Crimea, it was able to cope thanks to the strength of the economy, and made improvements: in 1855, better transport, medical provisions and logistics helped the army's health, while military intelligence also improved.

Allied strategy occurred almost by accident, there was an absence of purposeful planning, and the Allies were fortunate that the Russians lacked modern rifles and good commanders, appropriate doctrine and training, effective logistics and the necessary communications. There were no railways south of Moscow, and the army had to walk and be barged the whole way. The Russians also had to keep much of their army in the Caucasus, where conflict was waged with the Ottomans, as well as in Poland and the Baltic region in order to deter possible Austrian, Prussian and Swedish intervention. Yet, it is possible to underrate the Allies' achievement in deploying, supplying and controlling large forces. The Allies kept their forces in Russia until they had achieved their task, a goal that had eluded Napoleon I, although, unlike in 1812, the Allies of course struck at a peripheral target.

The Treaty of Paris of 30 March 1856 achieved Allied war goals by severely limiting Russian naval forces on the Black Sea. The long-term effects, however, were different, for Russia was able to resume expansion at the expense of the Ottomans in the 1870s, and successfully so. Moreover, the war breached the Austro-Russian alignment, and this weakening of Austria provided the opportunities for Italian and German unification.

The Russian failure in the Crimean War punctured the impression of military proficiency that had prevailed since victory at Poltava in 1709. The failure can be explained in part by the inroads of disease, notably cholera, but also by the severity of the challenge posed by Britain and France. The limitations of the earlier reforms under Nicholas I were also significant. Nonetheless, these reforms helped ensure that the very process of reform became normative and foreshadowed the more significant Russian military reforms later in the century, especially under Dmitrii Miliutin, Minister of War from 1861 to 1881. Russian military leaders were determined not to rely on numbers alone.

In place of a large standing army, it was decided to move to a reserve system wherein soldiers would serve only a few years on active duty and then return home for posting to a ready reserve status, but this posed the problem of serfdom: the authorities believed that after military service, a discharged serf-soldier was now a free person and his status would demoralise village morale and lead to unrest. The solution had to be the abolition of serfdom.

The Crimean War, the accession of Alexander II (r. 1855-81), and a reaction against Nicholas I's autocracy encouraged liberalism and an interest in reform as a liberal project. Much of the intelligentsia, many of whom were of the nobility, was increasingly critical of the imperial system. This attitude, which focused on Moscow and St Petersburg, drove forward reform views in government, and contributed to a sense that existing systems required change, so pressure for reform in part came from within the ruling élites. This led to the abolition of serfdom in 1861 (outstanding redemption payments were abolished in 1907), legal reforms in 1864, including new courts, the formation of a legal bar and real lawyers, as well as trial by jury, the encouragement of industrialisation and railways.

Serfdom no longer seemed so relevant, economically or militarily. The emancipation was a major change in society. About 80 per cent of the population in 1860 were serfs. The emancipation, which was to be gradual, was directed by the central government and, thanks to noble obedience, peaceful. It involved peasants receiving land, for the government did not want a destabilising landless emancipation, The government paid the nobles for land by means of bonds. Three years later, the establishment of meaningful rural institutions in the shape of village councils began the building of more roads and schools and the training of more teachers and medical personnel. Peasants were still essentially tied to the land, but the emancipation helped introduce a considerable fluidity to a society that was anyway to be transformed by a massive rise in population, which nearly trebled between 1860 and 1913.

From the late 1860s, however, liberals faced a stronger conservatism as problematic as the revolutionaries. In 1866 there was an attempt to assassinate the Tsar, the first by an ordinary Russian wishing to overthrow the system, and therefore very different to the killings of Peter III and Paul I in 1761 and 1801 respectively, and to attempted coups, all of which had been high-level affairs. Opposition to liberalism was an obstacle to liberal support for local self-government and a measure of electoral activity as part of a system of responsive as well as representative government. There was also a Slavophile reaction against what was held to be a rejection of traditions by Alexander II. In contrast, the conservatism of his two predecessors was more easily linked to Slavophile views.

Meanwhile, renewed opposition in Poland in 1863-4 was again crushed, maintaining the territorial order at the same time as it was being overturned in Italy and then in Germany. France was interested in the idea of an independent Poland, but this was unwelcome to Russia whose government took the view that the insurrection was simply an internal affair. The Polish situation ensured that the local self-government introduced elsewhere in European Russia in 1864 was not implemented in the former Polish lands until 1911.

The changing international situation meant Russia became less consequential. Whereas Russia had played a major role in negotiating a settlement to the Austro-Prussian war of 1778-9, rapid Prussian victory over Austria in 1866 and France in 1870-1 gave the Russians few opportunities to play a role in producing a settlement that maintained their interests. On the other hand, Russia became more favourable to Prussia thanks to Otto von

Bismarck's offer of help in Poland in 1863-4, while Russia exploited the Franco-Prussian war by renouncing the Black Sea clauses of the 1856 peace treaty.

Instead, Russia attacked the Ottomans in 1877, to protect the Bulgarians against harsh reprisals for their Russian-encouraged insurrection the previous year. Pan-Slavism had already led to many Russians volunteering to help the Serbs when they fought the Ottomans in 1876. Unwilling to accept the guarantees against repeated atrocities in Bulgaria as offered by the Ottomans at an international conference, Alexander II launched his forces against the fortress of Plevna, which fell in 1877 after very heavy casualties from poorly prepared frontal attacks with the Ottomans using Martini-Henry rifles, accurate at long distances. The Russians advanced in 1878 to within 15 miles of Constantinople, dictating to the Ottomans a peace at San Stefano creating a large Bulgaria that would stretch to the Aegean; only for British diplomatic and naval pressure on Russia to shrink it back down.

The war contributed to a strengthening of Russian nationalism. A self-conscious intellectualism was part of the process, linked to radical ideas. In the last part of Tolstoy's novel *Anna Karenina* (serial form 1875-7, complete publication 1878), the writer Sergei Koznyshev declared:

> Every member of society is called upon to do his proper task and intellectuals perform theirs by expressing public opinion... Twenty years ago we should have been silent, but to-day the voice of the Russian people is heard, ready to rise as one man and sacrifice themselves for their oppressed brethren.

His half-brother Nikolai Levin responds: 'But it's not a question of sacrificing themselves only, but of killing Turks.'

Meanwhile, the Russians were expanding rapidly in Central Asia. Historical centres of significance fell, Tashkent in 1865, Bukhara and Samarkand in 1868, Khiva in 1873 and Merv in 1884. Occupying Khiva, the Russians liberated 30,000 slaves, some of whom were Russians, although many were Persian. This was a projection of the Russian self-image as enlightening and civilising Central Asia, an approach also taken in the Caucasus. It could of course be interpreted as to the benefit of particular groups supporting expansionism.

In 1885, as Russian forces pressed on to probe the northern borderlands of Afghanistan, the British and Russians came close to war in the Penjdeh Crisis. In 1889, at the height of the 'Great Game' for predominance in Asia, Colonel Grombtchesky boasted to Francis Younghusband that his Cossacks would be able to cross the mountains into India. Further east, Russia took over the Amur valley in 1858, founding Vladivostok in 1860 (meaning 'Lord of the East', officially proclaimed a city in 1880). The expansion was an assertion of Russia's interest in the future of China.

Conversely, Alaska was sold to America in 1867. This was scarcely the product of pressure, which the Americans were in no position to exert. Instead, for $7,200,000, they bought the territory which the Russians were keen to sell, not least because the Russian-American Company, the finances of which had long been precarious, was close to bankruptcy. After the Russians sold Fort Ross in California in 1841, largely due to the decline of the local population of sea otters with their valuable fur, as well as the limitations of agriculture, Russian Alaska lacked the poor supply of grain from there and from 1838 obtained grain from the British in British Colombia. Critics in America condemned both the acquisition and the expense. There were only 2,000 European settlers in Alaska. The Russians were far more interested in China.

Russia as a great power meant the need for troops. Conscription focused on serfs, but could also be used as punishment, as it was in 1831 when defeated Polish rebels were conscripted into the Russian army and sent to serve in the Caucasus. In 1874, as a consequence of the end of serfdom and of the related conscription of peasants, more general conscription was imposed: six years in general, four years for those with an elementary education. This was a strengthening of the state after the end of serfdom, although the Muslims of Central Asia were exempted. The social politics of the army were such as to replicate serfdom in many respects, with the officers drawn in large part from landowning gentry and operating in a hierarchical and disciplinary system that carried forward aspects of serfdom, not least harsh physical punishments, including executions. Old habits of subordination remained.

Russia was a complex interaction of imperialism with nationalism. The imperialism was that of the Russian élite, while the nationalism was both Russian and, dangerously for the empire, the rise and expression of national consciousness by other peoples that were part of the empire. This was the case in particular with the Poles and later the Finns: Jean Sibelius' music included symphonic poems based on episodes in the *Kalevala*, the Finnish epic published in 1835, and his symphonic poem *Finlandia* (1899) was treated as akin to a national anthem. In part, Russification policies were also a response to concern about spreading German influence in the Baltic Provinces, especially Latvia, and in Finland. The Latvian language acquired a substantial number of German words, unlike the Lithuanians who shunned the incorporation of outside vocabulary.

The process of proto-nationalism establishing a history extended to Jewish intellectuals advancing a call for Zionism, in part in response to the rise of antisemitism. In 1897, the General Jewish Labour Union of Lithuania, Poland and Russia, known as the *Bund*, was founded. Antisemitism led to pogroms, large-scale antisemitic violence that notably occurred in 1881-2 and 1903-6. Pogroms were especially frequent during Easter Week. Although the immediate causes and contexts were the pressures of change in towns, particularly competition over housing and jobs, as well as specific political crises, notably the assassination of Alexander II in 1881, the more general context for antisemitism included the ethnic policies of Alexander III (r. 1881-94), which were directed against non-Russians.

The very conservative Alexander III replaced his more liberal father, Alexander II, who was assassinated in St Petersburg by nihilist bomb-throwers who hoped it would lead to revolution.

This assassination was widely seen as a sign that reform would lead to chaos. Following the stance of Nicholas I, but in an increasingly complex and changing society, Alexander III was deliberately reactionary and sought to limit elective parliamentary and autonomous practices in Russia. This was seen with a more persistent standardisation of regulations, as with the municipal statute of 1870, which was then introduced into the Baltic provinces in 1877. Police systems were also standardised. Russian became the general language of instruction in schools, and non-Orthodox and non-Russian subjects faced increased and sustained discrimination.

His Russification policies were continued by his conservative, bigoted and antisemitic son, Nicholas II (r. 1894-1917), consolidating the state around the Russian nationalism seen in bodies such as the Union of the Russian People. Nicholas read to his family *The Protocols of the Elders of Zion*, an incendiary 1902-3 forgery by the *Okhrana* (Russian secret police) that reported Jewish plans for world domination. In 1906 he turned down ministerial suggestions for a moderation of the harsh restrictions on the Jews, who were officially limited in residence, employment and access to education. Jews initially could only live in a 'Pale of Settlement' established by Catherine the Great, essentially Russian Poland, and were obliged to reside in towns there; although Alexander II had allowed them to move more freely outside the Pale.

Russian consciousness, and thus identity, if not nationalism, was seen across the arts. Mikhail Glinka employed folk themes in his operas *A Life for the Tsar* (1836) and *Ruslan and Ludmila* (1842). This was followed from 1856 by the impact of The Five: composers who presented themselves as distinctly Russian, not least in incorporating peasant and Church themes, such as the sound of Church bells. The key figures were Mily Balakirev, Modest Mussorgsky, Nikolai Rimsky-Korsakov and Alexander Borodin.

There was a greater cultural interest in the countryside, which was presented as linked to a cause of Russianness and an expression of it related to that of a distinctive people. In the depiction of peasant life, the painter Vasilii Pukirev built upon the earlier work of Aleksei Venetsianov, while natural countryside scenes were offered by Ilya Ostrukhov and Vasilii Polenov. This interest was associated with the emancipation of the serfs. There was also an emphasis on the Orthodox faith, with cathedrals constructed in Helsinki and Tallinn. In contrast, Catholicism was seen as linked with Polish and Lithuanian separatism and, in response, there was a stress both on the use of Russian in Catholic services, notably in Lithuania after 1863, and also on Orthodox proselytisation.

Nationalism was an aspect of a rising literacy associated with the expansion of the middle class, increased prosperity, the end of serfdom and a degree of urbanisation. Thus, the population of Riga rose from 102,000 in 1867 to 507,000 by 1913, with a major movement of peasants from the countryside. This was a process that was scarcely controlled by government but that depended on its attitudes: the situation was very different to that during the Soviet era, when the state was far more in control and when a very negative account of pre-Bolshevik social trends was advanced. Thus, the degree to which a large, self-confident and assertive middle class developed prior to 1914 was neglected. This middle class owed much to industrialisation, for, despite the combination of government and the private sector in establishing large industrial concerns, the industrial sector was not under the general control of the state.

Prior to this industrialisation, it was the lack of a middle class, alongside serfdom and autocracy, that were most apparent to critical Liberal thought elsewhere in Europe, and that helped ensure that this thought was generally hostile to Russia. In contrast, conservatives elsewhere in Europe could look to Russia with approval, although the absence of Catholicism was a complicating factor, as was a degree of autocracy that left scant role for an independent nobility. However, the nationalist cultural turn was of interest to conservatives elsewhere.

When Alexander II emancipated the serfs in 1861, practices of labour control gave way to the opportunities opened up for workers by industrialisation, urbanisation and internal migration, although, as later with the abolition of slavery in Brazil, it was the very existence of these trends already that encouraged the decision to emancipate. Although there had been plentiful serf-labour in industrial enterprises on noble estates, emancipation eventually meant that industrialisation benefited from the availability of more labour, for there was no immigration comparable to that in America. The emancipation was seen by Abolitionists elsewhere as a key move in their struggle and led the Union during the American Civil War mistakenly to hope for Russian support.

The crucial significance of government can be seen in the development of railways. Franz Anton Ritter von Gerstner was commissioned in 1834 by the Russian government to oversee the building of a line between St Petersburg and Moscow, although it was not completed until 1851. Nicholas I very much supported this line, in part as a means to stimulate economic growth. The army provided relevant personnel, but some of the advanced equipment and personnel was foreign. Initial plans for trans-Siberian rail links were advanced from the 1850s, construction beginning in 1891.

The key figure was Sergei Witte (1849-1915), who in 1889 became Director of State Affairs within the Finance Ministry, moving on in 1892 to be first Transport and then Finance minister, before becoming Chairman of the Council of Ministers (1903-5) and the first Prime Minister (1905-6), replacing the Emperor as head of the ministry. Witte was committed to the expansion of rail and to making it a state monopoly. The rail system was linked to Russian expansionism. From 1879, the Trans-Caspian Railway was constructed from Uzun-Ada (later Krasnovodsk) on the eastern shore of the Caspian Sea, reaching Merv in 1886, Samarkand in 1888 and Tashkent in 1898, with a permanent bridge over the Oxus (Amu-Darya) in 1901. This link was seen as consolidating Russia's recently established position in Central Asia and was to be important in the development of cotton growing and manufacturing.

Further east, by the 1896 Li-Lobanov Treaty, the Russians obliged China to grant a concession for a Russian-gauge railway to Vladivostok across Manchuria, which was a more direct route than one restricted to Russian territory. Witte was instrumental in the negotiations, which included Russia having the right to station troops in order to protect the railway. Railways established an interest that had to be protected, which underlined the nature of international competition. The railway was constructed in 1897-1904.

Industrialisation, which Witte pressed hard for in the 1890s, led over a longer period to the transformation of some regions such as the Donbass, where it was based on iron and coal. A very different industry developed in Baku, where oil wells, which had begun earlier, expanded in mid-century, as did refineries, with Russia's first pipeline system in 1877, and in 1897-1907 a large kerosene pipeline constructed to Batumi on the Black Sea. By 1901, half of the world's oil production came from the region. Around Moscow, there was a major expansion in textile manufacturing, while St Petersburg, Warsaw and the Urals all saw significant industrial activity. Riga became a major industrial centre, notably from the 1890s, with mechanical engineering, metalworking and chemicals all important. In Estonia, there was a significant growth in textile manufacturing, particularly in Narva, while Tallinn built ships.

There was a divide between grain importing regions, essentially northern Russia, the Baltic provinces, and Russian Poland, and grain exporting areas to the south, which fed the major growth of Odessa, a key export-port. The area of greatest grain export was in southern Ukraine, Crimea, the Kuban, Moldova and the southern Volga area, the regions with the highest increase in sown area. In terms of population density, Ukraine and Russian Poland were highest, but there was also a shift of population to Central Russia, Siberia and Crimea, in particular from the Baltic provinces where agricultural opportunities were limited. This process was encouraged by the differential regional pressures on the population of the famine of 1867-8, as well as by the wish to escape rapacious landowners.

Dynamism could be seen elsewhere, as in the expansion of cotton cultivation in Central Asia. Entrepreneurialism was a marked feature of the Russian economy in this period, and at all levels. Urban growth provided more of a market for rural output, not least from the peasant communal villages which proved more effective and less backward than was often argued. There was also a greater exposure to the opportunities and crises of a cash economy, and this affected the large numbers of urban clerks and workers who were linked to often cyclical economic movements. Their employment was more necessary, as there was significant population growth, from 59 million in 1857 to 175 million by 1914, with only a small part of this growth due to territorial expansion. Rising food production was a major reason, although better medical care helped explain a marked rise in the percentage of peasant children reaching adulthood.

Industrialisation was a source of both prosperity and instability, as well as of environmental transformation in particular regions. This instability troubled not only conservatives but also reformers keen to encourage a stronger and more liberal Russia that was a central part of the international order. Liberalism encouraged the idea of the public, as both goal and means of social and political improvement. The legal reforms of the 1860s advanced the ethos of equality before the law and access to it, an equality that extended to members of ethnic and religious minorities such as (Muslim) Kazan and Crimean Tatars. As a consequence, there was considerable engagement with the agencies of the state. The public had many different political manifestations, but in essence it qualified the role of the tsar, and certainly the traditional role.

Russia could be at the cutting edge, as when Dmitri Mendeleev (1834-1907), Professor of Chemistry at St Petersburg from 1866, devised the periodic table that grouped chemical elements – as well as criticising the popular world of occultism. Imperial society showed growth, but the base rate was low, and aggregate improvement was hit by a rising population, such that per capita income continued to be low, at about 20 per cent of that of Britain and 40 per cent that of France and Germany in 1900. Social capital was inadequate. Infant mortality was over 200 per thousand and only half of adult males were literate according to the 1897 census.

Governmental attitudes were conservative. Konstantin Pobedonostsev, the Procurator of the Holy Synod and thereby head of the Orthodox Church from 1880 to 1905, was a key ideological figure under Alexander III, hostile to Western influences, democracy, and Jews, and in favour of tradition and social conservatism. Under Alexander III, censorship was enhanced and police authority greatly increased by the far from 'Temporary Regulations' of 1881, which lasted until 1917. This was scarcely conducive to democratisation. So also in 1884 with the restrictions of the new University Statute, and in 1889 and 1890 with an undermining of the 1864 measure to introduce local peasant organisation and representation. 1892 legislation did the same with reference to the urban reform law of 1870, restricting the franchise allowed by the latter.

At the governmental level, there was an uneasiness that helped cause the Russo-Japanese War of 1904-5, about apparently rival powers, Austria, Britain, Germany and Japan, as well as a fear that the rural uprisings of the past might be transposed into an urban setting. Signs of instability included assassination attempts against tsars and prominent figures, the student protests of 1899, and the sense of failure provoked by the famine of 1891 and by the deadly chaos surrounding the coronation of Nicholas II in 1894. In reality, however, there were relatively few radicals and it was understandable that Karl Marx saw Germany and Britain as more likely sites of revolution.

There were signs of weakness, even failure, underneath a façade of progress, as in the fictional Mutual Credit Society bank in Anton Chekhov's farce, *Jubilee* (1892). Yet, that was true for all countries. There was no reason to believe that Russia was particularly weak. Indeed, between 1900 and 1914 there was the violent overthrow of the governmental system in Portugal, Turkey, China and Mexico, but not in Russia.

{ 7 }

CHAOS AND CONFLICT
1900-23

October 17, 1905, Ilya Repin's 1907 painting of a crowd joining figures from all parts and ages of society, celebrated the Tsar's proclamation 'For the Improvement of State Order' of that date, seeking to address revolutionary tendencies by promising liberty and parliamentary government. Yet due to censorship, this was exhibited in Russia only in 1912, and many of the promises were unfulfilled. Other images, of course, can be offered. The World Exhibition in Paris in 1900 saw a major promotion of Russia's transcontinental rail project. A carriage from the line proved an attraction, not least because a diorama of over 100 metres depicting the journey was drawn past the window. In 1904, Halford Mackinder, the leading British geopolitician, argued in a lecture to the Royal Geographical Society in London that the railway had moved the balance from sea to land power. He particularly justified the argument in terms of the Russian construction of the Trans-Siberian Railway on the pattern of transcontinental lines in North America, but which was, he argued, because of the Eurasian context, of greater geostrategic significance. To Mackinder, this railway made possible the movement of forces rapidly around a Eurasian 'Heartland' and 'pivot', such that Russia could threaten its opponents, whether Japan in the Far East, or British interests in India, or European rivals.

Chaos and Conflict: 1900-23

Russia's status as a great power was clear in the opening years of the century. In 1900, when the Russians successfully advanced against the Chinese in Manchuria, the Chinese Eastern Railway for which China had granted a southern extension to the port of Dalian (Port Arthur) in 1898 served as an axis of movement. In 1900-6, the Trans-Caspian Railway was linked to the Russian system by the Tashkent or Trans-Aral Railway, from Kinel to Tashkent. This could move troops to Central Asia and cotton from there to mills in Moscow. Although in 1904, the Trans-Siberian, itself only single track, was incomplete at Lake Baikal, requiring the use of ferries until the Circum-Baikal railway was completed in 1905, the Russians transported 370,000 troops along it to the east during the Russo-Japanese War of 1904-5.

This war was one that reflected Russian strength and weaknesses, the former seen in the bellicose response to Japanese interests. There was a foolish unwillingness to accept Japanese strength, views and determination, and the perception in certain Russian governmental circles that victory would enhance the internal strength of the government. Engaged in a complicated struggle for power and influence in St Petersburg, the Russian ministers and military chiefs were too divided among themselves and too intent on their own power struggles to have a coherent Far Eastern policy. Commercial interests played a major role, the influence of Alexander Bezobrazov and his Yalu River Timber Concessions resulting in a more hardline attitude towards the Japanese, and the bribery of leading figures was important in this instance and others.

The government was split. Whereas the Finance Minister, Witte, was very opposed to war, some of the military had served in the Far East, were linked to commercial adventurers with interests there, and were close to Nicholas II. He and his advisers did not think the 'yellow devils' would dare to fight, but Russian behaviour and arrogance helped create ultimate unity in Tokyo behind war. Nicholas was a ruler without intelligence or energy.

The Russians were heavily defeated at sea, the battle of Tsushima in 1905 proving very different to Cesme in 1770 and Sinope in 1853.

On land, the Japanese drove the Russians back in Manchuria. This was a war widely seen in terms of Russian failure, although, in practice, there were two rapidly industrialising powers fighting a war for which neither was prepared, but, crucially, doing a better job than it had been reasonable to anticipate. Russia faced serious financial problems, but its economy proved more durable than its political system and the forces in Manchuria were sustained.

Japanese victory owed much to political weakness in St Petersburg. The Russian government had a revolution to confront in 1905, one to a degree fostered by Japanese military intelligence and affecting part of the army. 'Bloody Sunday' in St Petersburg (9/22 January 1905) saw the Imperial Guard shoot down peaceful demonstrators singing patriotic songs and carrying religious banners en route to present a petition to Nicholas II, leading to maybe 140-240 deaths. In response, there were widespread and persistent strikes. The government sought to end these with concessions in the October Manifesto, notably offering an elected *Duma*, a national body that could present a new analysis, narrative and prospectus for national life, as well as civil liberties, freedom of speech, assembly and publication.

However, as a product of the strong autocratic tradition and the strength of bureaucratic service, as well as in response to a general strike, the government rolled back and turned to large-scale repression, with many killed and exiled. In some areas, there was a nationalist dimension, with the burning down of manor houses in Latvia and Estonia, leading from December to a military response and disproportionately more executions. Martial law was imposed on the Baltic provinces until 1908. More generally, there was significant radicalism including terrorist attacks on officials. The war was brought to an end by the Treaty of Portsmouth mediated by America in a significant expansion of its influence. To obtain peace, Russia ceded southern Sakhalin, its lease of the Liaotung Peninsula and its position in Manchuria, and Japan also gained a free hand in Korea.

This might seem a clear precursor to the revolutions of 1917, but in practice that of 1905 was suppressed and followed by a period in which the government sought with some success to stabilise its domestic position and to strengthen its international one. The attempt by revolutionaries to overthrow the government was held at bay by the *Okhrana* (State Security), which succeeded in undermining the dynamism of underground Russian groups. It is likely that the revolutionaries would have continued to have had no success had it not been for the total disruption caused by defeat and instability in World War One. Even had the Allies been successful and Germany been defeated as a result of failure on the Western Front with Russia still in the fight, nevertheless the strains of the war were very serious, although also different to those of the pre-war years.

The possibilities for change offered by the inexperienced *Duma* were counteracted, not least but not only by the autocratic tendencies centred on Tsar Nicholas who, under the Fundamental or Basic Laws of April 1906, retained control of foreign policy, the military, the Church and two-fifths of the budget. Moreover, there was a bicameral legislature with the *Duma*, the lower chamber, balanced by the State Council, the upper chamber, half of which was appointed by the Tsar and half elected by large landowners and prominent businessmen. The limitations on the power of the *Duma* helped explain the rising discontent of various groups across society who had placed hopes in it and were disillusioned by its inability to enact real change. Meeting first in April 1906, the *Duma* did not enact measures that were discussed to reform the laws on religion. Orthodoxy remained strong, even if it was challenged in reform circles where a civic view of national identity was being developed.

Agrarian reforms supported by Peter Stolypin, Prime Minister from 1906, showed however how the 'system', itself changing significantly, tried to respond to the 1905 Revolution not just through force but by major agricultural reforms. These were designed to foster a class of propertied (and hopefully prosperous) peasants who would become more natural supporters of the status quo and the regime. There was the consolidation of peasant strips of land into more viable homesteads. By 1913, perhaps one-eighth of Russian farms consisted of single plots of land instead of the scattered plots customary for peasants. Though many peasants hated those peasants with consolidated plots, as this was a new practice contrary to the small-group psychology of the peasant community where everyone was expected to be equal. The Bolsheviks were later to exploit this resentment.

This was a period of great experimentation in art, as with the Blue Rose, a Symbolist artist association in Moscow from 1906 to 1908 that very much emphasised colour and rhythm rather than shape, the Jack of Diamonds *avant-garde* group of painters in Moscow, launched in 1910, and the Donkey's Tail group that followed in 1912-13. Key figures included Mikhail Larionov and Marc Chagall, and their Neo-primitive style sought to link elements of modern art with traditional themes from Russian folk art. In music, Igor Stravinsky offered a distinctive tone that captured Russian themes in the ballets *The Firebird* (1910), *Petrushka* (1911) and *The Rite of Spring* (1913).

There was to be no war of *revanche* against Japan (until 1945), and, instead, an easing of tension with Britain in 1907 and a strengthening of the 1894 treaty with France. Peacetime government expenditure on the military rose, with the percentage of total expenditure increasing from 23.2 in 1907 to 28.3 in 1913. This was thanks to economic growth and French loans. However, the majority of Russian officers remained unable to put men and equipment to good use, while, encouraged by Nicholas II, the Russo-Japanese War led to a conservative reaction in military circles against attempts to reform operational practice. More generally, Nicholas was an obstacle to the grounding of the constitutionalism introduced in 1905 and stood against the attempt to create a Western-style civil society and government, as well as being opposed to the radicals. He dissolved the First *Duma* in July 1906 and the second *Duma* in July 1907, and a more conservative electoral process with less representation from non-Russian regions was introduced in June 1907. This led to a *Duma* that was more conservative and thus had easier co-operation with the government. Half the delegates to the Third *Duma* were nobles and a quarter peasants. The Third (1907-12) and Fourth (1912-17) *Dumas* backed Nicholas in part because of the impact of the more restricted representation, and in part thanks to the Socialist Revolutionaries staying away.

In 1911, the Prime Minister since 1906, Peter Stolypin, who was increasingly sceptical about Nicholas, was assassinated by a revolutionary during a performance at the Kiev Opera House. From then, Russia was under a more interventionist and aggressive government, one that was less willing to subordinate geopolitical goals to domestic issues. Russia became Serbia's protector, with the religious dimension of shared opposition to Islam and Catholicism. Russia sought to create a Balkan alliance that would weaken Austria, at the same time risking war for a nationalism that it opposed within its own dominions. To a degree, Russia bears part of the responsibility for the outbreak of World War One, although less so than Austria and Germany. In 1912 and 1914, Russia and Austria mobilised in response to Balkan crises. Allied to Austria, the Germans believed it necessary to defeat the Russo-French alliance: there was fear of Russians, not Serbs, in Berlin. Fearing war on two fronts, the Germans planned to defeat France before focusing on slower-moving Russia.

Ironically, although the Russians had built up an army superior to that of Austria and had quickly recovered from defeat by Japan, the Russian attack on Germany was to be defeated easily in 1914, and much of Russian Poland was conquered by the Germans in 1915. The Germans, both military and politicians, had consistently overestimated Russia's military potential. They exaggerated the quantitative indices of army strength at the expense of qualitative criteria, and irrational fears overshadowed practicalities and reinforced aspirations for war.

In Russia, there was a wish to support Serbia, to gain control over the German and Austrian portions of Poland and, once the Ottoman empire joined in on the German side, Russia also sought to win control of the Straits (the Bosphorus and the Dardanelles). Instead, major German gains in 1915, including Brest Litovsk and Vilnius, as well as heavy Russian casualties, notably large numbers of prisoners, increased pressures within the country. Amidst rising inflation despite the attempt to fix prices, social discontent and political pressure for change, Nicholas II in August 1915 dismissed and replaced his uncle, Grand Duke Nicholas, himself impressively incompetent, as Commander-in-Chief, and greatly compromised his reputation in consequence.

Rumours circulated, notably that the German-born Tsarina was pro-German. She was certainly under the thumb of a charlatan, Grigory Rasputin, a mystic who claimed to be able to cure the Tsarevich's haemophilia. The only way to stop his influence turned out to be assassination in December 1916, but that action by monarchists keen to strengthen the dynasty did not bring cohesion to the royal family, or government. Indeed, the myopic Nicholas lost support across the political class. He could not match effectiveness to authority. There was nothing inevitable about the fall of the dynasty, but Nicholas helped make it likely.

The economy was poorly managed and wasteful, with industrial production and transport both in grave difficulties. A serious munitions crisis affected Russia in 1915, and there was dependence on French supplies. The War Industries Committees that had been set up accomplished noteworthy feats, but in 1916 state monopolies took over coal and oil production.

In 1916, the Germans switched to focus on France, attacking at Verdun, and this enabled the Russians under Aleksei Brusilov to attack the Austrians in southern Poland, making impressive gains as a result of innovative tactics and because the Austrians had transferred forces to the Italian front. Brusilov, however, was hindered by an effective German response, and by the incompetence of Russian generals on other fronts, for example Aleksei Evert, the Commander of the West Front, who was close to Nicholas II. The Russian army proved inadequate to the challenge, in part because its command culture remained anachronistic. Although the General Staff graduates were a meritocratic group, exposed to a scientific approach to war, they were also a small one. In general, the army was characterised by an emphasis on lineage, connections, and character, which did not guarantee an informed response to the problems posed by machine guns and entrenched defences.

Yet, there is the problem of teleology: the conflict was to lead to revolution, but in 1916 the Russian military effort had still not collapsed (indeed shell production rose) and, at the end of the year, German gains did not match those achieved by the spring of 1918, let alone in 1941. Indeed, in 1916, there were major Russian gains against Ottoman forces in the Caucasus including the capture of Erzerum and Trebizond.

There was rebellion in 1916, but it was very different to the revolution that was to follow. In Central Asia, a widespread Muslim revolt that drew on anger over the Russian appropriation of land and water and more recent wartime seizure of goods such as livestock, was spurred by the introduction of conscription, especially for labour battalions in the army. In Kazakhstan, organised rebel forces reached a peak strength of about 50,000 men. They suffered from a lack of organisation, training and arms, and were defeated with great brutality and heavy casualties. This was the first serious crisis of the imperial regime in the mid-1910s.

1917 saw two revolutions that reflected the wartime strain on society. This included 1916 food shortages and riots in Petrograd (the renamed St Petersburg to remove a German name), the shortages due to government requisitions and peasant hoarding. The strain was accentuated by the pressures of the winter. The organizational weakness of the Russian state was particularly clear in transport and food allocation, and the resulting pressures were concentrated in the cities as the demand for food was greatest there, a demand driven up by the large number of refugees from the massive war zone. There were over six million refugees, and their movement contributed to a general sense of disorder. Thus, Russia's failure to protect its territory from invasion contributed directly to the socio-economic crisis. Peasants hoarded grain as the requisition prices set by the government were too low.

Food shortages became more serious in the context of irrational fears that drew on a lack of national unity and on related political and social tensions, with 'speculators' supposedly holding the populace in thrall while 'Germans', including the Tsarina, betrayed them. In practice, the 'betrayal' linked to the Germans was that obtained by the latter's skilful use of subversion, notably arranging the transportation of the Bolshevik leader, Vladimir Lenin, to Russia.

Alongside popular discontent, there was significant disillusionment among the élite focused not only on Nicholas II but also on Tsarism. The extent of radical opposition to the Tsarist regime played a part in its fall, but it was not the sole element. Lenin sought to offer a fusion of Marxism with Russian conditions. In 1903, the Russian Social Democratic Party (a Marxist body) had divided between the Mensheviks (the Minority) who continued the Western European Marxist tradition, and the Bolsheviks (the Majority) who sought to adapt Marxism to Russia with a powerful Party organisation able to prepare for revolutionary change. Lenin very much opposed parliamentary systems and liberalism, for he argued that the majority could be misled and difficult to mobilise, and that it was necessary to direct the state rather than indulge in politics. In 1902, Lenin created the Bolshevik Party, later renamed the Communist Party.

A popular demonstration in Petrograd against the price of bread on 8 March 1917 focused discontent, the police failed to control it and the government turned to the army. Disaffected, the troops on 12 March (27 February old style) refused to fire on the crowds and went on strike. The following day, the troops and the factories elected representatives for a Soviet, or council, the Petrograd Soviet of Workers' and Soldiers' Deputies. In the face of mounting chaos, some politicians and generals thought it necessary to act, and did so by determining to get rid of Nicholas II, who lacked the drive in this crisis to develop necessary links with at least part of the army. The *Duma* established a Provisional Government under the reformer Prince Georgy Lvov, Prime Minister from 15 March to 20 July. Arrested by the Bolsheviks that winter, he was able to escape and died in France in 1925. The term Provisional Government was intended to signify a temporary situation until an election could be held.

The refusal of the *Duma* to disband provided another focal point for discontent. Soldiers had played a major role in the overthrow of Nicholas II, not so much that some units demonstrated for change, but rather that there was also a lack of willingness to fight for the Tsar. There were divisions within the officer corps. He abdicated on 15 March and his brother, Duke Michael, did not want to succeed him.

The establishment of the Provisional Government unleashed political debate, some of a radical character, and with ideas of government by means of representation, for example through an elected Constituent Assembly, increasingly to the fore, although because of the wish to wait for peace, none was to be elected until November 1917. Women were given equal rights. Discriminatory laws against the non-Orthodox and non-Russians were abolished, trial by jury was restored, and capital punishment was temporarily abolished.

Yet these ideas could not solve the problems of a state that could not wage war effectively, nor of a society under tremendous pressure. Inflation continued to bite, while the transport system remained hamstrung. The war went on, without success. Indeed, the eventual fall of the new government in November owed much to its failure on the battlefield; or alternatively its failure to pull out of the war altogether.

The Western Allies hoped that the change in government would make Russia a more liberal state and acceptable ally, and would revitalise the Russian war-effort, and the Russian General Staff pressed for an offensive in order to help France and Britain on the Western Front. On 1 July, Brusilov, now the commander in chief, launched an offensive into eastern Galicia, winning a breakthrough success at the expense of the Austrians. However, announcing the summer offensive in advance was a mistake, while limited resources and motivation hindered the advance. A rapid German counter-attack on 19 July led to Russian defeat, heavy losses, retreat, and the collapse of the Russian army. Much of it anyway did not wish to fight and deserted. Brusilov was replaced on 1 August.

This failure contributed greatly to the weakness and lack of prestige of the government, which had faced a series of crises within Russia, political instability and armed uprisings. There was a tendency for regions and communities to be forced to a degree of self-reliance which, in turn, contributed to a sense of breakdown; and reality increasingly matched this sense, including peasants seizing land. To a degree, the Russian Civil War began in the summer of 1917 when the countryside started falling apart.

From 21 July, the government was headed by Alexander Kerensky, a Socialist who had played a leading role in the March Revolution and thereafter served in the government. However, despite its composition shifting leftwards, the Provisional Government proved unable to satisfy demands on the left. This paved the way for the Bolsheviks: the weakness of the government provided them with an opportunity to seize power after the army's new commander-in-chief, General Lavr Kornilov, had failed in September to overthrow the Petrograd Soviet in an abortive advance on the capital. This was a confusing episode that radicalised the Bolsheviks and led to an increase in the influence of men like Kerensky, who took the attitude of 'no enemies on the left', and cast around for support. There was a more general sense that counter-revolution was a threat.

As part of the process by which Bolshevik leadership drew extensively on *émigré* experience, Lenin had been returned to Russia from Switzerland in April, helped by the Germans in an attempt to sow disaffection, while, en route to Petrograd, Leon Trotsky was arrested and detained by British naval authorities at Halifax for a month because they believed he was a German agent. Lenin, who was against the war and confident that it would pull down the Provisional Government, more than fulfilled German hopes and justified the tens of millions of marks provided to further his activity.

At the same time, social tension increased, with support for the Provisional Government shadowed by divisions between the propertied and urban workers. These divisions were accentuated by the continuation of war and by economic strains. The government could not master the situation. Such strains were to be seen with the collapse of Soviet Communism culminating in 1991.

The sense of crisis increased when after an intensive but short bombardment a German offensive across the River Dvina above Riga, the largest city in Latvia, launched on 1 September, broke through the Russian positions and led the Russians to abandon Riga. The Bolshevik influence in the St Petersburg Soviet increased, and on 7 November, in the midst of radical turmoil in the capital, there was a coup by the Bolsheviks who were responding to developments as well as shaping them. Lenin sought to take the opportunity to seize power, but did so in part for fear of losing control of possibilities. This led to the overthrow of the government with little resistance. Albeit drawing on a degree of popular support, indeed a euphoric commitment by some to transformative change, this was essentially a revolutionary *putsch*. The government was unable to rely on the military because the governmental willingness to fight on against the Germans compromised military co-operation. Alongside disaffection among the soldiers, some of the senior commanders were unwilling to fight for the government. The Communists made a major effort to seize and make use of the telegraph, telephone and postal services, while the killing of opponents began at once.

The Constituent Assembly was dissolved in January 1918, in large part because the Bolsheviks saw it as a rival source of authority to that of the Soviets or workers. The Constituent Assembly had been put off until January and then, with its majority rejecting the measures of the Bolshevik government and the Decrees of the Small Congress, it was dispersed. This was a rejection of the political promises of 1917 and a closing down of possible avenues of development, making constitutional definition dependent on force, and debate a matter of resistance.

Nationalist opposition to the Imperial centre played a significant role in the collapse of the Provisional Government. Both Bolsheviks (radical Marxists) and nationalists (many of whom belonged to Socialist movements as well) were products of Russia's fast but uneven industrialization and incomplete agrarian reforms.

Although the principal industrial centres in the periphery like Baku and the Donbass were highly Russified, they housed the nationalist intellectual activists, while the agrarian areas provided mass support. The Bolsheviks addressed the working class of the industrial centres but also sought there to ally with the nationalist intellectuals. In all the *Dumas* the nationalists had strong groups that demanded administrative and cultural autonomy for their provinces. The activism of the peripheral nationalists during the Revolution pushed the former Russian Empire to become the federative Soviet Union and not a unitary state after the Civil War.

After a Russo-German armistice in December 1917, Lenin hoped that the spread of revolution to Germany would make negotiations unnecessary, but when the Bolsheviks refused to accept the terms offered, the Germans resumed the offensive. Their rapid success forced the Bolsheviks to accept even harsher terms in the Treaty of Brest-Litovsk signed on 16 March 1918. The Bolsheviks agreed to cede sovereignty over much of western Russia, lands inhabited by about 34 per cent of the pre-war population in Russia, including territory that had been Russian since the seventeenth century, as well as over half the industry and over two-thirds of the coalfields. Subject to a referendum, the Russians were to return to the Turks the lands they had gained in 1878.

The situation in these areas remained unclear, and the Germans moved forward to seize control. In April 1918, they overthrew the democratic government that had gained power in Ukraine and installed a puppet regime, although its protection then led to a commitment of many German troops. German pressure in the former Russian empire meanwhile continued, much of it motivated by the economic requirements of the war effort, requirements that also led to a determination to retain the labour of Russian prisoners of war. Georgia, Armenia and Azerbaijan declared independence from Russia in May, following Finland, Estonia, Latvia and Lithuania. Germany and its opponents saw opportunities from these new states and manoeuvred for advantage.

In addition to their own efforts on the ground, the Germans sought to manage the situation by agreement with the new

Bolshevik regime, prefiguring the situation during the Nazi-Soviet Pact of 1939-41. On 27 August 1918, Lenin accepted trade terms with Germany, providing grain and other economic concessions. The benefits the Germans appeared likely to derive from the changing situation in Eastern Europe led the British and French to support plans for overthrowing the Bolsheviks, regarded as a way to prevent Russia from falling under German control.

The revolution led to idealism, optimism, hope, and legislation for establishing freedoms, such as abortion, as well as to experimentation in social goals and means. In the first years of Bolshevik control, the peasants were given land, as by the Communists in China in 1948-9. Although with very many individual exceptions, women as a category also benefited from the Revolution. Yet, the revolutionaries' transformative aspirations were inherently based on the violent seizure of power that characterised policies and responses, with utopian desires linked to the rapid turn to terror as a means of policy. That this use of power by the Communists included censorship and excluded Anarchists, were demonstrations of its statist character and its rejection of libertarianism. So, also, with the revolutionary tribunals created to attack whatever could be seen as 'counter-revolution'. Russia was about to be plunged into a civil war on top of the already-destructive world war in which it had lost 1.81 million troops dead and 2.4 million captured, as well as massive civilian loss due to destruction, disruption and disease.

In the civil warfare that began in 1918, the failure of the anti-Bolshevik forces owed much to their serious internal divisions and lack of cohesion, notably in advancing from the east and the south, as well as to their political and strategic mismanagement. These forces ranged from the Whites on the Right to the Socialist Revolutionary Party and others on the Left. The Bolsheviks suppressed their former allies; the Anarchists in April, many being killed or imprisoned while some others fled or joined the Bolsheviks. This was followed two months later by a purge of Socialist Revolutionaries and Mensheviks, and in July, by a Left Socialist Revolutionaries uprising that was suppressed.

The multiparty system had gone. The Bolshevik leaders used democratic language but without democratic intent. By the standards of the age, that was not surprising. Democracy was not easy to introduce, and should not be regarded as the automatic outcome, the failure of which has to be explained.

The military opposition was dominated by the Whites. The Bolsheviks' central position was crucial. They had control of Moscow, which became the capital, and Petrograd, the vital populous and industrial areas, as well as of key arms factories around Moscow, and of rail links and internal river and canal systems. The industrial centres, where Bolshevik support was greatest, were also the hubs of the transport system. As a result, the Bolsheviks fought on interior lines, which a British General Staff report saw as a major advantage enabling the Bolsheviks in a very changeable conflict 'to concentrate at will' against individual opposing armies. Thus, in 1919, the White advance under Nikolai Iudenich on Petrograd was thwarted in large part because the failure to cut the railway from Moscow enabled the Bolsheviks to bring up large numbers of troops, as well as Trotsky, who proved an effective commander.

The Bolsheviks ruthlessly mobilized all the resources they could for the war effort, although that also harmed their support. Conscription was pushed hard, businesses were nationalized, grain seized, and a firm dictatorship imposed with opposition brutally suppressed. The size of the Red Army rose to five million men by the end of 1920, the result of reflecting harshly effective conscription. Such a large force of the people under arms corresponded with Bolshevik ideas about mass mobilization and also provided troops for the number of military challenges that the Bolsheviks had simultaneously to confront. The adoption of an equivalent to the *levée en masse* of Revolutionary France was in part due to necessity, but also reflected how the Bolsheviks were looking over their shoulders for guidance, to see how the French Revolutionaries had handled matters, to be copied or adapted.

Like the French Revolutionaries from 1792, the Bolsheviks overcame their oppositional tendencies and, while benefiting from taking over the established governmental infrastructure, created a new state and military system reliant on force and centralized control in order to direct resources ruthlessly. The Red Army gave force to this internal transformation and also represented it. A brutal secret service, arbitrary imprisonment, concentration camps, large-scale torture, and the mass killings of those suspected, were all integral parts of the Bolshevik system, encouraged by Lenin. He had a belief in the inherent necessity and value of violence, not only to transform society but also to maintain the cohesion and purity of a movement that was focused by his leadership.

Bolshevik violence contributed to a general social and political fragmentation and a destruction of the social and ideological resilience that might have helped to sustain resistance. This, alongside famine and exhaustion, was to help Communists suppress opposition on many occasions. Monarchy was ended, the imperial family slaughtered near Yekaterinburg in July 1918, and its past expunged. The statues of Tsars were destroyed or removed, one of Alexander III, for example, being hidden from view at the Russian Museum.

The Bolsheviks were assisted in Russia by the extent to which the rival Whites (or conservatives) proved unable to win and sustain peasant backing, whereas a very different situation was encountered when the Bolsheviks sought to advance into Poland, the Baltic Republics and Finland. Widely grounded opposition in these areas, especially Polish victory in the battle of Warsaw of August 1920, ensured Bolshevik failure. In contrast, the Bolsheviks succeeded in Central Asia, the Caucasus and Ukraine. Georgia was a Menshevik republic during the Civil War, which the Bolsheviks were fixated upon bringing down. Whereas the Western Powers supported Poland, there was no comparable backing for Georgia, Armenia and Azerbaijan. Failure and success defined the borders of the Soviet Union formed in 1922. The Union of Soviet Socialist Republics created a federal system and government for what had hitherto been *ad hoc*.

Lacking a broad social base and largely failing to see the need to create one, the White Russian governments were selfish, greedy, factious, and incompetent. The British General Staff was pessimistic about the prospect for a leading ally, Anton Denikin, the White commander in the South:

> Unless he can offer to the wretched inhabitants of the liberated districts ... conditions of existence better than those which they suffered under the Bolshevik [Communist] regime, he will in the course of time be faced with revolt and hostility in his rear just at the time when the Bolsheviks will be concentrating large numbers of troops for a counter-offensive.'

Foreign intervention on behalf of the Whites suffered from a lack of agreed aims and of resolve. The financial burdens left by World War One placed further limits on an interventionism that was far from popular in the countries intervening, underlining the broader international dimensions of the civil war. Thus, Britain and France in particular each had a range of onerous commitments, while Canada, Japan, and the United States were also under pressure.

Opposition to the Bolsheviks in Russia was also encountered from the Left, indicating the range of insurrection, the fissiparous character of revolutionary movements, the radical disruption caused by violent changes in authority, and the way it made renewed uses of violence seem normative. In February 1921, the sailors and workers on the Kronstadt island naval base to the west of Petrograd, the leading naval base, rose against the government and in favour of Soviet democracy, a rising the government falsely blamed on the Whites. After an initial attack on the island had failed, fifty thousand troops in an operation organised by Felix Dzerzhinsky covered by heavy artillery and supported by aircraft advanced across the ice and restored state control. Those who surrendered were shot without trial or sent to concentration camps. The Finns complained about the number of corpses of the executed that washed up on their shore.

The following year, Socialist Revolutionaries were attacked in a stage-managed show trial designed to present them as traitors, indeed 'enemies of the people'. The accused, in turn, charged the

Bolsheviks with betraying the revolution, which did not save them. In March 1921, the Bolshevik Party Congress had seen both the introduction of the New Economic Policy and the 'ban on factions' that restricted debate in the Party and paved the way not just for a one-Party state but also for a Party where debate was increasingly unacceptable and any opposing view targeted.

The Bolsheviks also faced peasant opposition, which reflected the burden of the civil war, the exactions of the new regime, notably its demands for grain and recruits, the former precipitating a serious famine in 1921-2, and opposition to its determination to control rural life. Much of this opposition, especially in the Volga valley, was large scale although poorly organized, like the Razin and Pugachev Revolts, and lacking foreign support. Its repression involved a significant deployment of government forces. Over 100,000 troops, supported by aircraft and using poison gas, were deployed in June 1921 to overcome the Antonov revolt in Tambov Province. In this case, as in others, there were mass internments, shootings, and deportations to concentration camps.

Islamic opposition was also crushed in the Soviet Union. The Red Army employed the brutal techniques already developed in the civil war, including mass deportations and executions, in anti-insurgency campaigns in Central Asia and the Caucasus. Overwhelming force, the use of artillery against mountain villages and the ability to call on some local support all played a role, as when the Soviets suppressed uprisings in the Caucasus areas of Daghestan and Chechnya in 1920-21, 1924, 1928, 1929, 1936, and 1940. These areas saw insurgencies anew from the 1990s.

During the Soviet period, insurgency and counterinsurgency, or, more mundanely, force and opposition, were linked to government social policy. This included not only social transformation seen elsewhere in the Soviet Union, notably the collectivization of agriculture, but also attempts at cultural revolution. Muslim courts were suppressed in Central Asia in 1926, followed in 1927 by Muslim schools and colleges, and there was an attempt to end the veil. In response, Muslims attacked women who unveiled, and the campaign to end the veil was called off in 1929. The closure of churches and monasteries led to an insurgency in Georgia in 1921-22. Another in 1924 was brutally repressed, with about seven thousand to ten thousand people killed, followed by large-scale emigration. In contrast, the scale of the antisemitic pogroms carried out by the Whites in 1919 helped encourage many Jews to seek protection from the Communists, although antisemitism was also a feature of Soviet attitudes and was to become pronounced after World War Two.

The Russian Civil War can be dated to 1918-21, not 1922, as far as Russia west of Lake Baikal is concerned, but to the east 1922 is the appropriate year for large-scale movements of troops because it was then that the Japanese, the largest of the intervention forces, withdrew, which enabled the Bolsheviks to take Vladivostok in October. The Okhotsk seaboard and Kamchatka, however, only came under Soviet control in 1923, Wrangel Island in 1924 and northern Sakhalin in 1925.

Yet, that account underplays the extent to which 1922, and, indeed, treaties such as those of 1920 and 1921 with Finland and Poland respectively, were seen by the Bolsheviks and their opponents alike as but stages in a longer-term conflict with non-Soviet powers. Indeed, Mackinder, then British High Commissioner in South Russia, had pressed the Cabinet in January 1920 on the danger of 'a new Russian Czardom of the Proletariat'. In 1923, the Soviets planned war with Germany in support of a hoped-for Communist revolution there, and efforts were made to win Polish support. In the event, there was no revolution and no Polish support. Yet, tensions continued.

So, also, in domestic policy. Although a measure of moderation was to be seen in 1921 in what was termed the New Economic Policy, Communism was inherently violent and committed to the transformative necessity of violence, as in the attacks on religion. In social matters, there was an emphasis on redistributive seizure, as in that of housing in order to create spaces for as many families as possible, and, in doing so, advance collective goals and solutions. This was designed to provide an exemplary communalism. Convinced that they knew the future and how to get there, the Bolsheviks sought to enable 'the New Soviet Man' by creating the utopia that was relevant, appropriate and possible. Throughout the 1920s, there was a significant 'Reds versus Experts' argument. Expertise, for many Party members, meant deviation from class consciousness, a bourgeois cover-up. Lenin propagated his belief that anyone can become proficient in whatever field if given the chance.

There was continuing difference over the organisation and the process of the Revolution. From March 1921 to October 1923, Lenin and Trotsky struggled with the concept of the 'Dictatorship of the Proletariat'. While Lenin believed that the Bolshevik Party must run it, Trotsky pressed for a reorganisation of the industrial workers to do so. In this period, Grigory Zinoviev, the head of the Leningrad Party branch, and Lev Kamenev, the head of the Moscow City Council, close Party allies of Lenin, promoted Joseph Stalin to be the Party's General Secretary in order to counterbalance Trotsky's authority as Commissar for Military and Naval Affairs. They also promoted Nikolay Bukharin and Alexei Rykov to be, respectively, the leading ideologue as editor of *Pravda*, the central Party newspaper, and the key government administrator as deputy to Lenin.

If civil war paranoia and mobilisation lent further energy to the elements of violence, they were inherent to Bolshevik ideology and practice. Any idea that the revolution was benign under Lenin, or at least had benign possibilities, and then was ruined by Stalin has to face the brutality of a terror already much in evidence under Lenin. Although the regime had its divisions over policy and practice, this was terror as intent and not as side-effect. The very absence of consent, and the lack of the ballast of continuity, meant that the regime operated to seek control through violence in what was a situation of change. War would be waged on 'anti-Soviet' forces throughout the succeeding decades.

{ 8 }

THE STALIN YEARS
1924-53

From Kartaly to Magnitogorsk, we played soccer along the tracks, then we ran to catch up with the train, which had gone only a little way.

American passenger, 1930, on a new rail line that was crucial to Soviet industrial plans.

Dying in 1924, Lenin did not leave a successor who was as powerful, but Joseph Stalin who was to take over was already General Secretary of the Communist Party from 1922. An ethnic Georgian, Stalin was educated at church school and trained as a priest before turning to violent radicalism. Aligning with Lenin's Bolsheviks, Stalin, who drew on the Caucasus background of gangsterism, used crime to raise funds, a form of political gangsterism, and was repeatedly imprisoned. An important Bolshevik propagandist in 1917, he was appointed the People's Commissar for Nationalities in 1917, and in 1918-20 played a role in the civil war, pressing for the execution of counter-revolutionaries.

Lenin came to distrust Stalin and express a degree of criticism. However, Stalin, a skilful organiser as well as an effective interpreter of Marxism, proved adept in the succession disputes after Lenin died. Initially, Stalin, Zinoviev, Bukharin and Kuibyshev, who each in effect led particular political/governmental groupings, remained sufficiently united to prevent Trotsky from gaining power. As Commissar for Military and Naval Affairs from March 1918 to January 1925, he was suspected by some of Bonapartist ambitions, but his grip on the army was broken and he was ostracised and replaced as Commissar by Mikhail Frunze, an ally of Zinoviev. Trotsky, however, remained on the Party's most senior body, the *Politburo*. Trotsky promoted the idea of ending the NEP and restricting the market economy in order to use resources to develop the heavy industry that was the basis of the proletariat. Bukharin defined this concept as being 'leftist', which led to Trotsky's group being called the Left Opposition.

Stalin allied with Bukharin in defending the NEP and together they also challenged the dominance of Kamenev and Zinoviev in the Party, turning its officialdom against them. Kamenev and Zinoviev composed the 'Leningrad Opposition' against Stalin's lead, and also allied with Trotsky, adopting his stance against the NEP, their alliance being labelled the 'United Opposition'. This was crushed at the XVth Party Congress in December 1927. The following July, he abandoned Bukharin, who was referred to now as the 'Right Opposition', and backed the First Five Year Plan and collectivisation.

Stalin characterised opponents as part of a Left Opposition or a Right Opposition, contributing to the fissures already present in the Party and government. At the same time, Stalin's own attitudes ensured that the leadership battles linked to the implementation of Stalinism took many years, for, repeatedly, he came to distrust officials he had put in place, for example in Moscow where the Party organisation was only really under control by 1930. This process was linked to a wariness about Party cells and a preference for organisational direction.

Stalin also pressed for a *realpolitik* in international relations that represented the normalization of relations with other states. This pressure was linked not to the abandonment of the international Communist cause, but to the pursuit of Socialism (ie. Communism) in one federal state (the Soviet Union), a course presented as leading to the strengthening of the cause and intended, in the long term, to be followed by the international expansion of Communism. This emphasis was associated with Stalin, who had little experience outside Russia, only knew Russian and Georgian, and was sceptical of the motivations and links of former *émigrés*. With the impatient and intolerant Stalin, scepticism meant extirpation.

Stalin, who became more powerful after Lenin's death in 1924 and controlled notably the Secretariat, was opposed by the more volatile Trotsky's demand for permanent and global revolution. At a meeting of the Politburo in 1926, Trotsky accused his rival Stalin of becoming 'the gravedigger of the revolution'. Trotsky, who had lost his military power base, was to be forced into exile by Stalin in 1929, and in 1940 was murdered in Mexico in a plot by the People's Commissariat for Internal Affairs, the secret police (the NKVD, 1934-46), the successor to the *Cheka*, the All-Russian Extraordinary Commission that operated in 1917-22.

This struggle over policy, control and personalities was also linked to questions of military organisation. Trotsky, who was never strong on consistency, had spoken in favour of a workers' militia, which he presented at the Party Congress in 1920 as appropriate for a Communist state and the way to use and retain class consciousness, and also backed technological modernisation for the Red Army. The Party Congress led to a militia alongside the regular army. The idea of dependence on a workers' militia was resisted with the argument that a standing army was the only way to defeat the regular forces of other states. A major element of Stalinist policy, both before and after World War Two, was suppressing those held to be Trotskyites, a policy that was linked to both antisemitism and hostility to what was presented as cosmopolitanism.

The search for Trotskyites was a rift that fed Stalinist paranoia and gave potent force to the idea of the enemy within. This idea was brutally enforced in Communist and allied movements abroad, as with the hunting down of those in the Republican camp considered suspect during the Spanish Civil War of 1936-9. That Stalin's paranoia in part came from misperceptions linked to flawed intelligence does not lessen his paranoid characteristics, because he had both established the relevant institutions and chose how to interpret what he received.

The Soviet Union was taken into state ownership, the country was forced into centrally directed industrialisation with the first First Year Plan of 1928-32, and, in place of the willingness to allow peasants to trade in food under the New Economic Policy of 1921, collectivisation was imposed on the countryside, notably in 1929-33, with not only land and production but also livestock collectivised. This was another form of serfdom. Only in 1976 were collective- and state-farm peasants given the right to have internal passports. Prior to then, if they wished to leave the farm to travel somewhere, they needed the permission of the collective or state farm chairman to do so in the form of a *spravka* (permission slip) that the peasant had to take with him on his journey in order to get travel tickets, stay in a hotel, or display to a policeman.

Furthermore, longstanding economic practices that did not fit into Soviet ideas were hit hard, for instance the Siberian fur trade. More generally, both agriculture and industry became spheres of (unrealistic) aspiration and coercion, rather than of achievement in terms of productivity, effectiveness or consumer satisfaction. Ideological considerations were important in limiting the supply of consumer goods, more of which could have been produced had emphases been different. The attitude of the Soviet system to the outside world encompassed a form of economic isolationism, with no convertible currency and, instead, barter. As a result, foreign investment was absent, which ensured that domestic society had to be squeezed hard to produce resources. There was a lack of links with innovation elsewhere in the world economy, and that at a time when an openness to American models, notably 'Fordism', mass production, was important to the other European economies. The Soviets by the late 1920s were committed to both economic and cultural autarchy and wished to cut themselves off as much as possible from the contaminating influence of the capitalist world.

Already hit hard by killings and seizures, the Orthodox Church was further devastated by Stalin. The discrediting of the

Church included the opening of tombs containing the supposedly uncorrupted bodies of the saints. Church bells were seized as a way to extend the control over communities and their practices. The bells were taken down to be melted for industrial and public-sign usage. Muslim courts and schools were suppressed. The Soviets simultaneously 'dereligionized' Muslim culture while building up and promoting a secularised version of inhabitants' cultural traditions. These were aspects of a determination to control cultural production and ideological commitment.

The secret police were a crucial prop to the state, for example in the expropriation and exile of *kulaks* (wealthier peasants). However, it would be mistaken to ignore the extent to which agency was shared: while totalitarian, the Soviet state was also influenced by its perception of public opinion. Moreover, Stalin could be seen as a helper against aspects of government that were disliked, as well as an opportunity to those seeking upward mobility in and through the Communist Party. Stalin also benefited greatly from collectivist and autocratic traditions and practices in Russian society and government.

Nevertheless, whatever the extent of support or compliance, surveillance was important to reshaping as well as scrutinising society, and, indeed, acted as a regulator for a state-controlled society that otherwise lacked them. This included as a regulator of economic affairs, both prices and labour. The government's manipulation of public information, so that it served the purposes of propaganda, was linked to its control over the means of information. Everybody lived in an information void, unsure of events. At the same time, the government found it difficult to gain reliable information and to direct associated systems, such as the registration of residency and control over movement. Control over identity was part of a comprehensive Soviet direction of movement and residence that was registered with a passport and residency system. This direction ensured that people could not re-create their own identity but were fixed at the disposal of the state. However, the system did not work well. There was considerable chaos and subversion in the passport system.

Information more directly served the purposes of Soviet government. Planning and statistical agencies had a symbiotic relationship. Thus, in 1932, TsUNKh (Central Administration of the National Economy), was separated out from Gosplan, the state planning agency. The command economy required information on the location of the means of production, as well as on numbers and dynamics. Gosplan played a major role in producing the statistics, but was also therefore subject to intensive political scrutiny, notably with the purge of 1929. There had already been a purge in 1924 in the Central Office of Statistics in Moscow, which reflected the tension between the use of statistics for narrower political purposes and for the wider goal of a state supposedly managed on a scientific basis.

Stalin believed that the implications of statistical findings were not independent of Party doctrine. This last was the purpose and method for the Communist state, but it was repeatedly limited by the extent to which poorly conceived policies of all types were implemented through bureaucratic systems that, in seeking to adapt these often highly naïve polices to circumstances and interests, also counteracted them. Statistical falsification at every level was part of this process, and an aspect of propaganda as government and government as propaganda. Partly as a result of the provision of reports on the exact lines of what was expected, the opening of archives in the 1990s has had only so much influence. There was also the more general character of bureaucracy: Soviet offices had desks jammed together, workers chatting, primitive office equipment, officials afraid to take initiative and constantly pushing matters up to superiors for decision-making, and general sloth and tardiness.

As another aspect of control, all collection of data relating to criteria such as prostitution, alcoholism, poverty and nutrition and infectious disease was halted on the grounds that, with Socialism almost achieved by the Communist state, such phenomena could not exist, or must be dying out and barely worth investigating. Seeing male homosexuality as a product of the capitalist past that could be linked to counter-revolutionary tendencies, Stalin made it a crime in 1934, and there was no decriminalisation until 1993. There was scant interest in the disabled who were considered not to be regular citizens and in some situations kept out of view, while the unemployed were increasingly treated harshly, as 'social parasites.'

In the background, propaganda was incessant. Nationalised in 1919, the film industry was used to propagate an exemplary account of recent history. This focused on the cruelty of the old order, as in Sergei Eisenstein's film *Strike* (1925), which depicted Tsarist troops shooting workers, and *Battleship Potemkin* (1925) which was produced to commemorate the 20th anniversary of the 1905 revolution. The tenth anniversary of the 1917 revolution was marked by a series of films that included Vsevolod Pudovkin's *The End of St Petersburg* (1927), Esther Shub's *The Fall of the Romanov Dynasty* (1927) and Eisenstein's *October* (1928). A usable past was constructed, albeit with considerable difficulty as Communism had to be imprinted on nationalism, identity and the past, with heroes and villains defined accordingly. Socialist Realism, a key cultural theme, in practice meant propaganda. Opening the first Congress of Soviet Writers in 1934, Andrei Zhdanov declared: 'Our Soviet literature is not afraid of the charge of being "tendentious" … in an epoch of class struggle there is not and cannot be a literature which is not class literature, not tendentious, allegedly non-political.'

The Soviet view of history combined established anti-Western Slavophile themes with more specifically Communist perspectives. Historians were expected to toe the party line as an aspect of the attempt to control what was defined as cultural production. The Soviets, for example, were resistant to the idea that early Russian towns, and the social developments represented by urban life, had been boosted by the Scandinavians. The control of the state over education was very tight, reflecting a strong belief in its ideological value.

Meanwhile, terror and government-tolerated famine killed at least eleven million in Stalin's 'peacetime' years, warped the lives of the remainder of the population, and made casualties of faith,

Poster for Sergei M. Eisenstein's docudrama (1928) *Oktyabr* about the 1917 October Revolution, re-enacting and celebrating scenes from the revolution. (Public domain)

hope and truth. During the 1931-3 famine, a national crisis, which owed much to drought, poor harvests, and government choices in food allocation, there were particular areas of devastation. Although estimates of deaths range up to ten million, probably about seven million died as a result in Ukraine (5 million), northern Kazakhstan (1-2 million), and southern Russia (1 million or fewer). Soviet policies towards the Ukraine famine which was, to a degree, a result of deliberate policies, notably taking food from the countryside to feed urban workers in favoured cities and thus help industrialisation, led to claims of genocide, both from within Ukraine and elsewhere, claims that were frequently expressed once Ukraine became independent in 1991. The Ukrainian term for this event is *Holodomor*, 'The Famine Epidemic'.

Far less attention in the Anglophone literature has been devoted to heavy losses in Kazakhstan, where the governmental policy was also brutal. There was a pressure to convert the nomads to a settled population, notably providing labour for collective farms, as an instance of Marxist social transformation. This was linked to a cultural assault on established social and cultural norms and practices in order to ensure 'civilised' Kazakh statehood.

The Soviet census of 1937, the first for eleven years, was suppressed, and the officials involved executed, probably because it revealed losses through famine earlier in the decade that, according to the government, had not occurred. Similarly, in 1936, the project for the mapping of the population density of European Russia was abandoned.

In Ukraine, the initial Soviet policy of 'national in form and socialist in content' and, in practice, a construction of a polity linking Ukrainian-speaking and Russian-speaking areas, had, in turn, become a deliberate assault on Ukrainian distinctiveness, with the use of the Ukrainian language seen in the 1920s replaced by an emphasis on Russian and a brutal reckoning with the Ukrainians who had done well there in the 1920s. In a classic instance of the tensions and inconsistencies central to Soviet nationalities policies, the emphasis from 1923 on 'indigenisation' in order to placate non-Russians and prepare them for Communism, was replaced and ideological purity, instead, in the 1930s equated with Russification. This was the case in Ukraine and elsewhere. There was also a cruel and controlling movement of people. There were deportations from Ukraine to provide labour for collective farms in Kazakhstan, or simply confinement in the open steppe.

Rather than seeing this in nationalist terms, it is necessary to note the Marxist ideological line. Stalin and other senior Bolsheviks believed that every 'Socialist' ethnic people needed to possess its statehood with elements of sovereignty and distinctive culture, and, at the same time, to be a part of the supra-national construction of the Soviet Union that must be the integrated Socialist nation. The Soviet leaders strove to keep this balance from the foundation of the Soviet Union until its final demise.

To Soviet leaders, Ukraine was part of a wider political geography of problems, one that in particular included areas where there were minorities judged a threat, such as Poles in Western Belarus, Germans in the Middle-Lower Volga region, and Muslims in the Caucasus. In the last, resistance to collectivisation in 1929-30 led to its suspension in mountainous areas until the mid-1930s. Peasant resistance on the Yenisei River in Siberia continued until 1932.

The large-scale deportations of *kulaks* or wealthier peasants linked to the collectivisation programme in the early 1930s hit hard at the communal continuity and sense of place of peoples such as the Don Cossacks, demonstrating a powerlessness and weakening a sense of separate identity. To put wealth in context, a wealthier peasant might own only one rake or one horse or one plough, whereas poorer peasants might own some or none of these, but in village society there could be differences and tensions that were open to exploitation.

Allowing for the multiple deceptions of Soviet propaganda and for the disaster of rural collectivisation and much else, there was also, however, important development in the Soviet economy, not least because there was continuing scope for recovery from war and revolution, as economic output in 1928 was still below that in 1913. There was a major expansion of the industrial sector and of electricity generation, albeit, as a result of the state-driven focus of resources on developing industry, at a heavy cost in terms of the everyday life of the population, notably in living standards, including food, accommodation and heating. The government understood the possibilities offered it in social policy through ruthless devaluation of the rouble. It had done so during the Civil War to impoverish the better-off city people and, from the late 1920s, did so to everyone, in order to squeeze resources to finance industrialisation through frequent price increases for staples. There was a decline in the rouble's purchasing power between 1928 and 1935. The forced labour of those made to work in harsh, often fatal, conditions on construction and other projects was another aspect of the more general pressure on living standards. The lives of those deemed enemies of the revolution were treated as valueless.

From the mid/late 1920s, Stalin was eager to back the industrialisation necessary for large-scale mechanisation. He regarded a powerful military as a way to defend the Revolution against capitalist states, which were seen as inherently opposed to the Soviet Union. Moreover, his support for Socialism (ie Communism) in one federal state (the Soviet Union) was not inherently pacific, as he used the idea of international crisis to press for an extension of state dominance, notably with the war scare of 1927, which he did not try to defuse.

In a clear parallel with the Soviet situation after 1945, industrial capacity was regarded as a basis for warmaking, both offensive and defensive. The theme of mobilisation was a potent one. It linked Soviet ideology to a consistent fear, indeed paranoia, that was integral to the character of Communism. Stalin was particularly prone to this paranoia, albeit with a blind spot as far as Hitler was concerned. Stalin's perceptions of encirclement, capitalist crisis, and inevitable, imminent war, generated his policies of breakneck modernisation.

Frustrated by the persistent gap between intention and implementation, the regime in the 1930s adopted more radical and totalitarian impulses and initiatives. In part this was a matter of Stalin's direction from the centre, but regional and local agencies also took a role that could include far more than just implementing the process. A lack of clarity over intention left much room for such initiative. So also did the links, from centre to localities and back, of rival institutions, factions and groups, notably between and within the Communist Party and the NKVD. In the Moscow Trials of 1936-8, Stalin sought to remove potential opponents, most of whom were longtime Bolshevik leaders. As part of the increasingly febrile atmosphere, Sergei Kirov, the Leningrad Party head, was assassinated in December 1934, possibly by the NKVD at the behest of Stalin, who got rid of a possible rival as well as using the opportunity to justify repression. In the Moscow Trials, torture and threats to family were used to extort confessions to ridiculous charges of treason. Subsequently, despite promises of mercy in return for these confessions, Zinoviev (1936), Kamenev (1936), Bukharin (1938) and others were shot.

The degree of violence was not simply transactional. There were also pathologies at play in the degraded viciousness of much of the humiliation and torture involved, as well as the deliberate destruction of families, with wives frequently arrested and killed and children sent to orphanages. The impact has understandably lasted to the present, and it makes a mockery of attempts to rehabilitate Stalin.

Attacks on Communists held to be suspicious expanded in the Purges or 'Great Terror', of 1937-8, alongside the confusion, indeed chaos, of a poorly planned and under-resourced, deadly but *ad hoc* repression, to the large-scale killing and imprisonment of those held to threaten the revolution or regarded as untrustworthy, although Stalin had already driven forward numerous arrests in a purge in the late 1920s. He was apt to present the opposition as Trotskyists, or Zinovievists, but criticism within the Communist Party was more wide-ranging and many were not accurately summarised in terms of these invented categories, or that of the 'Rightist-Leftist deviation', a label in use in 1936-8 to accuse the former members of the groups of Bukharin, Trotsky and Zinoviev, of an underground conspiracy against Stalin and the Party.

The 'Great Terror' is generally explained in terms of a number of overlapping and interacting tendencies and developments. The interaction of deliberate policies and the accelerators of implementation corresponded with the paranoia and cruelty that suffused Stalin's personality and characterised his policies. Alongside often highly fanciful reports of conspiracies and complaints, there was enough non-compliance to encourage Stalin to see evidence of active opposition, even if this just meant peasants killing their horses rather than giving them over to the collective farms.

Stalin's murderous paranoia was a key element, but so also was a chaos of slaughtering in which different groups and persons used the NKVD technique of framing suspects in order to remove those they opposed or just disliked and take over their offices and property. These were linked by the 'social engineering' deployed by Stalin and others. At the upper political level, Stalin killed the 'Old Bolsheviks' to establish an effective and controllable state bureaucracy in place of the experienced independently minded government administrators who had prior links separate to Stalin's dominance. At the lower social level, the victims were 'anti-Soviet elements' who belonged to what were seen as inborn class enemies, notably former rich peasants who, having been expropriated and imprisoned for a few years, had returned to their native villages by the mid-1930s. The rhetoric of the Party officials was directed against them.

There were also the dynamics within the Party, with younger 'Old Bolsheviks', such as Nikolai Yezhov, the head of the NKVD from September 1936 to November 1938, becoming key figures in a group that triumphed and gained promotion. The 'Great Terror' was both a social struggle and a political clash in the leadership linked to a generational change in power, away from the pre-Revolutionary Bolsheviks to the newcomers of the Civil War period. This was the generation to which the later Soviet leaders belonged, and, when this generation died out, the Soviet Union collapsed.

Military industry, the primary justification for the five-year plans for economic development and priorities, the first accepted in 1928 for 1929-33, was greatly expanded, due to its having a highly-placed patron – the Red Army – to push for investment and resources. The shift in Communist military thought from the early idea of the people under arms in the shape of a militia to the recognition of the need for a strong regular military and for comprehensive peacetime organisation for war, was highly important. Unlike in Western states, this focus on a military-industrial complex was a drive that was not restricted by meaningful pressures limiting investment, such as concern for consumer well-being. Military industry was encouraged by an ideology of hostility to foreign states that characterised even Communist moderates. Stalin's rise to power was supported by a military high command concerned by the efforts of the fiscally conservative Communist 'Right', such as Bukharin (also an opponent of collectivisation), to resist the rise in military spending. All these factors led to the extensive development of Soviet military industry. However, the rhetoric of a command economy and the practices of centralisation and surveillance could not preclude poor quality, waste, delay, corruption and a general sense of opportunism and deceit.

Stalin was eager to back the industrialisation necessary for large-scale mechanisation of the army. He regarded powerful military forces as a way to defend the Revolution against the allegedly implacably hostile capitalist states, especially Britain and Japan. An alleged plot to partition the Soviet Union to the benefit of Britain and Japan was among the charges against Bukharin, a prominent member of the Politburo in 1924-9, who was arrested in 1937, accused of conspiring to overthrow the state. Threats to his family were used to drive him to confess. After a show-trial, he was shot in 1938.

A type of defence Keynesianism had a stimulating impact on the Soviet economy, although it also distorted it by limiting the investment possibilities for other sectors of the economy. This factor remained pertinent until the end of the Soviet Union, and provided a clear and important continuity from the 'Cold War' that began in the 1920s to its close in the late 1980s. There were harsh consequences from the military industrial build-up for living standards. The deadly 1931-3 famine owed much to the disruption linked to agrarian collectivisation, but can in part be blamed on grain stockpiling and railway diversion in preparation for war. Such a liberal conception about living standards meant little within the authoritarian political parameters and opportunistic and paranoid culture of Stalin's Soviet Union. As with all 'totalitarian' states, there was a gap between what the regime wanted to happen and what actually occurred. In the case of the Soviet Union, the regime, frustrated by this gap between intention and implementation, was driven in the 1930s to more radical (totalitarian) impulses and initiatives, far more so than the authoritarian regimes that had gained power in former parts of the Russian empire, in Poland and Lithuania from 1926, and Estonia and Latvia from 1934. The Bolsheviks were formative for Italian Fascism, German Nazism, Chinese Nationalists, and others.

In the Soviet Union, ideological mobilisation, through Socialism (ie. Communism) backed by terror, was a keystone of the new society, seen in the trials of the critics of aspects of the Centrally Planned Economy instituted in the late 1920s. The trials of 1928-32 helped link the bloodletting of the early 1920s with that in the late 1930s. In the Purges of 1937-8, the political police used the details on everyone considered anti-Soviet that they had been building up from the early 1920s. The information was provided from outside, notably by denunciations, but also by the varied agencies and processes open to the political police, such as agents, informers, membership purges and verification procedures within the Communist Party. The gathering of data also threw up information on networks of acquaintances. In 1937, when the Purges were launched, it was easy with these records to link victims in supposed conspiracies. The Purges were joined by 'Mass Operations' against groups in the population at large, such as Poles. Both were linked to the belief that alleged dissidence within the Soviet Union was manipulated by hostile foreign forces. In July 1937 all frontiers were declared 'special defence zones' and ethnic groups in them considered threats were deported, the Koreans being moved to Central Asia.

At the same time, the regime experienced grave problems in its capacity to govern. Indeed, to a degree, the totalitarian dynamic was the response of the Stalinist regime to the problems created by the very nature of the political and governmental systems and the

The Stalin Years: 1924-53

cyclical nature of service-state rejuvenations. The manipulation of information was a key problem for the state as well as the means of operation. So also with factionalism and corruption. Belief in sedition directed against the Soviet system led to a search for supporting evidence, and to a treatment of information to the contrary as misleading. When information on sedition was not found, as was often the case, it was fabricated. Whereas, in its own eyes, Stalinism was a modern form of government, reliant on scientific planning and the expression of the direction of world history and human progress, in practice it was pre-modern and dependent on myth and faith. Combined with paranoia, this position left the system ripe for internal confusion and external manipulation, the very situation that was supposedly being guarded against.

In the case of the Purges of 1937-8, a regime willing and able to kill on an impulse found the process getting out of control, which, as later with the Maoist 'Cultural Revolution', led to a winding down of the Terror in 1938, with many NKVD appointees of the previous year in turn purged. This took place against a background of large numbers of letters of protest about wrongful arrest, but the key element was tension within the regime, and the invention accordingly of appropriate plots to destroy it. Yet again they were found within the regime. Genrikh Yagoda, the head of the NKVD from 1934 to 1936, was arrested in 1937, tried and shot in 1938. His successor, who took the Great Purges to a height and was known as the 'Bloody Dwarf', Nikolai Yezhov, was head of the NKVD from September 1936 to November 1938. In 1937-8, over 1.3 million people were arrested and close to 700,000 shot for 'crimes against the state' while at least 140,000 prisoners died in the *gulags*.

In an instance of the political coups Stalin frequently employed, Yezhov, in turn, was replaced by Lavrenty Beria, the Party Chief in Georgia, who became Yezhov's deputy in August 1938. Yezhov was arrested in April 1939, accused of the large-scale arrest of the innocent, and tried and shot in February 1940. Similarly, Yezhov's protégé, Aleksandr Uspensky, head of the Ukraine NKVD in

1938, was executed in 1940. The practitioners of Stalinist terror were also its potential victims, which greatly increased Stalin's control, enhancing the sense of volatility that was an aspect of this control. Despite the rhetoric of modernisation, this pre-modern form of government, one inherently divided as well as divisive and bureaucratic only in theory, remained a fundamental problem until the fall of the Soviet Union.

In the economy, there was a comparable situation, with surveillance, fabrication of data and alleged plots. Central planners set politically motivated targets, and factory managers lied about their available inputs and achievable outputs to maximise the former and minimise the latter, and then lied again when they failed to meet quotas, failures that were a reflection of a lack of realism in targets and of low productivity. The abolition of trade union independence weakened the levers available for winning worker support.

Regional Party and state bosses lied to cover up the lies of the big local factories. Industrial ministries, sensing that the information they were receiving from localities was false, lied so as to maintain a semblance of efficiency. All this misinformation was communicated back to the planning authorities, who lied to the political leadership about the fulfilment of the five-year plans. And the regime, realising things were seriously wrong, lied to the population about their triumphs, and set even higher targets for next time. This system, which remained the case throughout the Communist period, could hardly provide an effective background for policymaking.

The Purges of 1937-8, in which many of the senior employees of economic commissariats and major industrial plants, institutes and design bureaux were sent to prison camps (some were shot), encouraged the avoidance of risk. Moreover, censorship, the 'need-to-know' principle, and restrictions on travel and communications, all made it difficult to relate work to advances elsewhere, and thus to ensure productive synergies. A fear of denunciation made it hard for managers to direct their employees. Labour discipline was a problem in this totalitarian state, reminding us that behind the façade there were some workaday situations inherently incapable of correction, despite draconian Stalin-era regulations. This remained a problem in the 1980s, vexing Yuri Andropov, the head of government from 1982 to 1984.

Nevertheless, the defence Keynesianism, or stimulus through deficit spending, did bring important economic benefits, with the direction of resources leading to the major build-up of industrial, transport and energy infrastructure. Russia/the Soviet Union was perceived by Marx, Lenin and Stalin as a late developer having to try hard in order to catch up. In this race social engineering was regarded as essential, and for which the form pursued was 'revolution from above'. Elements of a similar attitude could be seen elsewhere, notably in Nationalist China and in Kemal Ataturk's Turkey, but, in neither case was this attitude linked to an ideology of global revolution. Although there was considerable violence, the degree of internal transformation in China and Turkey in the 1920s and 1930s, once Turkey's civil wars had finished and China's had begun to fade, was less dependent on terror than in the Soviet case.

In the case of rail, it is possible to adopt different emphases, as so often with the Soviet Union. The Civil War greatly diminished rail use, but by 1926 usage had passed the level of 1913. The network grew from 81,000 km in 1917 to 106,100 in 1940. A major new line, planned under the old order but built largely between 1927 and 1930, was the Turkestan-Siberia railway, linking Central Asia to the Trans-Siberian Railway and bringing to fruition an idea first proposed in the late 1880s.

There were certainly aspirations including classes of powerful locomotives, the *Joseph Stalin*, manufactured from 1932 to 1942, of which 649 were built, and the *Felix Dzerzhinsky*, built from 1931 (mass production from 1932), of which 3,213 were built, as well as stronger track thanks to heavier rails and better ballast, heavy rolling stock, automatic brakes and coupling, and better signalling. The importance of rail was shown by Stalin's close associate Lazar Kaganovich being People's Commissar for Transport in 1935-7 and 1938-42. Built in Russia by Krupp, the AA20 was a one-off locomotive named after Kaganovich's predecessor Andrey

Andreyev. In true Soviet style, it set out for superlatives, having the largest number of coupled axles on a locomotive (14), and being the longest rigid frame locomotive in Europe. It was too heavy, too large for turntables and subject to derailments and was withdrawn from service. Moisey Rukhimovich, the holder of the post in 1930-1 was executed in 1938, as was Alexey Bakulin in 1939, who held the post in 1937-8.

Rail construction faced many problems. In 1926, construction began on a line linking the 'Magnetic Mountain,' the iron-ore mountain that was to become the gigantic steel city of Magnitogorsk, to the rail system through a junction at Kartaly, 145 kilometres away. Steel production there depended on movement of coking coal nearly 2,000 kilometres from the Kuznetsk basin of western Siberia. The two were linked as the Ural-Kuznetsk Combine, but only 40 kilometres of track were constructed by the end of 1928. In 1929, the work was renewed and completed with military assistance, but the track was put down without ballast and due to repeated accidents, a speed limit of ten kilometres per hour was imposed. As a result of the poor state of the line, including a failure to use creosoted railway ties, there were major problems with capacity. Bottlenecks hit production: much of the rolling stock in the mid-1930s was inoperative, there was a severe shortage of rails and ties, and in 1936 it could take as long as two weeks for freight to pass from one shop to another. Quantity claimed proved no guidance to quality of output. Yet, however wasteful, there was output.

Force played a major role in the development of the Soviet rail system. Felix Dzerzhinsky ran the brutal secret police from 1917 and also, from 1923, was the founding Chairman of the Transport Commissariat. Forced labour served transport projects such as the Stalin White Sea-Baltic Canal built by manual labour in 1931-3 with about 100,000 workers of whom about 25,000 died. Peasants who were moved to perform forced labour in *gulags* proved a major source of manpower for new construction. This was especially the case with the Salekhard-Igarka Railway that was pursued, despite the problem posed by permafrost, from 1947 until 1953 as part of Stalin's plan for a line across northern Siberia.

The catalyst for full Soviet militarisation was Japan's conquest of Manchuria in September 1931. Manchuria was the part of China where heavy industry was most developed and this development was to be taken further by Japan, which also used Manchuria as an area for Japanese settlement. Seen as a strategic asset against the Soviet Union, Manchuria abutted the Soviet Far East as well as the rail route to it. This conquest, which accentuated Soviet anxieties about the fate of the embattled Russian Revolution as a whole, brought forward concern about Japan as a strategic threat in the Far East, to the Soviet Union as well as China. This concern was greatly strengthened by Japan's success in its 1904-5 war with Russia and by Japan's large-scale intervention in the Russian Civil War. The Soviet Union had hitherto been the dominant power in north Manchuria, but feeling vulnerable and wishing at this stage to avoid war, it proved willing to cede its interest before the Japanese advance.

Fears of Japan provoked a full-scale industrial mobilisation, which included expanding bases and forces in the Far East. The TB-3, the world's first mass-produced four-engine, all-metal bomber, was intended as a deterrent against Japan, and was part of the build-up of what, for a while, became the largest air force in the world. The heart of Soviet heavy industry was retooled for armaments production. The cost was immense, but levels of production far ahead of anything else in the world were achieved, notably 4,000 tanks annually, instead of about 1,000 until the end of 1931. Under Stalin, there was never any retreat from that level of production. Despite serious dislocation caused by German conquest in 1941, and allowing for the important help provided in 1941-5 by the Western allies, this economic growth in the 1930s was to sustain a large-scale military effort in World War Two and to be the basis of Soviet military strength in the Cold War.

The location of industrial development influenced Soviet strategic capability. Boosted in all regions, industry in the Urals and Siberia increased in the same proportion as elsewhere, but the already-strong metallurgical industry in the Urals served as the basis for an expansion of industrial production that was beyond the range of German air attack. This productive capacity proved a key strategic asset during World War Two. Major new industrial capacity was also developed near Novosibirsk in south-west Siberia, while new plants were built in Soviet Central Asia. This build-up of a large Soviet military-industrial complex was of great significance for the global arms race of the 1930s and for the development of the Soviet economy and system.

Reports in late 1935 about an Anti-Comintern Pact, which Japan was to sign with Germany on 25 November 1936, led Soviet strategists to fear a war on two fronts. This fear prefigured their concern in the 1970s and 1980s about conflict with both America and China. In January 1936, Marshal Mikhail Tukhachevsky, the commander of the Red Army (who was to be shot on the night of 12 June 1937), pressed the Central Committee of the Communist Party on the need to confront the danger of simultaneous war with Germany and Japan.

The Purges of the military from 1937 reflected the close linkage of force and politics in the Soviet Union and Stalin's determination to crush any potential form of dissidence. Claiming to discover a conspiracy between the Soviet and German armies, a belief fed by the German provision of forged information, Stalin, whose judgment was probably not determined by these documents, had the military heavily purged in 1937, the purges continuing until 1941. The claim by the Soviet leadership that there were plans for a military coup appears to have no basis.

In the Purges, over half the generals, including the vast majority of corps and divisional commanders, were killed, as were thousands of officers. An alternative basis of political power was thus ruthlessly crushed, while the purge of the military encouraged a more general terror against perceived opponents of the Revolution. Party control over the military was strengthened with the reintroduction, in 1937, of the system of dual control initially introduced in the Civil War. All military orders had to be countersigned by a political commissar. In 1938, military soviets, with a commander, a chief of staff and a commissar, were created to provide trusted leadership at army and corps level. The Purges hit the effectiveness of the military hard, as did the lack of education for the bulk of the army officers.

Yet, the innovative ideas of some of the purged and killed military leaders, such as the concept of operational warfare and mechanised annihilation offensive, did not die with their authors. Instead, they were used to great effect in 1944-5 by former pupils. Indeed, while ravaging the top leadership, the Purges mostly spared the middle level of commanders and opened for them prospects for promotion. Many of those replaced were old Civil War leaders. Foreign governments assumed that the Purges would greatly compromise Soviet military capability in any war. This affected attitudes to the possibility of the Soviet Union intervening effectively against Hitler during the Munich Crisis of 1938. Hitler's confidence about Soviet vulnerability when he launched Germany against the Soviet Union in June 1941 owed much to the Purges.

In the Popular Front Years of 1933-9, the Soviet Union had opposed Nazi Germany, but in August 1939 changed policy, in part due to perceived Anglo-French weakness which lessened the appeal of allying with these capitalist powers. A shared interest in revisionism and opposition to democracy provided a basis for agreement, however insincere, between Hitler and Stalin in 1939. Both reacted strongly against Enlightenment, liberal and capitalist values, and Stalin was more than willing to subordinate the cause of international Communism, about which he was anyway dubious, to that of state expansion in concert with Germany. Each man was responsible for massive slaughter. In the summer of 1938, Stalin planned to approach Hitler for an alliance. Later that year, the Czech crisis found the Soviets unwilling to give substance to their anti-Appeasement rhetoric even when given permission to transport troops and weaponry across Romania to help Czechoslovakia resist German pressure.

Indeed, the Soviet Union may in 1938 have sought to help cause a war that would exhaust other powers but one that it could then sit out, rather as Stalin succeeded in doing with the Korean War in 1950-3. Given the 1930s belief that a major conflict would be attritional, it meant that staying out for a while would give a power great superiority over the exhausted belligerents. Stalin was successful in this in 1939, only for France to collapse in 1940 and Britain to be driven out from Western Europe, which gave the Germans the opportunity to turn against the Soviet Union.

Earlier, far from seeking to protect neutrals when Britain and France guaranteed Poland and Romania on 31 March 1939 after the German occupation of Bohemia and Moravia on 15 March, Stalin had joined Hitler with the Ribbentrop-Molotov (Nazi-Soviet) Pact or Treaty of Non-Aggression of 23 August 1939. Stalin celebrated the Pact with a toast to 'the health of this great man', Hitler, and sent German Communists in the Soviet Union back to Germany to be killed. The Pact divided Eastern Europe into German and Soviet spheres of influence and expansion, and freed Germany in 1939-40 from the risk of a two-front war. The Pact also ended Soviet fears of Poland and Japan, fears that had encouraged large-scale and brutal action against Polish and Korean (Korea was then ruled by Japan) inhabitants of the Soviet Union. In April 1941, a non-aggression pact with Japan followed.

There was now a four-power Axis: Germany, Italy, Japan and the Soviet Union. On 17 September 1939, in accordance with the Nazi-Soviet Pact, Stalin joined in the German attack on Poland, although only after the Germans, who had invaded on 1 September, had already largely defeated the Poles. Soviet policy over Poland demonstrated Stalin's habitual pattern of allowing potential opponents to exhaust each other before deriving benefit.

The Soviets annexed eastern Poland after fraudulent elections had led to the election of 'People's Assemblies'. The latter voted in favour of incorporation into the Soviet Union, which thereby gained control of 77,500 square miles and 13 million people. The brutality of the Soviet system, and its treatment of all politics as social war, was seen in its occupation policy. In 1939-40, 1.17 million people, many from social categories deemed undesirable and reactionary, were deported from Soviet-occupied Poland to Soviet labour camps, the *gulags*, which were similar to the German concentration (as opposed to extermination) camps. A large number died on the long journeys. Many others who were not deported were slaughtered, and, although the degree of co-ordination is unclear, the NKVD shared information about Poles with the Gestapo. Those regarded as leaders of the community and as bourgeois were particular targets. These killings continued the 'peacetime' killings of many Poles within the Soviet Union, notably of about 111,000 in the 'Polish Operation', which began in 1937, as well as of other minority peoples, for instance Finns and Germans. In Belarus from 1988, mass graves at Kurapaty outside Minsk were exhumed: the NKVD had slaughtered at least 30,000 people there between 1937 and 1941. Some were Poles, others Belarusians , both those weeded to the idea of a a national culture, who had been purged from 1929, and those held to belong to unacceptable social categories. A quota system was used to ensure sufficient killings, most without trial.

The eastern Polish provinces were treated as an integral part of the Soviet Union and transferred to the local Soviet republics, Ukraine and Belarus. Nikita Khrushchev, a veteran of the Civil War, the First Secretary of the Ukrainian Communist Party from 1938 to 1947, played a major role in the resulting brutal transformation of government, society, business and culture, a transformation that was an aspect of the mass violence and destructive change of 1917-53, the legacy of which has lasted to the present. Later, Khrushchev was to succeed Stalin, though to disavow his legacy and methods. In 1939-41, the Soviet Union provided significant levels of economic support, notably with oil and grain, for Germany, helping the latter to overcome the blockading capability of British sea power.

In 1939-40, the Soviet Union invaded Finland, annexing ten per cent of the country including the province of Karelia. Most of the population of Karelia became refugees in Finland. Karelia was resettled by Russians and remained part of Russia after the collapse of the Soviet Union. In June 1940, the Soviet Union pressed on to invade and, after fraudulent elections, annex the Baltic Republics, as well as to take the regions of Bessarabia and Northern Bukovina from Romania. In each case, there was a brutal treatment of the population, with large-scale slaughter and the wholesale movement of people to labour camps. About 127,000 people were deported to the *gulags* from the Baltic States. This was part of the process by which Hitler and Stalin were each responsible for the slaughter of large numbers of people in Eastern Europe.

The Nazi-Soviet alignment was destroyed by Operation *Barbarossa*, the German attack on the Soviet Union, launched on 22 June 1941, to give effect to Hitler's determination to destroy Communism and Jews and to create a greater Germany. The defeat of the Soviet Union was also designed to put pressure on Britain. As a result of this surprise attack, an alliance of shared enmity to Germany replaced the earlier hostility between the Soviet Union and Britain.

Exaggerating their own capacity and underestimating Soviet fighting determination, the Germans sought to seize all objectives simultaneously. The Soviets were poorly prepared and deployed for the German attack as the extent to which the Germans would be able to advance had been underestimated. Stalin's instructions, that units hold their positions and not retreat, and his encouragement of counterattacks, ensured that the Soviets proved vulnerable to German breakthrough and encirclement tactics, losing heavily as a result, including many tanks. Aside from his complete and direct responsibility for the unprepared condition of the Soviet military at the outset of the war and, particularly, for the dire state of the command structure, Stalin had not appreciated that the Soviet army would suffer from *blitzkrieg*, and certainly not the degree to which it would suffer.

Stalin had a nervous collapse of will on 28-30 June, when the rapidly advancing Germans reached Minsk, the bombed capital of White Russia (Belarus). Indeed, there was possibly consideration on his part of a settlement with Germany, similar to the Treaty of Brest-Litovsk accepted by Lenin in 1918, a treaty that had enabled the Communists to consolidate their own position. This treaty might have been used to vindicate such an agreement in 1941. As another turning point, there was also a panic, involving popular disturbances, in Moscow in mid-October, as ministries and factories were moved in the face of German advance; but Stalin decided not to flee, and the ruthless NKVD was used to prevent anarchy and restore a murderous order.

The lack of Soviet collapse in late 1941 was a key moment in the war, and one that brought together a number of strands. Stalin's attitudes were a crucial element, and help explain his subsequent and present-day eulogisation by Soviet apologists and Russian nationalists in a Stalin cult. However, these eulogies ignore the extent to which, in trusting Hitler, he was largely responsible for the plight facing the Soviet Union in 1941, as well as for much else that ruined the life of his contemporaries, including a collectivisation of agriculture that contributed to the terrible shortage of food during the war that was partly responsible for so many civilian casualties.

The role of the pre-war Purges and of continuing and large-scale wartime slaughter and repression in ensuring that Stalin was able to pursue his course – first alliance with Hitler and then resistance to him – was important, but is difficult to evaluate, all sorts of counterfactuals come into play. Nevertheless, in the absence of political collapse at the top, the state maintained its control. With the exception of the early days of the war, when there was resistance to the Soviets in advance of the German conquest, for example in Lithuania, where members of the Lithuanian Activists' Front seized the city of Kaunas, this control generally only broke down in areas occupied by the Germans. Communist cadres in these areas found it difficult to inspire and lead resistance until German atrocities helped provide them with support.

The emptiness of German claims, at the time and subsequently, to be leading Europe against Communism was shown by the situation in Lithuania. The provisional government established by the Lithuanian Activists' Front on 23 June 1941 restored the administration before the Soviet occupation in 1940, but it was expected by the German occupiers to act as a puppet government and swiftly disbanded. Instead, German rule meant the exploitation of the population for the war effort. Thus, the property nationalised by the Soviet Union when Lithuania was occupied was not restored. After the initial stages of the German advance, there was no comparable development to that in Lithuania. In part, this was because with the exception of Ukraine, the Germans advanced into areas with a Russian majority. In addition, the ruthless determination of the Soviet system came into play after the initial shock was over. For example, on 4 October 1941, General Georgy Zhukov, the commander of the Leningrad Front, announced to Stalin's approval that the families of all those who surrendered would be shot.

Soviet (and Allied) propaganda made much of the resolve of the Soviet population, as also of that of the Red Army, each of which faced appalling circumstances. The Soviet Union lost about 28-34 million military and civilian people in the war, maybe 13.5 per cent of the pre-war population of Russia in June 1941. There was extraordinary devastation in its western lands, notably Belarus, which lost about a quarter of its population. Of the 34 million in the army, about eight million died (of whom 3.3 million were prisoners of war), and many were injured. In contrast, America lost 418,000 men in the war, 417,000 of whom were military.

Resolve was doubtless a factor, not least due to Stalin's skill in playing on nationalist themes, including Christianity and history; although there has also been scepticism about the effectiveness of Soviet propaganda. Stalin evoked memories of Russian nationalism, including in film, even though this nationalism entailed a patriotism that did not centre on Communist ideas and, indeed, involved respect for Tsars, especially Ivan IV (the Terrible), Peter I (the Great), and Alexander I, the opponent of Napoleon. Ivan's cruelty, not least his use of the *oprichnina*, his private army, for harsh repression, was presented as necessary patriotism in order to protect Russia, a parallel apparently justifying Stalin's Purges. Ivan's responsibility for expansionism toward the Baltic and into Siberia also ensured that he was praised. The film *Alexander Nevsky* was re-released in 1941 after the German invasion and the Order of Alexander Nevsky, one based on the Imperial Order of Saint Alexander Nevsky bestowed from 1725 until the Revolution, was established in July 1942 as a military honour.

The brutality of German occupation politics, integral to German policy and far from 'collateral damage', also contributed to Soviet resolve. The German Armed Forces Directive of 19 May 1941 declared:

> Bolshevism is the deadly enemy of the National Socialist German people ... this struggle requires ruthless and energetic action against Bolshevik agitators, guerillas, saboteurs, and Jews, and the total elimination of all active or passive resistance.

This was a direct encouragement to large-scale slaughter by the military, alongside the greater number of killings by German police units. Such killings were exploited by Soviet propaganda and played a role in popular resolve, or at least fatalism.

These arguments can be pushed too hard. For example, the heroic stereotype of the Red Army soldier bore scant reference to the reality, not least to the marked contrast between nationalities: the Central Asian recruits had little understanding of the causes or purposes of the war effort. As with the Germans, the Soviets, due to distrust and a measure of racism, made insufficient use of the subordinate peoples within their empires: a similar point can be made about African-Americans. In the Soviet case, heavy casualties ensured that many Central Asian recruits, initially in construction battalions and logistics, in part due to racism but also because their Russian-language skills were not seen as good enough for combat service, were moved into combat divisions. The war, to an extent, 'Sovietized' the constituent republics.

Helped by the coercive powers of his brutal state, Stalin proved an effective war leader. A dictator, he took a significant role in strategy, although frequently with dire consequences, as in early 1942. He was even more important in the mobilisation and production of resources, notably through the State Defence Committee. Totalitarianism was not incompatible with conflict effectiveness, although this did not extend to agriculture, while it is important not to forget the extent to which the Soviet war effort depended on the supply of British and American *matériel*. This theme was very much downplayed in Soviet-era history, but this supply was crucial at the key moment of the Battle of Moscow in December 1941, when the Soviets made extensive use of British tanks.

Soviet mobility greatly depended on the supply of American trucks, and this mobility was important as the Soviets advanced because they were not able to rely on rail links in reoccupied areas. The rapid Soviet advance in 1944 owed much to such mobility, although, like the Germans, the Soviets also made extensive use of horses for transporting supplies. Large numbers were deployed when Germany was invaded in 1945, although the Soviets did not put such horses in their celebratory parades and films. Lend-Lease helped the Soviet Union to focus on what it did well – building T-34 tanks and artillery barrels – by giving it what it could not make. Food was a significant part of Lend-Lease. The Americans also provided many non-ferrous metals.

The Soviet Union proved better able to cope with the demands of mobilizing resources than Germany, which, of course, also had to support the war against the Western Allies and cope with strategic bombing. Once relocated beyond the range of likely German advance or air attack, in areas where there had already been considerable investment in the 1930s, Soviet industries turned out vast quantities of military *matériel*, out-producing the Germans in tanks and artillery. The Soviet commitment to quantity rather than quality, which was more generally true of the practice of Soviet government, proved particularly well-suited to the equipping of the large Soviet armies, and, crucially, to their

The Stalin Years: 1924-53

re-equipment as ordnance etc. was destroyed. Like the Americans, the Soviets concentrated on a few basic designs and did not focus on perfection and producing large numbers of prototypes, characteristics of the Germans.

The aftermath of the Communist destruction of intermediate institutions and the brutal treatment and cowing of the population in 1917-41 helped ensure that the economic system responded to the particular requirements of state-directed mobilization. One symptom was the production of large quantities of *matériel* by the inmates of Soviet *gulags*; their camp commanders ran their own local economies. The *gulags* were characterised by inadequate care, food, sanitation and housing and overcrowding prior to the war. All of these problems increased greatly during it, with many prisoners in effect worked to death. This situation continued after the war when Stalinist controls were harshly reimposed in the Soviet Union, weakening the sense of national unity that had developed in the furnace of the struggle.

The strength of the Soviet state, including a centralised system for allocating resources, combined with its substantial military industrial complex, ensured that the Soviet military system had more durability than that of Russia in World War One. In 1941, Soviet resistance rapidly became more effective, causing heavier German casualties than anticipated, and costing the Germans time they could not afford. The Soviets created a multifaceted defence-in-depth that included military reorganization and rebuilding, the movement east of industrial plant, and an eventual political resilience that owed much to the lack of any viable prospect for a compromise peace. Initially built in Leningrad, production of the KV-1 was moved east to Chelyabinsk, which became known as Tankograd. The Kharkov tank factory moved to Nizhny Tagil, that from Kolomna to Kirov, and that from Moscow to Sverdlovsk.

In contrast, wartime food production relied on private and local enterprise, notably with individual allotments and the establishment of the black market. Food rationing combined with the requisition of draft animals, tractors (women could and did pull ploughs), and resources in general, hit the agricultural economy and civilian population across the Soviet Union, leaving a bitter memory of the war and also ensuring hostility toward refugees and other displaced people.

Suspicion about others was not only directed at these people The paranoid Stalin was suspicious about the failure of Britain and America to launch a large-scale ground attack on Germany by opening a Second Front in Western Europe. In particular, Stalin exaggerated British hostility to Communism, just as he had earlier neglected British warnings about likely German attack, as well as those from his own agents. When, in May 1941, Rudolf Hess, Hitler's deputy, flew to Britain on an unauthorised, uninvited and unsuccessful attempt to settle Anglo-German differences, this mission was seen by Stalin as a possible means of negotiation designed to isolate the Soviet Union. This may, indeed, have been the intention, but was certainly not Churchill's response.

Again, in the autumn of 1942, Stalin discussed whether Churchill wanted a separate peace with Germany so as to leave the latter free to oppose the Soviet Union. When probing the possibility of a separate peace with Germany, the Soviets mentioned their suspicion of the Anglo-American failure to open a Second Front in Western Europe. These probings led to a Soviet peace offer to Germany in September 1943. The Germans had lost tremendously in their failed offensive against the Soviets that led to the battle of Kursk (5-13 July), as had the Soviets and, well aware of the costs of continuing the war, Stalin sent out feelers for peace negotiations, with the intent of having the Germans withdraw from the Soviet Union and ending the war. Hitler was not interested in pursuing the offer. While allies, the Soviets mounted a major intelligence offensive against Britain and America, one that laid the groundwork for the acquisition of American nuclear secrets.

Major German defeats at Stalingrad (1942-3) and Kursk (1943) were followed by a series of Soviet offensives. These became increasingly effective in 1944. Because there was no single-campaign end to the war, it had an attritional character. This accorded with the authoritarian nature of the Stalinist regime and its focus on the production of military resources.

For Jews, the occupation was genocidal. 2.74 million Soviet Jews (Soviet as of June 1941) fell under German occupation, of whom 2.62 million were murdered. However, post-war, the Soviet government presented wartime civilian casualties as Soviets and did not focus attention on the extent to which the victims were disproportionately Jews. 'Death to the Murdering Judeo-Bolsheviks,' a German poster of 1941 that was published in many languages, including Polish and Ukrainian, showed an animalistic diabolical Jewish Bolshevik slaughtering women and children, but about to be killed by a German soldier. Bolshevism was seen by the Nazis as the product of Jews and as an antithesis of Nazi ideology, in its support for revolution and its commitment to class war within races. In fact, there was a small minority of Jews among Bolshevik leaders, most prominently Trotsky, a minority that saw Zionism as parochial and their radicalism was attracted by the egalitarian ideology of Bolshevism and its explicit modernism, and had been alienated, like the Zionists, by the pogroms. In practice, the Bolsheviks closed places of worship, nationalised businesses large and small, expropriated savings, attacked small-scale trading and peddling and drove Zionism underground as anti-national. Yet, there was an official rejection of antisemitism, Jews had opportunities (circumscribed in Poland and unthinkable in Romania), and roughly a quarter of civil servants were Jews by 1930, in part due to their greater literacy, including about 39 per cent of NKVD leaders by 1934.

Stalin, who gained power in part through purging others, changed much of this. He had a deep suspicion of Jews, although he allowed Yiddish language theatre to continue until after World War Two. There were fewer Jews in leadership positions under Stalin and Stalin was anti-Zionist. But the perception was that the Communists were Jews. In part, this was a consequence of the large-scale internal migration of Jews into Soviet cities. This was a major change from the situation in Imperial Russia. 'The Trotskys launched the Revolution and the Bronsteins paid the price' was a

Jewish expression, referring to Trotsky by his adopted name and his original one.

In Eastern Poland, many Jews welcomed the Red Army in 1939, for example in Lviv (Lwów, Lvov), because the *Wehrmacht* was far worse. Many Jews fled from the German zone of conquest to the Soviet one: 'We had traded a death sentence for life imprisonment' one commented. There were also new opportunities under the Soviets that were unheard of under the Poles, for example as medical students at the University of Lviv. This was very unpopular with local Poles, Ukrainians and Lithuanians. In practice, of the one million people deported from Soviet-occupied Poland alone, 20 per cent were Jews, some because they were adjudged Zionists.

In addition to German slaughter and devastation, the recapture of regions by the Red Army was very destructive. The territory regained in 1943-4 had largely non-Russian populations, notably Ukraine, Belarus and the Baltic Republics. German occupation there had been brutal and murderous, but there was the complication of nationalist opposition to a Soviet return, notably in the Baltic Republics and western Ukraine. The equivalent to these nationalist movements was the 'Russian Liberation' movement of Andrey Vlasov, a Soviet general captured in 1942, who from 1943 founded a pro-German movement. He was executed in 1946. However, the war against the Soviet Union was conceived from the outset by the Germans as a genocidal war, and there was planning for thirty million Soviet deaths. This death rate estimation was part of plans for a complete ethnic and geopolitical recasting of the Soviet Union, and in part to ensure food for the invaders.

Although there was at the outset little real partisan threat, the Germans used indiscriminate brutality against those whom they alleged to be partisans or their supporters. In areas with a largely Russian population, for example around Smolensk, there was a murderous occupation, which, therefore, is part of the history of modern Russia. In Smolensk itself, due to flight as well as the slaughter principally of Jews, the population fell from 160,000 to about 30,000, most of whom were the elderly and women. Part of the German-occupied Soviet Union was under 'civilian' administration and part under the army. Civilians in reconquered areas were suspected of collaboration, and there was much murder, deportation to *gulags*, and rape. Jews again were victims.

After the war, the Americans and British handed over about 4.25 million people to the Soviets, in accordance with the agreement at the Yalta Conference of 1945, those captured who had been Soviet nationals before the Nazi-Soviet Pact of 1939. A large number were sent to the *gulags*, but many were killed at once, including the Cossack prisoners handed over by the British. The latter step caused much post-war criticism. In practice, the action was in accordance with the spirit as well as the letter of the Yalta agreement. Those who had not been Soviet nationals before the Pact, for example citizens of the Baltic Republics, were not handed over. The handing over of prisoners to the Soviets was encouraged by a need to ensure the return of the large number of British and American prisoners taken by the Germans and then in Soviet hands, and by the huge problems facing Britain, France and America, especially with displaced persons in their own areas, as well as dire warnings of famine and deaths for the winter of 1945.

Stalin was convinced that capitalism was doomed. His assumption that the wartime Grand Alliance could not be sustained after the war, itself almost the definition of a self-fulfilling prophecy, left him determined to extend the Soviet sphere of influence and obtain direct territorial control through annexations. The latter would show that Stalin could reverse the losses Lenin had had to accept in 1918, and then again in 1920-1. Stalin saw such expansion as a way to limit the risks from any later sudden attack comparable to the German invasion of 1941. Thus, Soviet expansionism was in part defensive in ethos and intention, although other elements were involved, including acquiring strategic points from which further gains could be pursued.

Territorial changes and those in political systems were a major issue in Allied politics in the last stage of the war. In 1944, as Britain responded to Soviet demands on Poland's frontiers, Anthony Eden, the Foreign Secretary who had been a critic of

Chamberlain and had accordingly abstained in the Commons debate over the 1938 Munich agreement, asked 'If I give way over Lviv, shall I go down in the history books as an appeaser?' The advancing Red Army did indeed ensure that Lviv became part of the Soviet Union, as part of what is now the independent state of Ukraine.

Whatever the views of Western leaders, the central role of the Red Army in destroying the German army ensured that the Soviet Union would dominate Eastern Europe, as it had sought without success to do in 1920. The reality of the Soviet advance to a considerable extent undermined subsequent claims that Roosevelt and Churchill sold out Eastern Europe to Stalin at the Yalta conference of 4-11 February 1945. In practice, Poland was already occupied by Soviet forces, and eastern Germany soon would be. Warsaw in 1944, and Berlin, Prague, Vienna and Budapest in 1945, all fell to Soviet forces, and not to their American or British counterparts; and after the rapid defeat of Japanese forces in August 1945, Manchuria, northern Korea, Southern Sakhalin and the Kuril Islands. Leadership, violence, willpower, and improvisation had all played a role in Soviet success; as had the mistakes and weaknesses of other powers, notably Hitler's Germany but also his Eastern European allies, such as Romania and Hungary.

The political rivalries that followed the Soviet advance into Eastern Europe, Manchuria and North Korea in 1944-5 led directly to the Cold War. This advance was a resumption of the Soviet expansionism displayed in 1939-40 when Stalin was allied to Hitler. However, the context was different as a result of the destruction of independent states, Poland and the Baltic Republics, in 1939-40. In 1944-5, in contrast, the Soviet Union was conquering the territories of the rival German and then Japanese empires. This process provided the opportunity for Soviet expansionism and preceded the process of new state-building. Although much of the population was still in place, the slate seemed wiped clean, an attitude that took precedence over pre-war legalities, not that these were of great concern to Stalin.

The Stalin Years: 1924-53

From the Soviet perspective, the creation of new client states provided the opportunity to consolidate their military success. As the situation in the Balkans, where existing states continued, showed, the Soviet determination to establish control was not simply a matter of drawing new territorial lines against a background of the destruction of the vicious German and Japanese empires. Nevertheless, such a process was seen in the major redrawing of Poland's frontiers and in the partition of East Prussia between the Soviet Union and Poland. The Soviet Union retained all of the gains it had obtained in 1939-40 (from Poland, Romania and Finland, as well as the Baltic Republics in their entirety). Thus, most of Lenin's losses were reversed. The Soviet Union also added part of Czechoslovakia that had been annexed by Hungary in 1939, which was called Carpatho-Ukraine; as well as the northern part of the German province of East Prussia.

Poles were moved out of the territories gained by the Soviet Union in the western Ukraine and were resettled in lands cleared of Germans. Soviet policy became more ethnic in its character. As a consequence of such movements, cities changed. The replacement of Poles, following on the German slaughter of Jews, made Lviv and Odessa Soviet cities. Cities that had been lost by the Soviet Union in 1941-4 were brought back under Soviet control, with policing accordingly, as well as other means of favour such as the allocation of apartments. 'Ethnic cleansing' was a product of the interaction of ethnic nationalism and ideological strategies. The previous situation of stratified ethnic incorporation in the towns was destroyed. 'National Communism' became a policy, as when Vilnius was allocated to the Lithuanian part of the Soviet Union. Stalin supported ethnic homogeneity.

Königsberg, the capital of East Prussia, was renamed Kaliningrad, honouring Mikhail Kalinin (1875-1946), the former head of state, first as President of the Soviet Central Executive Committee (1919-38) and then of the Praesidium of the Supreme Soviet (1938-46). As an aspect of his fearful loyalty to Stalin, Kalinin in 1938-9 had to accept the arrest, torture and imprisonment of his estranged wife, Ekaterina Kalinina, as a punishment for her criticism of Stalin.

The Ukrainian question was a key aspect of the post-war settlement of the Polish border, and one that saw a determination by the Soviet authorities to suppress Ukrainian nationalism. There was a link to the situation before 1914 when Ruthenian (Ukrainian) nationalism was a source of great concern to the Austrian empire. As the republics of the Soviet Union were then under firm central control, the extension of Ukraine into former Poland was not regarded as an aid to this nationalism. So also with the annexation of part of Slovakia (pre-war Czechoslovakia) to the Soviet Union and its allocation to Ukraine. Albeit in a very different context, this annexation throws instructive light on the positive remarks frequently made about opportunities for co-operation with Stalin both at the time of Munich and subsequently.

In the Baltic Republics there was a resumption in 1944 of the opportunistic Soviet expansionism of 1940, one again accompanied by the large-scale deportation of local people to *gulags*. Such deportation, and the more general process of oppressive control, were designed to make the clean slate a reality. In the Balkans, where the Soviets created a new indirect empire, their objectives took precedence over consideration of local political interests and wishes.

The Soviet dominance of Eastern Europe through client Communist regimes encountered growing Western opposition, notably from 1948 when a coup was mounted in Prague and West Berlin was blockaded by the Soviets. That year, Stalin attacked what he called 'nationalist-deviationist' Communist leaders, notably Josip Tito in Yugoslavia. Stalin was determined to control Communism and to set the line on foreign policy. This inflexibility was to be repeatedly a problem for Communist ideology and governance.

The Soviet Union treated the Great Patriotic War with Germany of 1941-5, its term for the conflict with Germany (and not a World War Two that included a Soviet-German alliance in 1939-41), as the vindication of Stalin and Communism, and as justifying the extent of postwar Soviet power and influence. The wartime popular resolve was supposed to inspire later behaviour. The traditional Victory Day parade in Moscow on 9 May included the march of the Immortal Regiment, which allowed people to hold up pictures of dead World War Two relatives.

In the memorialisation of World War Two, Stalin, in a Moscow speech on 9 February 1946, referred to the 'inevitability of war with the West'. This underpinned the use of violence to suppress real and alleged opposition, notably anti-Communist nationalist guerrilla movements in the Baltic Republics and Ukraine, especially the Ukrainian Insurgent Army. The resistance drew on opposition to resettlement policies. These Soviet campaigns involved substantial forces and heavy casualties, especially in Ukraine, from which over a quarter of a million people were sent to Siberia in order to weaken the alleged nationalist threat. Disoriented by the killing and seizure of activists, opposition was demoralised, worn down, and eliminated by 1957. The imposition of Soviet control included attacks on the personnel (clerical and lay) of the Catholic and Ukrainian Uniate churches, with the Russian Orthodox Church advanced as the expense of the latter. There was also the suppression of Chechen guerrillas, consistently pursued from 1942.

There were three arenas of Soviet strategy, all of which overlapped but stood out separately in various degrees. First was a philosophical strategy that emanated from the basic ideological worldview (*ideologicheskoe mirovozrenie* – mirroring to some extent the German *Weltanschauung*, although the two are not quite synonymous) of the Soviet Communist Party. Soviet *mirovozrenie* ardently postulated an elemental struggle between the third stage of history (capitalism) and the fourth (Socialism) and argued that the Soviet Union and its guiding Soviet Communist party were destined to lead this struggle against capitalism and to see it through, and with inevitable success. This view was consistent, despite the later shift under Khrushchev in the mid-1950s to the doctrine of 'peaceful co-existence'. This ideology manifested itself politically in the domestic, foreign, and military policies of the Soviet Union.

Second was diplomatic strategy. This advanced the basic ideological world view. The strategy had to reckon with the non-ideological criteria (pre-Marxist or un-Marxist) of states and non-state actors. These criteria would include cultural and socio-economic developments, political structures and military strength. This face of Soviet strategy, combining as it did ideology and pragmatism, was the one to which Westerners were most exposed. They tended to equate the postures and actions of Soviet diplomacy with Soviet ideological direction as a whole, but more than once, this was a fallacy. The Americans did not understand the ultimate aims of the Soviets.

Third was military strategy. The strong engagement with counter-insurgency was largely handled by security agencies, not the military, but it was an important aspect of strategy. The numerous stages in Soviet military development from the Russian Civil War to the 1980s responded first to variable inputs of ideology and external conditions (the latter focusing on the location of Soviet borders, and on the military capacity and friendliness of bordering countries, and of main adversaries further afield); secondly, to the legacy of the world wars; thirdly to atomic weaponry; fourthly to trans-oceanic possibilities; and, lastly, to Soviet inter-service co-operation and rivalries.

Post-1945 Soviet military publications – newspapers, journal articles and books – believed in the implacable hostility of the Western countries toward the Soviet Union and this belief was incorporated into Soviet military training and planning. Thus, Soviet strategy was long-term; incorporated a variety of domestic and foreign inputs, which were refracted through Marxist-Leninism; and exhibited, in its pronouncements and actions, earnestness and deception.

Alongside an ideological commitment to an international mission and to the inevitability of Marxist victory, came a strong sense of vulnerability. In part, this sense reflected real threats. These included serious challenges to territorial integrity and interests, notably from the late 1910s to the mid-1940s from Japan in the Far East. There were also threats to the very existence of the Soviet regime, particularly in the Russian Civil War of 1918-20, and then again from Germany in 1941-2. Yet, there was also a

The Stalin Years: 1924-53

paranoid concern about threats that were non-existent or greatly overplayed. This sense of vulnerability can be traced back to the early seventeenth century. More recent events, and the perception of them, were significant. These included foreign intervention in the Russian Civil War, the working of the Leninist-Stalinist political system predating the Second World War and its consistent belief in conspiracies linked to foreign powers, the experience of unexpected German attack in 1941 of course, and the American development and deployment first of the atom bomb and then of the hydrogen bomb, before then of submarines armed with ballistic missiles.

Central to Soviet strategy, this sense of vulnerability encouraged a major stress on military expenditure as well as a return to the garrison state of the 1550s-1762. The Soviet Union sought an all-round capability to match that of the United States, developing for example the world's second largest navy, even though that was marginal to the Soviet focus on land, air and rocket power.

There had been some hopes that the war would be followed by a loosening of government control or at least methods, but Stalin rejected any such ideas and instead pressed the need for his versions of Communist orthodoxy and security to continue. He faced staggering World War Two losses, and his perception of his regime's unpopularity. His goals were re-establishing control over the countryside, reinstituting the five-year plans and collectivisation, and intensifying dictatorial control, not least for fear of regime collapse.

A cultural challenge was to confirm a new nationalism. In 1946, the Central Committee of the Communist Party decided to free Soviet culture from what it termed 'servility before the West'. Cosmopolitanism and Westernism were attacked, while Russian origins were found for Western inventions and scientific theories. This campaign, which was particularly associated with Andrei Zhdanov, the Central Committee Secretary and Stalin's likely successor, who died in 1948 as a result of alcoholism, continued until Stalin's death in 1953.

All branches of culture were controlled and scrutinised carefully, with writers such as Anna Akhmatova and composers such as

Dmitrii Shostakovich criticised accordingly. Zhdanov and his protégés attacked in particular Ukrainian writers, condemning their alleged separateness from Soviet themes, but it was also as a way for Ukrainian-born Zhdanov to protect his position. Volodymyr Sosiura, a Ukrainian poet and Communist who had been 're-educated' in a factory in 1930-1 for his nationalistic themes, won the Stalin Prize in 1948, but after a Russian translation appeared in May 1951, his poem *Love Ukraine* (1944) was bitterly attacked in *Pravda* on 2 July 1951 for praising the Ukraine landscape and not the new Soviet Ukraine of industry and workers. This escapism was considered 'vice-ridden'. Sosiura was denounced as a 'bourgeois nationalist', the poem banned from publication, and more 'fraternal' wording inserted.

Jews were presented as unpatriotic cosmopolitans, the wartime Jewish Anti-Fascist Committee was suppressed and its Chairman, the actor Solomon Mikhoels, murdered in 1948 when its other prominent members were arrested; they were executed in 1952. The following year, Jewish doctors were denounced in *Pravda* as a 'Zionist terrorist gang', anti-Semitic attacks occurred, and it is possible that this campaign would have led to the deportation of Soviet Jews to Siberia, possibly to murder there in boxcars run into Lake Baikal, but Stalin's death cut short the idea. Sport was very much mobilised for the purposes of the Soviet state and represented accordingly across the fields of culture and media, as in Aleksandr Deineka's painting *The Goalkeeper* (1936).

Science was also in the front line. Stalin was commited to a reliance on work by Communist scholars, an attitude that affected the treatment of foreign work, for example by Albert Einstein, although the institutional and factional politics of Soviet scientists were also significant to responses, both positive and negative. In biology, the official adoption of Lysenkoism in 1948 was part of the war of ideas, as well as a major aspect of public policy. Lysenkoism reflected the Marxist optimism that man could dominate nature. This ideology was advanced in conscious rivalry with genetical theories that were dismissed as bourgeois and were criticised as linked to racism. The Imperial Russian geneticists had been world leaders, but accused of supporting the Trotskyist-Bukharinist opposition, were purged in the late 1930s, Georgii Nadson being shot in 1939 for participation in a terrorist organisation, while Nikolai Vavilov was imprisoned in 1940, dying in 1943 as a result of harsh conditions.

In their place, Trofim Lysenko (1898-1976), the much-decorated Director of the Institute of Genetics of the Soviet Academy of Sciences from 1940 to 1965, rejected the accepted theory linked to Gregor Mendel, and instead drew on the thesis that genes could be altered during one's lifetime. Indicating close interest and personal commitment, Stalin edited Lysenko's key speech himself, and those who opposed Lysenko were arrested and executed, or saved themselves by publicly rejecting the theory of the gene and genetics, which was banned. The treatment of Lysenko's critics scarcely matched ideas of the Soviet Union as a scientific society and, therefore, more advanced. At present, many Russian nationalists praise Lysenko.

Lysenko's argument that environmental determinants could be changed was conducive to Soviet plans to expand arable production greatly in areas not hitherto under the plough, notably to the drier south and south-east of the existing cultivated area: for example, in Kazakhstan. Lysenkoism proved a serious mistake and hopes of greater arable production were not fulfilled for many years. This failure was serious not only because of an eventual need for Western grain imports, but also because the Soviets had hoped that grain exports would win influence in the Third World, for example in Egypt. This was an instance of how the Soviet Union found itself trapped in propping up the misfiring statist economic policies of its allies, who themselves were selectively imitating Soviet policies.

Transport was part of a strengthening of the state. The idea of a rail tunnel between Siberia and Sakhalin was revived in 1950, again for military purposes, as Japan was now an American ally. A tunnel along with connecting rail lines on both sides was planned for completion in 1953 and full operation in 1955, to be built by forced labour; but the project was abandoned in 1953. This abandonment reflected the little that had been completed, but also was due to a lack of drive after Stalin's death in 1953, to inherent seismological dangers suppressed under Stalin, and to the post-Stalin amnesties reducing the labour force.

Khrushchev was to remark that foreign policy for Stalin meant keeping anti-aircraft batteries around Moscow on 24-hour alert. Indeed, Stalin's often-paranoid perceptions of encirclement, capitalist crisis and inevitable imminent war generated his policies of breakneck modernisation as well as the brutal and bloody internal repressions; although his chosen course also had to do with domestic political struggles. Schoolchildren frequently were shown maps of 'capitalist encirclement' to drum into their heads that their country was living in a siege environment. Marxist-Leninism always saw, from day one, enemies without and enemies within.

The test explosion of a Russian atomic device in 1949 encouraged Stalin to take a more bellicose attitude, encouraging Kim Il-Sung to attack South Korea in 1950. He subsequently provided a measure of air support. However, in the Korean War (1950-3), Stalin showed his marked preference for exploiting advantages rather than facing risks: he did not wish to take the chance of formal Soviet entry into the conflict. At the same time, his period of power saw a major expansion of the Communist bloc from 1939 to 1949, with much of Eurasia taken over or threatened. This posed a serious challenge to Western interests.

From 1945 to 1955, during the Fourth and Fifth Five Year Plans, the emphasis was on rebuilding the country, heavy industry and preparing for war. This rested on the developments already made in the recent conflict. Stalin was not much interested in light industry, the standard of living or consumer concerns. There was a continuation of the attempt to develop industrial production in areas distant from hostile air power, notably the Urals and south-west Siberia.

The development of Siberia was pursued by the use of forced labour, with *gulags* providing a workforce analogous in many respects to the Nazi concentration camps. Political, social and cultural outcasts from Stalinist rule, plus those who had been captured by the Germans in the recent war and were therefore suspect, German and Japanese prisoners, as well as deported minorities such as Crimean Tatars, Volga Germans and Kalmyks, were held in large tracts of Siberia designated as labour camp or isolation camp administrative regions. The novelist Alexander Solzhenitsyn (1918-2008), who had been in prison camps from 1945 to 1953 while an artillery officer for making critical remarks in private letters about Stalin, set the novels *Cancer Ward* (1966) and *The First Circle* (1968) in the dehumanising institutions of the Soviet police state. In the latter, he captured the uncertainty of transferred prisoners and the cruelty of their treatment:

> Will they stop his correspondence for years on end, so that his family thinks he is dead? ... will he die of dysentery in his cattle truck? Or die of hunger because the train does not stop for six days and no rations are issued?

Stalin dominated the period through the divisive and disorientating use of arbitrary violence. At the same time, the Communist state entailed a coalition of interests shaping policy and dividing privilege, in secret. Intimidation, protection and brutal trade-offs were the means of politics. Zhdanov was a rival of Beria and Georgy Malenkov. After Zhdanov's death in 1948, the Leningrad affair of 1949-50 saw Leningrad politicians and other figures purged and replaced by Moscow-based figures, with many imprisoned and some killed, including Mikhail Rodionov, the Chairman of the Council of Ministers of the Russian Republic in 1946-9, and Nikolai Voznesensky, the Chairman of the Soviet State Planning Committee from 1938 to 1949, Deputy Chairman of the Soviet Council of Ministers and a protégé of Zhdanov. Voznesensky was too statistical and straying too far from party-mindedness in Stalin's view, who was suspicious of Leningrad politicians. Beria and Malenkov organised the purge, but their victims were rehabilitated during the Khrushchev era.

Differing interests could be more easily accommodated as long as there was not opposition, open or suspected, but rivalry led to such killings. Secrecy and the absence of accountability very much encouraged a corruption that was central to an

Stalin voting in a 1950s propaganda poster by Victor Ivanov. (Public domain)

authoritarianism that had power and controlled a populace that could not match the dictates of its ideology, not least because there was public compliance and conformity alongside individual evasion. The people did not meet the ideology. There was a deep Party suspicion of people: no matter how compliant, an individual always remained a suspect and was subject to arbitrary power. This remained the case after Stalin: the methods changed, but not the context.

{ 9 }

FROM STALIN TO THE FALL
1953-91

A disaster that left both real decay and a feeling of decay, the fire at the nuclear power station of Chernobyl on 26 April 1986 arose from poorly prepared tests and lasted for weeks. In accordance with the usual Soviet preference for secrecy, there was no publicity, while contamination was treated in an incompetent fashion. The Chernobyl episode indicated sub-optimal Soviet management. The plant managers decided to run a safety test by withdrawing all primary and secondary safety back-up measures, including lifting the lead rods from the old-fashioned water containment cylinders. As a result, the air pressure inside the dome increased 1,400 times within four seconds and the dome exploded. The Soviets waited eighteen days before reporting the accident, ensuring that the necessary precautions against radioactivity could not be taken. About 600,000 people suffered as a result of radiation, and crops and animals were affected over a wide area. There was subsequent criticism of nuclear power in the Soviet Union and the mass demonstrations that helped bring about the end of Communist rule included a big march through Kiev on the third anniversary of Chernobyl.

Although shot through with the rivalries, contradictions, ambiguities and secrecies of Kremlin politics, there was a significant reaction against Stalinism after his death in 1953. Aside from changes in personnel and the struggle between factions, this reaction focused on a wish, alongside maintaining military effectiveness, to shift some expenditure from military to domestic purposes, including the consumer goods that would secure domestic support.

The Soviet Union enjoyed appreciable growth during the global 'Long Boom' after World War Two, although there is room for considerable scepticism about the growth figures. In part, growth was a consequence of recovery from the war, but agricultural mechanisation, industrial modernisation, and the large-scale transfer of labour from agriculture to industry were all significant. However, the emphasis was on heavy industry, which diverted resources and goods from consumers.

Communist state control and planning were an attempt at modernisation in a period of competing modernisations. Despite considerable propaganda to the contrary, this state control and planning and the wiping out of the pre-existing economic systems that went with it were to prove unsuccessful and widely unpopular. The Communist era also saw terrible damage to the environment, which was repeatedly subordinated to economic goals and affected by poor management. The dumping of waste poisoned waterways and seas, while the tundra of Siberia was hit hard by mineral and oil exploitation.

A key instance of the difficulty of responding adequately to new possibilities was provided by cybernetics, a term coined in America in 1947 to mean the science of communications and automatic control systems in both machines and living things. Military needs in the Cold War spread the new practice of systems thinking, although the term cybernetics was banned from Soviet universities until the 1970s, as it was associated with non-Marxist-Leninist, falsely 'objective' (ie. bourgeois) criteria. In the 1960s, the Scientific-Technological revolution (NTR) was meant to cure all the ills of the Soviet Union. It was hoped that computers might help with central planning and thus realise the great promise of Communist progress. However, the possibility of new analogies and unauthorised answers offered by cybernetics led to its bureaucratic stifling in the Soviet Union, because of a determination to restrict the unpredictable element of computers. This apparent triumph of dialectical materialism was to be short-lived, and the resulting lack of engagement with the possibilities offered by computers was to be regarded as a major weakness of the Soviet economy, notably so by the mid-1980s.

A sense of instability and flux after Stalin's death arose from uneasiness among the Communist élite as political links were tested and new policies suggested. Lavrentii Beria, the head of the Soviet security systems, failed in an attempt to take over the leadership, in part due to the opposition of Marshal Zhukov, the Deputy Minister of Defence. Beria was imprisoned and shot. There were survivals from the old Stalinist system, not least Lazar Kaganovich and the continuation as Foreign Minister of Vyacheslav Molotov, and his effort to create a unified, neutral Germany. This was an attempt that ignored both West Germany's commitment to the Western bloc and the commitment of the bloc to West Germany. Georgy Malenkov, the Chairman of the Soviet Council of Ministers, in contrast, was more conciliatory to the West and partly as a result fell in 1955. He lost a power struggle with Nikita Khrushchev, the Party First Secretary from 1953 to 1964. Khrushchev's headship of the Party apparatus gave him a key advantage. A committed Communist who advanced Soviet interests in the Third World, notably through arms sales to Egypt and industrial assistance (mostly building factories) to Algeria, Ghana and Nigeria, Khrushchev sought to achieve Soviet goals in Europe by demilitarising the Cold War and making Communist rule more attractive. Under Khrushchev, the military enjoyed less favour than had been the case under Stalin.

The 1955 creation of the Warsaw Pact, which supplanted the bilateral military pacts the Soviets had with the individual Eastern European countries, gave Khrushchev leeway for the withdrawal from Austria. In 1955, he began articulating the doctrine of 'peaceful co-existence', an expression drawn from Lenin's canonical writings. This was a major change from the Stalinist doctrine of the inevitability of war between Socialism and capitalism, a doctrine that had helped lead to the Korean War. What Lenin and Khrushchev both meant was that while the ultimate outcome of the fourth stage of history in terms of the success of Communism was never in doubt, that did not preclude peaceful relations between the two blocs. In the West, this approach was seen as duplicitous.

Once Malenkov had fallen, Khrushchev, a repentant Stalinist, tried to strengthen the Communist bloc itself through de-Stalinisation. Economic growth was to safeguard living conditions and thus enhance popular support for Communism. Labour heroism was important to Khrushchev's vision, and labour was to be encouraged and rewarded. Far more than admonitions were to be on offer. There was to be a 'guaranteed tomorrow', as well as an equality of living space and income, and a modest standard of living. Khrushchev's 'thaw' influenced a generation of people in their late teens, twenties and thirties who in the mid and late 1980s were to press change much further. However, Khrushchev was a devoted Communist. The central-planning system and the collective farms were Stalinist and remained unchanged until well into the Gorbachev period in the late 1980s, when they both began to fall apart.

The Twentieth Congress of the CPSU (Communist Party of the Soviet Union) in February 1956 witnessed a denunciation by Khrushchev in his report 'On the Cult of Personality and its Consequences' of the crimes committed by Stalin but not of the basis of the Soviet system. Khrushchev argued that the Party had deviated from its 'historic course' due to Stalin. This denunciation weakened his rivals, notably Kaganovich and Molotov, who were far more compromised by their role in Stalin's purges, although Khrushchev himself had actively supported them. Thousands of political prisoners were released in the 'thaw', and many were found posts by Khrushchev, uneasily coexisting with those who had sent them to the *gulags*.

As a major aspect of the break from Stalin, there had already been an attempt at reconciliation with Yugoslavia, leading on 2 June 1955 to the Belgrade Declaration, in which the Soviet Union accepted that relations with other Communist states should be guided by the principle of equality. In June 1956, Tito visited Moscow, and Party relations were officially normalised, although Tito refused to return to the fold by following Moscow's lead.

Only limited de-Stalinisation was on offer with Khrushchev. In Hungary in 1956, this led to the brutal crushing by Soviet troops of a reform Communist movement. In the Soviet Union, repression was far less violent than under Stalin but still incessant. Culture continued to be political. Finished in 1955, Boris Pasternak's novel *Doctor Zhivago* was refused publication the following year due to its rejection of Socialist Realism, and because of its criticism of Soviet norms. The novel was banned in the Soviet Union and he was not allowed to receive the Nobel Prize for Literature when it was awarded in 1958.

On 4 October 1957, the Soviet Union launched a missile that carried Sputnik I, the first satellite, into orbit, where it circled the world at 18,000 miles per hour. The launch did not mean that the Soviets had intercontinental ballistic missiles able to carry atomic bombs, but it meant that such missiles might soon be close. Sputnik appeared to prove Soviet claims of technological superiority, not simply in military hardware but also in technological capability, as well as in standards of living. Indeed, the Cold War was, in one respect, a battle over technological modernity. In 1961, the Soviet Union sent the first man into space, Yuri Gagarin. Competition over living standards reflected the increasing sense in the late 1950s that the Cold War was a battle for the hearts and minds of consumers on the home front as much as of armed forces. A spirit of can-do optimism was propagated in the Soviet Union.

The public relations coup created round Sputnik was totally misleading. Soviet economic statistics were manipulated and there was a systemic Soviet failure to ensure that accurate figures were obtained and that proper balance sheets were produced. For example, in Uzbekistan (a republic in the Soviet Union) under Sharav Rashidov (1959-83), the figures for cotton production were persistently grossly inaccurate. Nevertheless, Western concern about Soviet economic growth added to anxiety about its apparent expansionism and military capability.

Soviet growth was important in the propaganda war, which increasingly focused in the late 1950s on the living standards of consumers. If the Soviet system could provide better outcomes, then surely, it was believed on the Soviet side and feared in the West, workers around the world would opt for it, as would newly independent Third World states such as Egypt. This approach represented a challenge to capitalism, but also to the Socialist parties that the Communists presented as tarnished by their willingness to compromise with capitalism. In short, the Soviet project was relaunched on the competitive world stage in a fashion very different to its earlier versions in the years of the Revolution and the successive attempts under Stalin. The Soviet modernity under offer was part of a new political struggle. Peaceful co-existence was to be 'won' by the Soviet Union.

Khrushchev had won the struggle to dominate the Soviet regime. Having compromised his rivals with his anti-Stalinism campaign in 1956, Khrushchev faced their counter-attack and attempted coup in June 1957 when the 'Anti-Party Group', led by Malenkov, Molotov, Kaganovich and Dimitry Shepilov, gained a majority in the Politburo for his dismissal. However, allied to Georgy Zhukov, the Minister of Defence, who provided vocal support, and to the KGB, Khrushchev insisted that the decision be ratified by the plenary session of the Central Committee. That overturned the Politburo's decision. With the unspoken consensus among Presidium and Central Committee members that there would be no return to Stalin's deadly purges, Khrushchev then removed his opponents, sending Molotov to be ambassador in Mongolia, Malenkov to manage a hydroelectric plant, and Kaganovich to run a potash factory. In October, accused of pursuing a personality cult, Zhukov was dismissed in order to strengthen Khrushchev's position.

Competition with America was to the fore under Khrushchev as it represented the capitalist dream. Khrushchev saw 'a race to see who could do the best job at supplying the ordinary fellow on the beach with his cold drink'. Impressed by American consumerism, Khrushchev regarded it as the challenge now that the Western colonial empires were fading: 'The Americans got it. They understood that if ordinary people were to live the way the kings and merchants of old had lived, what would be required was a new kind of luxury, an ordinary luxury built up from goods turned out by the million so that everybody could have one.' In the event, however, the Americans could deliver rockets and consumerism while the Soviets found the latter an impossible goal, in large part because of the serious deficiencies of a Communist-controlled economy and the degree to which the throttling of consumer products resulted not only from command-control economic tactics but also from genuine political-ideological concerns.

There was a long tradition of using Western visitors to showcase Soviet achievements. In July 1959, Richard Nixon, the Vice-President, and Khrushchev significantly squared off in a kitchen in the American National Exhibition in Sokolniki Park, Moscow, to debate the virtues of the two systems, Nixon boasting about colour television. Khrushchev criticised the 'gadgets' of the capitalist American home, but set out to ensure consumer satisfaction, although the Socialist consumerism that was to be on offer in the East, for example sensible 'Socialist fashions', suffered from a serious lack of understanding of the market mechanisms of consumerism.

Thus, in housing, there were often poorly produced urban apartment blocks that proved a dispiriting environment, and there was no choice about where to live. Many apartments were communal and that was key to the Soviet urban experience. Nor was there advertising in the Soviet Union anywhere near approaching the scale in the West. There was a lack of marketing expertise, competition, and quality control. The only billboards were Party slogans, such as 'Glory to the CPSU' and 'The Party and the People are United.' The Soviets, with their fixation on urbanisation and tall blocks of flats, were incapable of understanding that the fairly roomy Russian peasant houses were actually acceptable and only required the installation of water pipes and indoor toilets.

Khrushchev was compromised by the risk of war in the Cuban Missile Crisis of 1962, being perceived as erratic by his Politburo colleagues. He had to hold them at bay by reputation; there was no equivalent to the role of terror and fear in the maintenance of Stalin's position. He was also hit by the poor grain harvest of 1963, which meant buying Canadian grain. Thereafter, the Soviets never ceased purchasing Western grain. This situation rested on more profound problems with the collective farms, and with agriculture as a whole; the drive to improve diet by growing maize to feed animals that could provide meat and milk faced repeated setbacks.

When Khrushchev was removed from office by the Central Committee on 14 October 1964, being accused of risking war over Berlin and Cuba, a collective leadership emerged. The main figure until his death in 1982 was Leonid Brezhnev, the Party leader, a protégé of Khrushchev. Brezhnev was determined to avoid war, in part because of his experience of World War Two as an army commissar. The prospect of cutting defence costs was attractive, as was importing Western technology. *Détente* therefore appealed to different constituencies in the Soviet Union. Soviet interest in stability was revealed in 1971 in Brezhnev's speech to the 24th Congress of the Communist Party, in which he called for international security and devoted scant space to the international cause of 'national liberation'.

The Soviet position meanwhile deteriorated as a result of a rift with Mao Zedong that gathered pace from 1960, and by the outbreak of local frontier fighting in 1969, fighting with China that was not kept secret. From 1960, the Chinese denounced the Soviet Communist Party for revisionism, trying to curry favour with Western imperialists and, in general, for retreating from Stalin's line.

As the Soviet Union was a major oil producer, the marked rise in the price of oil from 1973 greatly helped Soviet finances. This enabled the Soviets to invest more heavily in exporting their brand of Communism to Africa, notably to Angola and Ethiopia, as well as sending arms to Egypt and Syria. However, the financial improvement encouraged a complacent failure to address serious structural problems in the Soviet economy. The benefits of the oil price hike came on top of the improvement in Soviet economic performance in the late 1960s, which engendered some complacency. There appears to have been significant improvement in the economic lot of Soviet citizens during the Brezhnev period (1964-82), notably in housing and the provision of goods. Much of the period was one of moving forward, of progress, in which Soviet society as a whole, bearing in mind the basic constraints of its being a police-state, was becoming more open. The Brezhnev years saw a significant improvement in investment into the Soviet social welfare system. Wages increased by 50% between 1967 and 1977, and a five-day working week was introduced. The rise in wages permitted only a modest standard of living, but it represented a huge improvement from the 1930s and 1940s. The wages of collective and state farm workers rose above the average wage. Although the Soviet cult of statistics incorporated major problems with manipulation and accuracy, production figures suggested genuine improvements.

The Brezhnev government, however, lacked an effective response to economic issues, with the role of state planning, particularly by Gosplan, the State Planning Commission in the Soviet Union, proving inadequate. There was a failure to develop the consumer spending that was so important to economic activity and growth in America and Western Europe. This was a political decision, lest consumerism lead to the fetishisation of things and to bourgeois attitudes. The dour Politburo member Mikhail Suslov was the key figure. An ideologue of the Stalinist school, he had played a major role in overthrowing Khrushchev and continued in office until his death in 1982. Conventional Communist ideology was underlined in 1977 in the new Soviet constitution, which essentially confirmed that of 1936 produced under Stalin, and asserted without hesitation the role of the Party. It was declared both the leading force of Soviet society and the force that determined the course of Soviet domestic and foreign policy. The 1977 constitution declared that the Soviet Union now had 'developed Socialism'.

Economic innovation failed to make traction. In 1965, Prime Minister Aleksei Kosygin had tried to push through a modest move back from centralisation that would have enabled factory managers on the spot to determine within limits the amount of production they wished to pursue. This move had been blocked by middle-ranking administrators in many of the industrial-production ministries.

Moreover, the increase in output figures for the five-year plans showed a clear decline over the decades, and more than could be explained by the base being quite large (unlike in 1928) and gradually becoming larger. The Brezhnev era was not characterised by economic stagnation until the pace of growth slowed from the mid-1970s. From 1950 to 1965, the annual rate of increase in GDP varied between 4.5% and 5.5%, but the trend was then downward:

Five Year Plan	Years	Annual Rate of Increase in GDP
8	1966–70	4.8
9	1971–75	2.9
10	1976–80	1.8
11	1981–85	1.7
12	1986–90	1.3

The productivity of Soviet workers was not really increasing, and Soviet machinery was aging and not being replaced. The Soviets regarded industrial machinery as a wasting asset to be used until it wore out, whereas other industrial societies had a time- and profit-based, technologically sensitive approach towards depreciation. In the mid-1960s, machine tools in America could be totally depreciated in tax terms after seven years, which acted as a stimulus for technological innovation. In contrast, Soviet machine tools, the foundation for any kind of industrial sophistication, were being fully depreciated over a thirty-year period. More generally, the resources, cheap and plentiful labour, and government confidence that all marked the Soviet Union in the 1950s were no longer there by the 1970s, although the product mix was far greater than it had been in the 1930s.

The Soviet failure to fulfil the goal of agricultural self-sufficiency ensured that grain had to be imported, notably from America, which was a striking instance of economic and political failure as the free market remedied the failings of the command economy. In large part, the Soviet failure was due to the inability of collective forms of management (that in practice represented central state direction) to realise the potential of Soviet agriculture. Managerial quality and peasant motivation were greatly lacking on the collective farms, and the use of student workers in the summer did not greatly improve the situation. By the late 1970s, the Soviet Union had easily outproduced the Americans in the production of farm machinery, and in the black-soil region of Ukraine they had a rich arable resource, but American agriculture was more productive. Collectivisation was a harmful legacy in the Soviet Union: there was a lack of private agriculture and little incentive on the part of collective farm members to work hard on public farmland. Due to central planning there was an acute shortage of spare parts, which meant that much farm machinery was not usable. In addition, there was a very high spoilage rate for Soviet agricultural products. A lot of produce rotted in rural warehouses or at train stations where it would not be picked up in time, and that was after substantial damage from the farms as the lorries bounced along ill-maintained dirt roads.

The Virgin Lands project to create ploughed lands in Kazakhstan, which started in 1954, eventually straightened itself out and that republic became a major grain-producing area. However, the deeper one goes into the territory of the Soviet Union, the drier and colder it becomes, while rainfall is less predictable. Furthermore, the demand of the populace for beef increased as the urban population expanded. More grain was needed as feed grain for cattle as opposed to grain for people, although that also was a factor. From 1963, the Soviet Union imported grain from several Western countries, first Canada and later America. The Soviet government in the late 1950s had committed themselves to sharply increasing meat production, giving rise to Khrushchev's 1958 remark that the Soviets would overtake the Americans in meat production by 1960. To increase the number of livestock meant a significant rise in the amount of feed grain required, which affected the availability of grain for humans. Two-thirds of the revenue from the oil exported by the Soviets was being used by 1982 to purchase grain from the West, which was not the profile of a balanced industrial economy.

Some of the biggest planning disasters in the world occurred in Soviet agriculture, notably with cotton production in Soviet Central Asia, a sphere in which rampant corruption and the serious misreporting of production statistics, notably from Uzbekistan, vied with fundamental environmental degradation due to excessive irrigation that caused the astonishing exhaustion of the Aral Sea. These problems were a major issue for Mikhail Gorbachev, appointed to the Secretariat for Agriculture in 1978 and from 1980 the Politburo member responsible for agriculture. Environmental issues included the release into the air as injurious dust of dried-out soil contaminated by chemical fertilisers. This led to an increase of birth defects among Uzbek and Turkmen children, while the children living in eastern Kazakhstan were afflicted with such horrors due to the aftermath of nuclear bomb tests.

Given problems with environmental degeneration, alcoholism and cramped living space, it is not surprising that infant mortality and life expectancy were high and low in the Soviet Union. This discredited claims about the superiority of the Soviet system and also fed through into economic problems, for a decline in population growth hit the increase in the labour force in the 1970s and even more in the 1980s. Soviet labour needs had, in part, been met by high employment rates among women, but by the 1980s there were fewer new female workers that could be added to the workforce.

Labour issues were seriously compounded by the scale of underemployment that resulted from a failure to allocate resources in accordance with market mechanisms. The Soviets were trapped into under-employment, for that was the only means of hanging onto the ideologically driven nostrum of full employment. A failure to accept the reality of unemployment, which did exist, exacerbated the problems of economic management.

The Soviet Union was in a very difficult situation by the mid-1980s. Economic downturns interacted with already pronounced systemic faults. There was a failure to ensure adequate mechanisms for incentive, which meant lack of entrepreneurship. With bright people unable to follow the Western pattern of raising money for investment and generally excluded from state monopolies governed by timeserving and unimaginative bureaucrats, it was not surprising that the Soviet system could not engage adequately with change. This inability to engage was seen dramatically in the failure to produce sufficient computers, which was indicative of an unwillingness to put an accurate cost on the use of human time, and a reluctance to depart from paper records.

This unwillingness was a symptom of a more systemic management incompetence and planning failure that helped ensure that the commitment of resources and effort did not yield qualitative improvement. The focus solely on output, or rather on claims of output, was misconceived. Communist economics entailed scant concern for the free market, and this situation led to numerous instances of the supply of only part of the process: shaving cream without razors, for example.

Economic and other statistics from the Soviet era are unreliable. Nevertheless, there is little doubt that measures of economic growth show a fall in the Brezhnev era (1964-82); with earlier rates of increase, in national income, production, productivity, and return on investment, not being sustained. This fall represented a serious failure in the planning set out under the five-year plans, and the mismatch between these plans and the reality of often lacklustre outcomes helped discredit Communism as a system of economic analysis, a guide to planning, and a means for social progress. The conceptual problems were serious. Alongside state bureaucratic control, there was a difficulty in understanding time and value in economics, as well as the energy and labour inadequacies and insufficiencies of Soviet manufacturing, the growing impracticality of the centralised monitoring of the ever-escalating product mix, and the general realisation that the implications of opportunity costs arising from technological innovation conferred economic benefits that were not the same as those connected with the maintenance of wasting, depreciated capital assets. The Soviets appeared unable to visualise economic reform.

The economic impasse of the Soviet Union was reflected in the lack of alternative plans. There was no longer any lived business experience. When these aggregate failures were combined with a lack of innovation and new product ranges, then the situation was indeed serious. The command economy, with its micromanagement in planning and execution from the centre, was failing. Limited growth, moreover, intensified competition for resources, and the state lacked an adequate mechanism to cope with this competition which, anyway, it did not understand fully. The nostrums of Marxist-Leninism offered no help and decreasing inspiration.

The situation with railways was instructive. They were crucial to an economy that did not rely heavily on road transport, despite the availability of oil. This role reflected legacy factors from earlier Soviet history, as well as the ideology of Communism. The system was, at 147,400 kilometres (91,600 miles), the largest in the world, although the size of the Soviet Union meant that its density was low, certainly compared to the rest of Europe. This, however, looked somewhat different if attention was devoted solely to European Russia, where the density was higher. Post-war expansions were at the annual rate of 639 kilometres from 1965 to 1980, and notably so in Siberia, where the existing capacity was limited. Bringing new rail capacity to areas with developing oil and mineral extraction was crucial. Driven by strategic considerations, not least concern about possible hostility with China, the Baikal-Amur Mainline parallel to the Trans-Siberian to the south was a key addition. However, that new line suffered greatly from poor management and congestion and thereby highlighted more general issues for the Soviet network as a whole. In 1974, Brezhnev presented this railway as 'the construction project of the century'. It certainly overcame a harsh terrain, notably permafrost. Building on land affected by permafrost was difficult and raised the question of climate change causing damage through the melting of the permafrost layer. The railway has numerous bridges and tunnels, all of which increased construction and maintenance costs. Much of the labour force was provided by professionally inexperienced volunteers from the Young Communist League. The railway was declared complete in 1984, when it wasn't, and, again in 1991. Many mining and industrial projects were linked to the railway, but it did not match expectations in terms of revenues.

Low productivity and massive under-employment meant that per capita GNP was very low compared to the West. Combined with the high rate of military expenditure, these economic problems limited the funds available for social investment and consumer spending. Unlike in the West, economic growth in the Soviet bloc did not lead to personal prosperity, and certainly not by the standards of the West. This limitation increasingly compromised popular support for the system. The government pushed 'Socialist social policies' as it sought to reconcile economic with social policies and to use social welfarism to enhance labour productivity. Instead, this welfarism, designed to create the 'guaranteed tomorrow', proved a drain on the economy, while also failing to satisfy rising popular expectations, and actually undermining the incentive to work. Falling life expectancy, which owed much to pollution, was a clear symptom of the social failure of economic management and challenged the state's legitimacy, which the Communist government based on social progress including good universal health provision.

Political failure was evident in corruption, not only for personal profit but simply in order to get economic processes to work. Unreported and illegal production and trades were necessary for the economy to function, not least through a large-scale barter system which encompassed industry, agriculture, the bureaucracy, services and individuals. This production and these trades led to the development of a parallel world of personal gain regulated by bribery. These practices made a mockery of Communism, not least as this parallel world included public institutions. The ability of Party officials to gain special privileges, notably in housing, the purchase of goods, travel, education and preference for relatives, further helped to discredit the Communist system. The manner of economic functioning was pre-capitalist and a regression from Marx's third stage of economic development, which followed what he called slave and feudal societies. Thus, the Communist Bloc's economic performance by the 1970s invalidated Marx's argument about a superior, fourth stage of history, Socialism.

With time, the sham character of Communist progress became more apparent, to the population and to foreign commentators. The failure to match Western European improvements in living standards helped cause widespread apathy, cynicism and disillusionment among the population. The inherent weaknesses of the Communist system, and notably its economics, were increasingly understood. However, in a serious failure of knowledge, analysis and assumptions, Western intelligence agencies were to be surprised by the speed of the eventual collapse of the Communist regimes. Practically no one in the Russian history field in 1985 predicted that the Soviet Union would fall apart. The seeming durability of dictatorships proved an *idée fixe* for Western observers. More predictably, Left-wing sympathisers continued to publish articles praising Communist states and, at the least, putting them on an equivalence with America.

The Brezhnev regime was increasingly characterized by incompetence, corruption and sloth. The sluggish and complacent Brezhnev, who failed to see the need for change and indeed sought to support the *status quo* and maintain continuity, neglected warnings of problems and proved particularly negligent in economic management. Subsequently, the disastrous explosion at Chernobyl and the dishonest and inefficient response of the government despite Gorbachev's championing of *glasnost* (openness to public scrutiny), suggested that the entire Soviet system was weak and negligent. This was true for example of the key element of the economy, defence, or more properly, war preparation. While apparently 'modern', notably with the missile and space programmes, these were poorly organised and prone to bitter disputes between competing individuals and groups.

Nevertheless, despite serious economic problems, the Brezhnev regime retained control because of the strength of the Soviet dictatorship. This strength was not simply a matter of coercion, although that was important. Much activity was devoted by the KGB to spying on dissidents and to persecuting them by methods such as imprisonment, internal exile, and consigning sane people to psychiatric hospitals to administer psychotropic drugs forcibly so as to severely damage their cognitive abilities or drive them into imbecility. Solzhenitsyn, who won the Nobel Prize for Literature in 1970, was arrested and exiled in 1974 for his description of Stalinist terror in *The Gulag Archipelago* (1973). The Soviet ambassador to America from 1962 to 1986, Anatoly Dobrynin, claimed that Brezhnev kept 800,000 political prisoners in prison or psychiatric hospitals. It was not enough just to act against those judged dissidents. Instead, the entire population was under surveillance, with informers in every workplace and apartment block.

Inertia, however, was more potent than coercion. There was a fatalist sense among the public that there was no alternative to Communist rule. This sense encouraged widespread despair and high rates of drunkenness, affecting health and life expectancy. Vodka was not drunk with mixers because that was regarded as unmanly and Western.

Alongside inertia and coercion, the state's ability to seem to offer some improvement or benefits was useful with particular constituencies of support, notably the bureaucracy and the military. Enthusiasm, however, was limited and the Communist Party, which did not succeed in inspiring, was pushed to the back by state bureaucracies that did not seek to inspire except in empty terms, such as the by-now formulaic Socialist Realism in the arts. Thus, in 1987, the Museum of Revolution was opened in Tallinn with a mural *Friendship of Nations, Depicting the Achievement of Peoples' Friendship and Socialism* painted by Evald Okas (1915-2011); he had painted the ceiling of the Estonian National Opera in a similar style in 1947.

Meanwhile, there was a widespread privatization of commitment at the individual and household level, and a focus on getting by. These shifts and expedients involved bartering, persuasive corruption, and often shoddy compromises. The Russian term for getting children into universities or institutions through connections, or doing anything and everything through connections, was called *blat* (pull). Personal integrity and the sense of self-worth were repeatedly bargained away to obtain benefits. Suicide rates among the young were high. This situation did not mean or lead to significant active opposition, but it left government and the Communist Party in a vacuum, with Party members largely cut off from the working class they were supposed to represent. There was also a disconnect from the peasantry and the intelligentsia. Political opposition, where it existed, could hope to win a measure of public acceptance, possibly support, but it was denied the means of political expression employed in the West.

Dying on 10 November 1982, Brezhnev was succeeded as General Secretary of the Communist Party by the 68-year-old Yuri Andropov, Soviet ambassador in Hungary in 1956 and the head of the KGB from 1967. He appeared to offer the possibility of a new start because he did not share Brezhnev's complacency and appreciated the need for improvement, becoming the mentor of Mikhail Gorbachev whose career he advanced in the Politburo.

However, Andropov had scant concept of improvement other than better social and work discipline. He had little notion of improving qualitative industrial output, or making radical changes. Policies included the dispatch of agents into cinemas in the early afternoon in order to check viewers' identities so as to establish whether they were absentee workers, and the decree that liquor stores had to open later in the day to prevent workers from leaving their jobs to buy vodka. As was true for many Soviet propaganda campaigns, after a short period, matters continued on their usual course and nothing substantive was done. Andropov was anyway increasingly ill with kidney disease.

On 17 January 1983, Ronald Reagan had approved National Security Decision Directive 75, which included the goal of promoting 'the process of change in the Soviet Union toward a more pluralistic political and economic system in which the power of the privileged ruling elite is gradually reduced'. There was scant sign of such a prospect under Andropov, and the Directive was correct in pointing out that 'Soviet aggressiveness has deep roots in the internal system.' Andropov died on 9 February 1984 and was replaced by Konstantin Chernenko, another member of Brezhnev's gerontocracy and, like Andropov, in poor health when appointed. Chernenko lacked even Andropov's energy and this contributed greatly to the sense of policy deadlock.

Andrey Gromyko, a key senior member of the Politburo, who had been Foreign Minister since 1957, maintained continuity in foreign policy. An expert on relations with America, where he served at Washington from 1939 before becoming Delegate to the United Nations from 1946 to 1949, Gromyko saw the world almost exclusively through the prism of Soviet-American relations. He did not seek a breakthrough with America. Instead, under Gromyko, Soviet foreign policy was nearly as rigid as he was unsmiling. Certainly, there was no bold initiative comparable to Richard Nixon's approach to China, nor, subsequently, any Soviet ability to retrieve the situation there. At the same time, there were changes and openings before the rise of Mikhail Gorbachev. In September 1984, Gromyko travelled to Washington to meet Reagan and in January 1985 the Politburo decided to engage again in arms negotiations with America.

A staleness was particularly apparent in the early 1980s, and notably under Chernenko, who died on 10 March 1985. An impression of stagnation, if not decay, became more insistent and was commented on both within and outside the Soviet Union. 'The patient had died already on the operating table' by 1985, although few of the top Soviet leaders understood that. Yet, underlying later counterfactuals about whether different outcomes were possible, very few commentators proved willing to predict that the Soviet bloc, let alone the Soviet Union, would soon collapse. There was an awareness in the West of its economic problems, but not of their consequences. The ability to suppress dissent in Poland in 1981 encouraged a sense that force would deal with problems. However, the combination of Soviet economic difficulties, Soviet political sluggishness, and a much broader and better educated Soviet citizenry, indicated that the country in 1985 was very different to what had been anticipated during the 1917 Revolution. Moreover, the citizenry was aware of this contrast. Although Party membership was often considered a wise career move, as reflected in figures for membership, Communism failed to engage the affection of most of the population.

A recognition of Soviet weakness was central to the change in policies introduced by Gorbachev. The youngest member of the Politburo (of which he became a voting member only in 1980), he became leader as General Secretary of the Central Committee of the Communist Party of the Soviet Union on 11 March 1985, at the age of 54. The first Soviet leader who was really a post-Stalinist, Gorbachev had joined the Communist Party in 1952 and had benefited from the Khrushchev thaw. His grandfathers had both spent time in labour camps.

Gorbachev's main rival for power in 1985, Grigory Romanov, a hardliner, would probably not have taken reform so far. Internal security in Leningrad where he was the Party boss was tight, as the place had a reputation as the Westernising city. A protégé of Andropov, he had been promoted thanks to his help to the post of Secretary of the Communist Party responsible for industry and military output. However, under Chernenko, Gorbachev had a more senior position and acted as Chairman when Chernenko was ill. Romanov was possibly affected by a scandal involving his commanding the Hermitage Museum to send valuable china to a family wedding, in which it was broken by the drunken guests hurling empty glasses at the fireplace, which is a Russian custom. This made Romanov look extravagant, and there were also reports of him having an affair with the famous popular singer Alla Pugacheva. Once Gorbachev was in power, Romanov was rapidly sacked from the Politburo and from office.

Gorbachev's key policy changes were domestic, as he sought to modernise Communism by introducing reforms; but there was also a drive for a less combative and confrontational international stance. Aware that he faced problems, Gorbachev put the difficulties of the Soviet Union and the Communist cause in a Marxist context, in which the strains of global capitalism were apparent. The notion of progressive crises in the capitalist order remained strong among Communist thinkers, and Gorbachev was confident that these economic and social crises would lead to political rivalry within the West, weakening America and helping the Soviet Union. Gorbachev initially pressed for a more coordinated and successful approach to the Third World, based not on the withdrawal of Soviet commitment but rather on appropriate policies by allies, combined with prioritisation by the Soviet Union. This approach meant stricter budgeting, as the Soviet government could no longer afford all its overseas commitments. This prioritisation was partly responsible for the decision to withdraw from Afghanistan. It would be mistaken, therefore, to use this (eventual) withdrawal to suggest that Gorbachev was unwilling to defend overseas Soviet interests and allies. In 1985, in response to an American trade embargo of Nicaragua, Gorbachev increased economic assistance to Nicaragua and promised Cuba help if it backed Nicaragua against an American military attack.

The reform policies of the Gorbachev government were, in effect, its attempt to create what had been termed, with reference to Alexander Dubcek and Czechoslovakia in 1968, 'Socialism with a human face'. The sham propaganda of Communist progress, however, helped ensure that these policies inadvertently destroyed Communism in Eastern Europe and the Soviet Union, as well as the Soviet state. It proved impossible, at yet another stage of the attempt to uplift the Soviet standard of living and thus promote the efficacy of Soviet ideology, to introduce a market responsiveness in a planned economy.

Consumerism was a Western bourgeois concept to the Soviet government, but nevertheless, there was a wish to win popular support through economic means. Efforts from 1985 to achieve economic and political reform faced the structural economic and fiscal weakness of the Soviet system, the preference for control as opposed to any price system that reflected cost and availability. The post-Communist dismantling of the old command economy was to expose the uncompetitive nature of much Soviet-era industry, both of individual enterprises and of the economy as a whole. By 1985, it took the Soviet Union three times as much electricity to produce one ton of steel as in West Germany, and at least twice as much time (ie labour) as in the West German and American cases. Soviet economic inefficiency and costs led to the moment of truth that Gorbachev faced in the mid-1980s.

Assessing the Soviet economy, and indeed the Cold War as a whole, means avoiding the trap of teleology: making the outcome appear inevitable. Ironically, such an approach was a characteristic of Communist thought. However, there was a total failure to predict eventual outcomes or to understand processes at work and changes that were occurring. All of this proved the case with the collapse of the Communist bloc. However, there are problems with the argument that the Soviet Union could not sustain its position as a great power because its economy was illiberal. Indeed, although the economy was not capitalist, it managed to produce sufficient material to underpin Soviet military strength to the degree necessary to make the Soviet Union a great power. Their opponents *might* have been victorious in the event of war, but the sheer size of the Soviet forces induced grave strategic concern in the West. More generally, the amount of Soviet production (not the means or efficiency of obtaining it) was significant; and the Soviet focus on the strength of the state and not on the wealth or well-being of the individual, was not inherently inefficient. An emphasis on per-capita GNP, which reflects both the quantity of goods brought to market and liberal economic views of the superiority of comparative advantage, is not invariably valid, as per-capita GNP does not determine power. Russia had demonstrated that in the nineteenth century.

These points about the amount of production, however, seem more valid for the 1930s than for the 1980s when the pace and nature of technological change suggested that the character of economic development was clearly moving away from a situation in which the process could be readily directed by government. Moreover, the fall in the price of oil and natural gas in the 1980s hit Soviet finances. The price of oil fell by nearly 80% between 1980 and 1986. But linking the respective significance of these points to the more general fashion in, and after, the 1980s for liberal economics remains fraught with interpretive danger. Aside from the economic situation, the international political and military environment was not auspicious: the Soviet Union was on bad terms in the 1980s with America, much of Western Europe, China and Japan.

The intellectual crisis of Marxism was not the reason for the collapse of the Communist states. However, the failure of what the Soviet Communists under Lenin and Stalin had fashioned and presented as the Marxist model for an economic system joined its political to its intellectual crisis. The Soviet Communist Party labelled Marxist-Leninist theory a 'science'. Marxist-Leninist theory could, allegedly, predict outcomes, but in practice, Marxist-Leninist thinkers faced philosophical, methodological, epistemological and psychological problems. There was no infusion into Soviet Marxism from the Frankfurt School, or the relatively liberal Italian Communist Party, or the British Marxist School, or Latin American Liberation Theology, or Chinese developments towards a more liberal economic order. Soviet Marxist-Leninism remained ideologically autarkic until the late 1980s and, when it faced crisis, it fell apart and Soviet Party members by the millions discarded their Party cards.

Nevertheless, the collapse of Communism was largely due not to this intellectual failure, but to the specific political and economic circumstances of the 1980s. The possibility of a different trajectory, and thus the value of counterfactual speculations that probe such possibilities, was exemplified by developments in China. There, the introduction of capitalism proved compatible with the Communist rule that was maintained by the availability of force and, in 1989, by the willingness to use it.

As a further reminder that ideological issues should be set in context, the problems of Soviet Communism were to be matched in post-Communist Russia. The situation then, now capitalist (of a type) and democratic (of a form), was, in practice, like the earlier Communist system. There was a reliance on informal networks, personalised loyalty, and the exchange of deals, all of which sapped institutional effectiveness. As under Communism, assets were not properly costed, while private property was at risk.

As far as the intellectual crisis of Marxist-Leninism was concerned, the commitment of much of the population to Marxist-Leninism as the basis for understanding themselves and their world was anyway limited; and debate among intellectuals was of scant relevance to them. Moreover, the crisis of Marxist-Leninism as a viable theory was not of great relevance for the government. Instead, its sense of change as necessary owed far more to pragmatic considerations.

The impact of dissidents was limited, especially in the Russian Federation, the major part of the Soviet Union. Although of considerable interest to foreign commentators, dissent there did not gather pace to become opposition. This failure was a reflection of the nature of Russian public culture, the dominant role of the Communist Party in education and among workers, the effectiveness of repression, and a marked degree of anti-intellectualism. The last included persistent and strong anti-Semitism: many dissidents were Jews. The Soviet government began selectively adopting anti-Semitism during World War Two, before becoming more persistent in the late 1940s and the early 1960s, and very much so after Israel's victory in the Six Days' War in 1967. There was certainly no comparison in Russia to the major impact of the opposition intelligentsia in Czechoslovakia, let alone in Poland. In each case, the intelligentsia expressed a degree of nationalism that was compatible with their calls for reformed Communism.

Among the Soviet élite there was a sense by the mid-1980s that change was necessary, which helps explain why Gorbachev was not removed by an indignant Politburo, as had happened in 1964 to Khrushchev. He did not come from the KGB, had few links with the military, and was not closely allied with the remaining members of previous generations of policymakers. In a continuance of Khrushchev's assumptions and policies, Gorbachev criticised Stalinist rule: 'We cannot and should not ever forgive or justify what happened.'

Critics of Gorbachev's changes were sidelined. Thus, in 1985, Gorbachev dismissed Nikolai Baibakov (1911-2008), a Stalinist who had headed Gosplan, the State Planning Committee in 1955-7 and from 1965, and had earlier served Stalin in 1944-6 and 1948-55 as minister for the oil industry, a crucial ministry. Baibakov's generation, which had dominated the ministries from the 1940s, was now superseded and was unable to move beyond a measure of criticism of Gorbachev. Unused to attacks from the leadership, Party ideologues were pushed onto the defensive, and this represented a fundamental split within the Communist Party and a loss of its legitimacy.

This leads to the question of whether a leader with views different to Gorbachev could have kept the Soviet system in place, as suggested by some commentators. Gorbachev saw liberalism as essential for a stronger Soviet Union, and he was willing to argue the case publicly, pressing for a 'Socialist pluralism' in 1987, and persuading the Party Conference the following year to support truly contested elections for a legislature independent of the executive. These elections meant Communists could compete with each other, and to do so push different policies, which was a rejection of the Leninist idea of democratic centralism. This was a reversal of Marxist-Leninism, as was Gorbachev's pressure for the subordination of the Communist Party to the law, and his call for checks and balances.

His public rejection of Party infallibility in February 1990 meant that the Soviet Communist Party had now become a Menshevik or parliamentary Marxist Party. His break with the authoritarian legacy of Communist rule included a sweeping relaxation of censorship, which made it far easier to question Marxist-Leninism, a process which rapidly had consequences that neither he nor most others anticipated.

Supporting *glasnost*, Gorbachev was confident that the Soviet Union and the Communist Party would not only be able to survive these challenges, but would be strengthened by them. He was to be proved completely wrong. Instead, economic reform, in particular *perestroika* (restructuring), the loosening of much of the command economy, the 'centrally planned' economy of the Soviet model, led unexpectedly to economic problems, including inflation, which caused much popular unease, as well as hitting economic activity. There was also a major rise in the budget deficit. Shortages resulted in the stockpiling of goods by individuals and factories and contributed to a breakdown in economic integration within the Soviet Union, and in the confidence on which systems of barter were based. There was nothing to buy.

Perestroika created pressure for political change. Gorbachev's economic and political reforms helped cause economic confusion and a marked increase in criticism that delegitimated the Communist

Party and affected the cohesion of the Soviet Union. Opposition to Gorbachev was not only mounted by Party ideologues unhappy with the content and direction of change but also came from reformers within the Party who were dissatisfied with the pace of change.

A key figure was Boris Yeltsin. Like Gorbachev born in 1931, he was a reformer brought into the Central Committee of the Soviet Communist Party in 1981. Promoted under Gorbachev, he became in 1986 First Secretary of the Moscow City Party Committee and a Candidate Member of the Politburo, both important roles. However, Yeltsin fell foul of Yegor Ligachev, who supervised Party organs from within the Central Committee secretariat. Yeltsin attacked Ligachev and also, in effect, Gorbachev, at the 70th anniversary of the October Revolution in 1987. Yeltsin was removed from his posts and clashed with Ligachev and Gorbachev when he pressed for political rehabilitation at the Party conference in 1988.

Gorbachev was far more successful in external affairs than in domestic policy, and notably in easing relations with America and ending the Afghan disaster. His commitment to good relations abroad greatly defused tension, although he was clear on the need to maintain the fundamentals of the Soviet position. Thus, the Warsaw Pact, then thirty years old, was renewed for twenty years in April 1985. However, willing to challenge the confrontational worldview outlined in KGB reports, Gorbachev was convinced that American policy on arms control was not motivated by a hidden agenda of weakening the Soviet Union, and this conviction encouraged him to negotiate. Gorbachev had been described by Margaret Thatcher in December 1984, when he visited London, as 'a man with whom I can do business'. Her opinion was influential with Reagan. Gorbachev was also prepared to abandon an approach to foreign policy suffused with the rhetoric of class, as well as to reject the vested interests of the powerful but costly military-industrial complex. His openness on policy helped ensure that his first summit with Reagan, at Geneva in November 1985, went well.

From Stalin to the Fall: 1953-91

In December 1987, the Soviet government accepted the Intermediate Nuclear Forces Treaty, which, in ending land-based missiles with ranges of between 500 and 5,000 kilometres, forced heavier cuts on the Soviets, while also setting up a system of verification through on-site inspection. Both of these were confidence-building measures. The entire range of arms limitation was now open to negotiations, and agreements followed. In 1990, NATO and the Warsaw Pact were able to agree a limitation of conventional forces in Europe. In July 1991, START 1 (Strategic Arms Reduction Treaty) led to a major fall in the number of American and Soviet strategic nuclear warheads.

In theory a federation, the Soviet state had sought to develop nationalism separate to that of its constituent republics, an idea expressed in a 1973 song by David Tukhmanov: 'My address is not a house or a street / My address is the Soviet Union.' Tukhmanov was also responsible for 'Victory Day' (1975), the World War Two celebrations. However, the state rested on a powerful degree of Russian as well as ideological imperialism. As a result, in some of the non-Russian republics, nationalism had long provided a popular and inclusive language for dissent. In contrast, dissent within the Russian Federation lacked such focus. Russian nationalism was not the theme of dissent there, in part because the Soviet system acted as the protector of Russian interests.

From mid-1988, the growing weakness of the Soviet state and the division and confusion of the government's response to nationalism was accentuated by the strength of nationalist sentiment, especially in the Baltic republics, the Caucasus republics, and the western Ukraine. This sentiment had been manifested from the mid-1980s in increased opposition to Communist rule. The waving of national flags and singing of national songs increased. On 23 August 1989, two million people formed a human chain between the capitals of the Baltic Republics. The Soviet idea of a limited flowering of national cultures as part of a wider concept of a unified Soviet people, a policy adopted in 1923, had proved a total failure.

During the late Soviet period, some Russians resented the 'internationalism' of the Soviet Union wherein resources, money and technical know-how were handed over by Moscow to the non-Russian sectors. The foreign accents of the non-Russians when speaking Russian in the army and elsewhere were treated with irritation, even suspicion. An explicitly conveyed sense of Russian identity had emerged by the late 1960s with the *derevenshchiki* (ruralists), Russian writers such as Valentin Rasputin. Without tackling the censorship head-on, what the *derevenshchiki* tended to do was to decry the baneful effects of Soviet Communist modernisation upon the older rural way of life and its values. By the later 1970s, different strands of Russian national identity, expressed in the form of resentment over the perceived shunning of Russian cultural values, were expressed by other writers.

Nationalism could also be expressed by continued commitment to religion in the most secularist of state systems, one that offered very different communitarian norms. The insecurity resulting from the arbitrary and harsh policy of the regime and its failure to fulfil promises of social security helped ensure a continued need for non-state systems of identity and support and, therefore, a powerful place for religion. Orthodoxy was strong in Russia, Islam in Soviet Central Asia, and Catholicism in Lithuania.

While separatist nationalisms developed and were increasingly expressed, there was no protracted attempt to use the extensive military resources of the Soviet state to prevent the collapse of the Soviet Union. Already in 1986-7, the government had refused to use force to support Party leaders in the Baltic Republics. When the crisis rose to a height, counter-reform attempts by the Soviet military, keen to preserve the integrity of the state, led to action against nationalists in Georgia (1989), Azerbaijan (1990), Lithuania (1991), Latvia (1991), and Moldova (1992). However, these steps were small-scale, and there was no significant violent supporting action by the 25 million Russians living within the Soviet Union but outside Russia, those, for example, who played a key role in crises in Crimea and eastern Ukraine in 2014.

Gorbachev, the Sorcerer's Apprentice of Marxism without there being any Sorcerer to restore order, had never sought the disruption he created. Article six of the Soviet constitution, which guaranteed the Communist Party a monopoly of power, was abolished in February 1990. The Party proved unable to compete effectively in the new political situation. Gorbachev wanted to preserve the Soviet Union, if necessary only as a loose confederation. Thus, when the republics declared their independence, Gorbachev supported the attempt to maintain the authority of the Soviet Union by sending troops into them in January 1991. This policy led to clashes in Riga and Vilnius, the capitals of Latvia and Lithuania. Fourteen unarmed people protecting the television tower in Vilnius were killed and five civilians in the seizure of the Interior Ministry in Riga. These steps did not intimidate the nationalists but led to the building of barricades in both cities. Iconic moments and locations were provided both for the nationalist movement and for post-independence memorialisation, notably in Vilnius.

Nationalism in the Soviet Union was directed against Soviet Communism but could also draw on support from Communist reformers and indeed cautious Party officials in particular republics. This nationalism culminated when Yeltsin, in effect, successfully launched a Russian nationalist movement against the remaining structures of the Soviet Union. While Russians did not feel the core-periphery tug of war in the same way that Ukrainians or Estonians did, since most of the Russians lived inside the core, in the end the Russian Federation was itself to secede from the Soviet Union.

In 1988, the Party Conference had decided that there should be competitive elections both for Party posts and for the Congress of People's Deputies, the new-style Soviet legislature. The latter, held in March 1989, enabled Yeltsin to show his popularity in Moscow by easily winning a seat there, that put him not only on the Congress but also on the Supreme Soviet. The problems of Soviet society were bluntly outlined from a populist perspective in Yeltsin's election manifesto, in which he attacked the unjustified stratification of the population and the privileges of the *nomenklatura*. Yeltsin won nearly 90 per cent of the vote in Moscow. Prominent in the Inter-Regional Group of Deputies, Yeltsin pressed for economic and political reform and also supported popular concern about environmental issues. In 1990, competitive elections were held for the first time for the legislatures of the republics in the Soviet Union, and Yeltsin was elected to the Congress of People's Deputies of the Russian Soviet Federal Socialist Republic, becoming Chairman of the Supreme Soviet of the Republic. In an instructive parallel to the relationship between England and Britain, the Russian Republic had had no real institutions of its own until 1990, being, instead, conflated with the Soviet Union. To Yeltsin, this was unacceptable.

Russian dissent contained explicit secessionist aspirations, while Russian sovereignty was in effect declared in June 1990 when Yeltsin announced that Russian legislation would prevail over Soviet legislation if the two clashed. As an indication of how changes in Russia interacted with those in some of the other republics, this was an approach also taken by the Baltic Republics. The greater Soviet Russia which protected Russians living in the other republics was thus replaced by a post-imperial Russian nation-state, a development about which President Putin was to complain publicly in 2014.

As so often in history, personalities played a major role in the developing crisis, in this case Yeltsin's unwillingness to co-operate with Gorbachev. So also did the staples of, first, the pressure of international competition, in the form of the strains arising from the Cold War and, secondly and more specifically, nationalism. Both undermined the Soviet Union as they had earlier done the Austro-Hungarian empire in the 1910s, and the British empire after the two world wars. In the Soviet Union the nationalists forces descended abruptly. Neither the Austro-Hungarian empire nor the Soviet Union had a Western-style political party capable of transcending ethnic lines. The Emperor in the one and the Communist Party in the other were the transnational symbols and reality that worked well for a long period, but, in the end, neither was capable of adapting sufficiently. The same was true of the British empire in the case of Ireland and India respectively after World War One and World War Two. Challenges themselves were not new. As a reminder of continuities, such as that of Russian/Soviet expansionism, Russian nationalism was in part another version of the Slavophile attitudes seen in the nineteenth century.

Nevertheless, as a political force during the Soviet period, this nationalism was new.

Yeltsin clashed with Gorbachev and Party conservatives and, in July 1990 announced that he was leaving the Communist Party, a course followed by other prominent figures in Russia, and one made possible by the Party no longer having a monopoly of power. In the late summer of 1990, Yeltsin and Gorbachev sank their differences to establish a committee to develop measures necessary for the transition to a market economy, but the 500 Days Programme it produced, which included privatisation and decentralisation, proved too radical for much of the government. Gorbachev backed away from his original support, harming his relations with Yeltsin. The two negotiated again in 1991 over a new Union Treaty intended to preserve most of the Soviet Union, which was the wish of 77.85 per cent of those who voted in a referendum on 17 March 1991, the only national one in Soviet history, although it was boycotted in six of the republics. Elected President of Russia that June, Yeltsin pressed for more rights for the republics than Gorbachev wanted. However, the latter was willing to go farther than many of his governmental colleagues, a difference that triggered an attempted coup.

Hardline Communists, organised as the State Committee for the State of Emergency in the Soviet Union, or the Gang of Eight, attempted a coup in Moscow on 19 August 1991. Motivated by loyalty to the Party and the state, they were also anxious to preserve their position and the Soviet Union. However, like the attempted right-wing coup in Spain in February 1981, this coup proved an abject failure that also greatly helped advance the change it had sought to stop. The coup encouraged opposition in the republics to the Soviet Union. More immediately, the coup boosted the prestige of Yeltsin, who played a prominent public role in opposing it, leading the protestors in Moscow's streets from the Russian Parliament and thereby providing a clear and effective symbol of popular constitutionalism. In street-fighting not seen in Moscow since 1917, three protesters were killed by the army, which was itself divided. Soviet citizens were no longer the supposedly supine creatures and docile masses that the Party leadership had taken for granted in decades past. Gorbachev, a prisoner in his summer retreat in Crimea, did not play a role comparable to Yeltsin and, indeed, was regarded as displaying a degree of ambivalence about the attempted coup.

The coup's failure was followed by Yeltsin deciding to sweep aside the old system, and by the marginalisation of hardline Communists and their power-centres: the activities of the Communist Party were suspended on 29 August and the KGB was abolished on 11 October. The Felix Dzerzhinsky statue in front of the KGB building had been destroyed on 24 August and the old imperial colours adopted for Russia's national flag. Moreover, Soviet Cold War foreign policy was abandoned. Gorbachev and Yeltsin yielded to American pressure to stop sending aid to Afghanistan and to withdraw all Soviet troops from Cuba. In addition, the Soviet Foreign Ministry largely abandoned Communist ideology.

The attempted coup had stopped the signing of the New Union Treaty that was due to take place on 20 August 1991. Instead, late that year, nationalism in the republics led to their independence and secession from the Soviet Union. Disintegration proved cumulative. The Ukrainian referendum of 1 December, which saw a 91 per cent vote for independence, was decisive and, thanks to the failed coup, a major shift from the situation in Ukraine earlier in the year. The Communist Party in Ukraine was now largely committed to independence and to holding power in that context. A week later, Yeltsin, as President of Russia, and his Belarus and Ukrainian counterparts, announced at Minsk, the capital of Belarus, that they were forming a Commonwealth of Independent States in place of the Soviet Union, and invited the other republics to join. Gorbachev protested the next day, but he was now without consequence. On 21 December, at Alma Alta, the capital of Kazakhstan, the heads of all the republics bar Georgia, Estonia, Latvia and Lithuania, which sought a more complete independence, endorsed the step taken on 8 December, joined the Commonwealth of Independent States, and declared that the Soviet Union had ceased to exist. Gorbachev resigned on 25 December as President of the Soviet Union.

From Stalin to the Fall: 1953-91

The new system was seen by Yeltsin as truly federal, but this was not the case as far as, most crucially, Ukraine was concerned. Most other republics followed its example of independence in action. Russia under Yeltsin accepted this situation. In 1994, Russia signed a treaty guaranteeing the borders of Ukraine which, in turn, gave up its nuclear weapons. The influence of the former Soviet Union, however, created serious tensions from the 2000s as Vladimir Putin, as President of Russia (2000-8), then Prime Minister (2008-12), then President again (2012-), sought to drive through political and economic coordination for at least part of the former Soviet Union under Russian leadership, and to limit links with the West, notably the accession of Georgia and Ukraine to NATO, and of Ukraine to the European Union.

The collapse of the Soviet Union is usually explained with reference to four elements. An economic explanation focuses on long-term economic difficulties, notably an autarkic economic system that did not adequately understand time and value. A military-economic explanation centres on the impact of Soviet military expenditure being far greater than that of America. A sociological explanation suggests that three or four generations after 1917, the élite groups had lost their enthusiasm for the cause, while other population sectors had become disillusioned and apathetic. The political explanation emphasises the degree to which Gorbachev's opportunistic and poorly planned strategies precipitated a series of crises for the governing élites of Eastern Europe and the Soviet Union that otherwise might have been avoided. In particular, the failure to sustain the Soviet system politically undermined the exchange networks of the centrally planned economy.

The account of Soviet collapse offered here does not put the Cold War foremost. It is possible to focus on the degree to which the arms race that was a central element in the Cold War inflicted economic penalties on the Soviet Union as it sought to match American defence spending, caused a sense of Soviet weakness, and resulted in a pressure for change there. This approach produces a top-down account that has value. However, it directs attention away from the view of the populace in the maintenance or otherwise of the Soviet system, and the related question of consent and opposition. Of course, to write of the populace and consent can imply a democratic aspect. This requires qualification as all consenters were not equal. Indeed, even more significant than the absence of support for the regime, important as that absence was, was the disengagement of Communist Party members, particularly those in their thirties and forties who had grown up in Party-controlled systems. They decided, correctly, that these systems were not working and that they could do better without existing governmental, political and economic arrangements. Their attempt to create a modified or 'reformed' Communist system of control helped cause the collapse of the system. This was similar to the rapid end of the right-wing authoritarian Francoist regime in Spain in 1975 after the death of the dictator: in both cases, the willingness of ostensible supporters to conceive of different arrangements, and to adjust accordingly, was crucial to the fall of an authoritarian system.

These specific factors in the fall of Soviet Communism are fundamental in explaining the crises of 1989-91, but it is also important to consider long-term problems, from grave economic mismanagement to stultifying military expenditure. Totalitarian regimes, such as the Soviet Union and Nazi Germany, were command systems that were inherently prone to impose inefficient direction, rather than to respond to independent advice and to independent popular demand. Nazi Germany was greatly weakened by this characteristic during World War Two and, had that regime survived that conflict, would have been harmed by it subsequently in the confrontations to which its ideology inherently gave rise. This outcome was, indeed, the fate of the Soviet Union. Although by then there was no comparison with the methods or ethos of Nazi Germany or Stalinism, 1989-91 saw a crisis of totalitarianism, a crisis that fortunately did not lead to war, civil, international or both. Gorbachev deserves praise for responding to the crisis and disintegration of the Soviet Union without recourse to international war or sustained repression.

From Stalin to the Fall: 1953-91

Alongside discussion of the collapse of the Soviet bloc in terms of the failure of totalitarianism, the fall of empires can be made more possible, as with Yeltsin, due to a lack of commitment to them. The Soviet Union was a military super-power that had an international mission but also lacked a solid basis of support for this mission, both domestically and internationally. The popular domestic support to fight a defensive struggle against Germany in 1941-5 had gone.

Nearly a quarter of state expenditure went to military purposes in 1952, when the Soviet Union was not at war, and this figure increased increased in absolute terms as greater nuclear and conventional capability was added to the arsenal. The Soviet Union sought an all-round capability to match that of America. By the early 1980s, defence expenditure was 15-25 per cent of the GDP of a significantly larger economy and may even have been higher. Like Khrushchev before him, Gorbachev and his generation correctly felt that any meaningful economic reform demanded cuts in this expenditure. This decline had a dramatic impact as far as the geopolitics of the 1990s was concerned, but it was to be rejected by Putin as he sought to reverse change.

Alongside an emphasis in explaining the Soviet collapse on the failure of the planned economy under the Cold War and on the collapse of an empire as the élites of republics, notably Ukraine, abandoned the imperial centre, it is possible to stress Russian nationalism, specifically the political élite grouped around Yeltsin, that did not support imperial ambitions and instead sought to make Russia independent. This group might be traced to the Leningrad affair of 1949-50 in which Voznesensky and others were accused of Russian nationalism and a coup to make Russia independent. Russia as the gravedigger of the Soviet Union might appear implausible from the perspective of Putin's recent attitude and policies but, as with Gorbachev, an emphasis on Yeltsin highlights the point of unexpected outcomes and, linked to that, the precarious nature of Soviet power.

❧ 10 ❧

A NEW RUSSIA
1992-Present

Global politics were reshaped in the early 1990s and Russia became weaker. Boris Yeltsin, its President from 1990 to 2000, remarking that trying to mix Communism and a free market was like trying to mate a hedgehog with a snake. If this, alongside the problems of seeking to match a planned economy with decentralisation and innovation, had been a cause of the problems facing reform in the late 1980s, the situation when Communism and the planned economy had disappeared was not a drastic improvement. The economy was hit in 1989-92 and thereafter by the disintegration of Eastern European economic ties, the collapse of the collective farm economy and of the powerful military market for industry, the disintegration of trade within the Soviet Union as the federation unravelled, skyrocketing inflation, the collapsing labour market, and the falling apart of allocation decision-making. Market reforms were introduced more effectively in China. In contrast, there was no rapid economic growth in the former Soviet Union, the successor parts of which were to prove less than the sum of the earlier whole. In particular, it proved very difficult to establish and sustain effective monetary and fiscal mechanisms.

There was no smooth transition to capitalism and democracy. Models of political society and economy with which the Russians had no experience proved difficult to introduce. In addition, turning to Western ideas on economic and financial policies contributed to a more general crisis in Russian self-confidence. A group of Harvard economists, notably Jeffrey Sachs, who knew little or nothing about pre-Soviet economic history, and who were unaware of the importance of cultural factors in the reception to economic planning, persuaded Yeltsin to embrace a 'shock therapy' of the instant mass privatisation of industry and the simultaneous removal of all price controls.

This led to chaos, with the rapidity of privatisation producing, in the type of society and politics Russian then had, the dominance of the economy by corrupt oligarchs. Moreover, the bankruptcy of large parts of the former command economy, much of which had been uncompetitive, as well as the dismantling of social welfare, led to a major rise in unemployment, poverty, social polarisation, and a rampant drunkenness that contributed to a marked fall in male life expectancy. Public culture was affected by disillusionment and corruption, the symptom of a wider disinclination for reform. Two besetting Soviet workforce problems, alcoholism and absenteeism, continued.

Western loans were necessary in order to prevent a total collapse of Russia in the 1990s, but Russian debt payments caused a severe crisis in 1998, leading to default in debt payment and devaluation. That default was to be overcome with Russia benefiting thereafter from the revenues produced by oil and gas exports.

Entrepreneurialism and crime filled the vacuum left by the collapse of the Communist state, but had to compete with the secret police, who had earlier been restrained by the close relationship between the Communist Party and the government. The massive transfer of assets involved in privatisation attracted the attention of profiteers. Soft loans from banks were used to finance the process but frequently became non-performing, putting pressure on the banking system. Under Vladimir Putin, who had served in the KGB from 1975 to 1991 and was Director of the Federal Security Service from 1998 to 1999, the secret police were to win the struggle for power, not least at the expense of oligarchs who were seen as hostile and were also political competitors. Some were killed, for example Boris Berezovsky in 2013, while Mikhail Khodarkovsky, a banker and oil magnate who had founded Open Russia in 2001, was imprisoned from 2003 to 2013. Some oligarchs, such as Roman Abramovich, who made his money in acquiring a large oil company and then in aluminium interests, however, were seen as supporters of Putin.

Competing interests ensured that the overlaps between crime, business and politics that Putin sought to control remained inherently unstable and even destabilising. These overlaps made the nature of Russian politics particularly opaque. Putin was surrounded by the *siloviki* (strong guys). These were the KGB friends and totally compliant oligarchs around Putin who controlled gas, oil and other assets. The shadow-establishment centred on the secret service and linked political and business interests was a continuation of the structure of the Communist state, albeit without the Marxist rhetoric, but with the same brutality. This was seen in the suppression of democratic movements in the 2010s and 2020s, not least the arrest, imprisonment and, in 2024, murder in prison of Alexei Navalny, the main opposition leader. In addition, over twelve (and by some accounts far more) journalists have been killed, notably Anatoly Levin-Utkin in 1998 and Anna Politkovskaya in 2006, civil liberties restricted, elections rigged, and independent radio stations and newspapers closed down.

This is not only the brutality of simple would-be totalitarianism, but also an aspect of the longstanding idea of a oneness of 'front' and 'rear' necessary to pursue a military effort. Internally, Putin's system rests on a power network in which 'crony capitalism' or rather, a spoils system, is linked to a use of force and intimidation. Opponents and critics were compromised, imprisoned or killed. Freedom was ended in the media and governmental authority centralised, with Putin announcing in 2016 the creation of a National Guard. The effective autonomy of the business 'oligarchs' in the now-privatised industries, as well as that of provincial governors, was brought to an end.

A New Russia: 1992-Present

Affected by crime, corruption and state intervention, the privatised economy of the 1990s also displayed a new vulnerability to international trends. In 1998, the currency collapsed to 8,000 roubles to a dollar, before stabilising at around 33 to the dollar and remaining within a stable range of 28 to 34 to the dollar for the next 16 years. In 2000, Russian GDP still showed a decline on the 1990 figure and there was certainly a significant decline in greenhouse gas emissions, in part due to the collapse of the industries in the Ural region producing for the military. The collapse of the collective farm system in 1991 was not followed by an increase in agricultural productivity. Yet, the extent of post-Communist decline assumes accurate GDP figures during the Communist period, which is problematic, not least as they included a substantial amount of fairly useless production. Moreover, there had been a significant and relevant change in incentive structures. Under Communism, the incentives were for producers to claim quality and quantity in production that they had not in fact achieved. Now, with taxation, the incentives were precisely the opposite, which meant that decline may have been overstated.

At any rate, economic disruption and problems affected political stability, although there were also the problems of establishing and bedding down new political and legal systems and practices, and a new civil politics in which nationalism could provide strength rather than simply Soil and Church nostalgia for pre-Soviet days or xenophobia. In 1990, Solzhenitsyn's citizenship was restored and he was awarded the Russian State Literature Prize. Returning from exile in 1994, Solzhenitsyn increasingly offered a Slavophile/Russian nationalistic viewpoint, to which Orthodox Christianity contributed greatly, that propounded a critique of both Communism and the West, especially of atheism and consumerism respectively. The government's focus on Russian national identity also led to a celebration of writers judged appropriate, as with the lavish Pushkin commemoration in 1999. There was also a nostalgia focused on the Soviet Union. Soviet films and songs enjoyed a certain popularity, not least with the television channel Nostalgiya, launched in 2004, which made the artefacts of Soviet life seem welcomingly familiar.

Censorship ended from 1988 onwards and was followed by an openness to the outside world and by a massive expansion in the number of publishing firms and magazines. Readers rushed to read genres hitherto unavailable, such as self-help books, religious literature and romances, for example novels by Barbara Cartland. The moralising, uplifting works produced (and then only in limited editions) during the totally controlled Communist years were no longer of great significance.

In turn, there was, in some former parts of the Soviet Union, an active depiction of the Communist oppression and a recovery of the history of the lost years. Cities were renamed; Mariupol in Ukraine, which had been renamed Zhdanov in 1948 after the Stalinist leader born in that city, reverted to its former name in 1989. Riga gained Latvia's Museum of Occupation, 1940-1991, while the townscape of Tallinn, the capital of Estonia, is a rejection of Communism. There is a Museum of Occupation, while the former KGB headquarters carries a plaque 'This building housed the headquarters of the organ of repression of the Soviet occupation power. Here began the road to suffering for thousands of Estonians.' In Freedom Square, which was used for military parades under the Soviets, the Freedom Clock was installed in 2003. It shows both the current time and the number of years since Estonia became independent. There were new names for streets, apartment blocks and much else.

The nationalism of former Soviet republics, what the Russians called the 'near abroad', was accentuated by the self-interested rule of Russia's leaders, not least Yeltsin, who proved only too willing to manipulate the Russian constitution to his own ends. Thus, the attempted pro-Soviet coup in 1991 was followed in 1993 by a violent political crisis in which Yeltsin used troops to storm the Parliament building, while Yeltsin's re-election as President in 1996 was criticised as corrupt. The marked revival of the nationalities question in both the former Soviet Union and in Russia itself also affected Russia's international influence.

A New Russia: 1992-Present

As a result of Soviet collapse, there was a dramatic change, amounting to a rupture, in the international situation. The Western powers, led by America, were able to intervene decisively against states that earlier would have looked for Soviet support, notably Iraq in 1991, in the First Gulf War, and Serbia in 1995 and 1999, in the Bosnia and Kosovo crises respectively. Indeed, when welcoming the annexation of Crimea in 2014 after a plebiscite of dubious legality, Putin complained about these earlier Western interventions, and particularly about that against Serbia in the Kosovo crisis. In addition, in the 2000s, as an aspect of the problems facing the former allies of the Communist bloc, Libya found it helpful to seek reconciliation with the West, although Colonel Qaddafi was overthrown with the help of NATO intervention in 2011. North Korea and Iran sought safety in developing their own nuclear capability, though a far more critical interpretation of their decisions is also pertinent.

The combination of Soviet collapse in 1991 and Iraqi defeats in 1991 and 2003 led to talk in America of a 'new world order' and of the 'end of history'. These triumphalist claims, which encompassed arguments on the cause, course and outcome of the Cold War, rested on the belief that Soviet collapse represented a triumph for American-led democratic capitalism, and that there would be no future clash of ideologies to destabilise the world.

Meanwhile, serving as a substitute for Marxist-Leninism as both ideology and social cement, the Orthodox Church, the Russian state Church, revived rapidly as a public force from 1991, with new churches, monasteries and seminaries, and with a major role in public memorialisation of the past. The calendar was no longer dominated by Communist celebrations, most obviously of May Day. Revolution Day, the anniversary of the Bolshevik Revolution, was renamed the Day of Accord and Reconciliation. In Leningrad, the secular 1970s monument commemorating the city's successful resistance to German forces in World War Two and the eventual relief by Soviet forces was joined, in the 1990s, in what was now renamed St Petersburg, by a church.

In 1998, with the support of Putin, the remains of those members of the Romanov dynasty slaughtered by the Communists during the Russian Revolution were buried in St Peter-Paul church in the eponymous fortress where nearby all Nicholas II's predecessors are buried. This reburial was an indication of a more general search for historical resonance as nationalism was pushed to the fore in the post-Communist years. The massive Cathedral of Christ the Saviour in Moscow, originally built in 1839-83 by public subscription to commemorate victory over Napoleon and demolished, with great difficulty, by Stalin in 1931, was rapidly rebuilt from 1997 to 2000, when it was reconsecrated on the Feast of the Transfiguration. Yeltsin was given a lying-in-state and funeral there, becoming the first Russian ruler since Tsar Alexander III died in 1894 to receive an Orthodox funeral. In 2007, Putin attended the Easter Vigil in the Cathedral and praised the role of the Orthodox Church, and on Ascension Day he attended a ceremony there marking the reunification of the domestic and exiled branches of the Church, thus associating the state with this act and with the legitimation it was seen to provide. Also in 2007, the Assumption Cathedral in Omsk was finished, replacing that demolished by Stalin in 1935. Religious validation was also sought and displayed elsewhere. When, in 2004, Mikhail Saakashvili became President of Georgia, he first went to a revered monastery, founded by Georgia's most famous monarch, in order to receive a blessing.

In Russia, the Orthodox Church provided support to the Putin government and, in turn, benefited greatly from its protection. The even-handed position of the Russian government toward different faiths in the early 1990s under Yeltsin was swept aside, and Protestants suffered in particular, while there was a significant growth of anti-Semitism in Russia, as well as war with Islamic independence movements in the northern Caucasus, notably in Chechnya in 1994-6 and 1999-2000. An emphasis on religion appeared to bring Russia into line with America, but the alliance between Putin and the Church was far closer and the social politics much harsher, as in the 'gay propaganda' ban of

2013 in Russia and the rejection of homosexuality as an aspect of Westernisation.

Putin's supporters and officials strongly opposed calls for reform, liberalisation and democratisation. Instead, cultural assertion included an attack on Hollywood's role. There was also the establishment of a quota system and funding from television channels, encouraged by Putin, that ensured a major revival in the film industry: from 2 per cent of the national market in 2002 to 23 per cent in 2006.

The American triumphalism of the early 1990s proved less durable than had initially appeared probable. In turn, the authoritarianism of Putin, who became President in 2000, led to a different perception of Russia. Its influence was accentuated by improved relations with China, as well as the increased value of its oil and gas. This helped ensure more wealth for the government and a rise in the average monthly salary, while the percentage of people living below the poverty line fell. Government wealth was crucial to the payment of pensions. Putin also used the supply and pricing of its natural gas to put pressure on other countries, such as Belarus in 2007, and permitted far more expenditure on the military.

Putin's popularity was relatively high, but the fraudulent 2011 legislative elections in which Putin's party, United Russia, won led to considerable criticism, with large protests, notably in Moscow and St Petersburg, against election fraud. There was talk of a possible 'colour revolution' against Putin, such as the Orange Revolution in Ukraine in 2004-5, but mass arrests were used to close down public dissent. Subsequently, Putin's unpopularity increased. This encouraged him to move further in a nationalist direction, leading in 2014 to a far more interventionist stance on Ukraine.

On 10 February 2007, Putin, at the Munich Security Council, decried a unipolar world in which America felt free to act as it wished. Russian ambitions and actions in recent years, notably in the Caucasus, where Georgia was successfully attacked in 2008, and more particularly, in Ukraine in 2014 and from 2022, have reawakened echoes of the Cold War and even led to questions of whether it is really over, or whether there is a new one in process. In 2017, Russia deployed 100,000 troops in the Zapad-17 ('West-17') military exercise, an intimidation of NATO in the Baltic sphere.

The nationalism was and is anti-Western, which encourages talk of a new Cold War launched by Russia. However, this nationalism is not linked to an account of global progress and strife, as had been the case with the Soviet implementation of Marxist ideas. Instead, peer-group competitiveness with America irrespective of ideology became a crucial driver for Russian military commentators.

Putin argues that many millions of Russians have been left living in foreign countries, and his interventions have fulfilled his sense of mission. Putin's backers present the invasions of Ukraine in 2014 and 2024 as defensive acts similar to the resistance to German attack in 1941, and describe Ukraine as neo-Nazi, which is a misreading of the past intended to validate action in the present. This was seen in Mariupol: seized by the Russians in early 2022 after a devastating three-month siege that involved heavy civilian casualties, in 2024 it became the site of a museum dedicated to Andrei Zhdanov, a Stalinist who had been born there in 1896, with an emphasis on his role in defending Leningrad against the Germans in 1941-4.

Teachers' manuals described Stalin as 'the most successful Soviet leader ever', and one who had to use force to mobilise the country. At a conference held at his presidential dacha in 2007, Putin referred to Stalin's Purges as terrible but also compared them to the American atomic bombing of Hiroshima as a necessary step. Putin's argument was not intended to argue an equivalence between all horrors, the route taken or implied by German and Japanese revisionists, because he continued: 'In other countries even worse things happened. We had no other black pages, such as Nazism, for instance.' Yet, his comparison of the Purges to the use of the atomic bombs was not one that would have commanded much confidence in areas that suffered Soviet occupation, notably Eastern Europe, and confused a key element of domestic policy (the Purges) with a strategic tool of war. Putin's argument, that internal control and violence was crucial to success in war, was one in keeping with Soviet ideology and Communist practice. Putin has argued that 'Historical memory is important for any people if it wants to preserve itself and have a future.'

There was a more positive re-evaluation of Stalin, in contrast to the view in the 1990s. The end of Communist rule had been followed by the establishment of a museum covering the *gulags*. Located on the site of a Stalin-era labour camp, Perm-36 recorded the fate of the dissidents incarcerated there. After 2012, when Putin became President again, a supporter, Viktor Basargin, was appointed the local Governor. Having cut regional finances and raised taxes, he removed funding altogether in 2014 and the museum, without water or electricity, closed. At the same time, there was scant public commemoration of the centenary of the October (1917) Revolution, due to an ambivalent relationship with the Soviet past. This was seen in the 'pick and mix' attitude toward the Stalinist legacy.

Approved by the government and published in 2023, the tenth grade (age 16) textbook, in its section on the Civil War, praises Felix Dzerzhinsky, the murderous founder of the Cheka secret police, for playing an 'enormous role … in the struggle against counter-revolution.' The nature of Russian textbooks may now well be less doctrinaire and tendentious than their Soviet predecessors, but are scarcely without flaws, not least in their presentation by omission of much Ukrainian history. Unlike in the Soviet period, a separate Ukrainian people is dismissed. Similarly, the takeover of the Baltic Republics in 1940 is presented as voluntary, which is totally misleading.

Putin's most reliable ally, Alexander Lukashenko, President of Belarus since 1994, took steps to limit the memorialisation of the Stalin-era repression at the Kurapaty NKVD killing site. A former Director of a state farm, Lukashenko continued Soviet-era government ownership in an authoritarian state. In 1999, based on agreements in 1996, 1997 and 1998, a Union State of

Russia and Belarus was created, a supranational union committed to integration. Subsequently, in 2014, there was an agreement to establish the Eurasian Economic Union, initially of Belarus, Kazakhstan and Russia, with Armenia and Kyrgyzstan following that year. More generally, Putin sought to re-create the Soviet Union.

In 2013, partly under Russian pressure, the Ukrainian President, Viktor Yanukovich, rejected an agreement for an association with the European Union. The linkage of Ukraine and Russia had become more important to the latter as Slavic identity, Orthodox Christianity, and opposition to the West combined in a potent ideology. Linked to this, the historic struggle between Russia and Poland, now in the European Union and NATO, appeared newly relevant.

In turn, large-scale Ukrainian popular anger with Yanukovich's action helped to provoke his overthrow, despite the killing of over 100 protestors, in February 2014, in the Maidan Revolution or Revolution of Dignity. Russian commentators repeatedly, and misleadingly, alleged a continuity with the willingness of some Ukrainians to cooperate with the invading Germans in 1941.

Putin responded in March 2014 by seizing Crimea, using disguised Russian troops plus sympathetic locals, and then annexing it. Reversing the handover of Crimea to Ukraine in 1954, this pushed Putin's approval rating up by 20 points. This was also presented as a rejection of recent humiliation: in the speech he delivered to Russia's Parliament on 18 March, Putin referred to the dissolution of the Soviet Union in 1991 as a mistake, adding a theme of blood-right:

> Crimea has always been and remains an inseparable part of Russia. This commitment, based on truth and justice, was firm, was passed from generation to generation. There are graves of Russian soldiers on the peninsula whose courage enabled Russia to make Crimea part of the Russian Empire in 1783.

Later, he told crowds in Red Square: 'Crimea and Sevastopol are returning to their home shores, to their home port, to Russia! ... Glory to Russia.' In turn, Putin was compared to Hitler. Hostilities in the Donbass, where Ukrainian rule was challenged by pro-Russian separatists threatened a wider war. Initially, the Minsk agreements of 2014 and 2015 seemed to promise peace, but the Russian-backed separatists breached their terms and this maintained local conflict and a broader tension. In February 2022, Putin declared that the agreements no longer existed, shortly before invading on 24 February.

The Ukraine war from 2022 indicated Russian determination, but also the extent to which that entailed the strains that the state could impose on society, even if in his State-of-the-Nation Address in February 2023, Putin declared:

> You know there is a maxim, guns versus butter. Of course, national defence is the top priority, but in resolving strategic tasks in this area, we should not repeat the mistakes of the past and should not destroy our own economy.

In 2022, as a result of inadequate Russian planning, notably poor intelligence and logistics, Ukrainian resilience and flexibility, and a lack of tactical competence on the part of Russian commanders, the Russians failed to crush Ukraine, although they did capture a significant amount of territory, notably to the north of the Sea of Azov. The war also served the interests of the Patriarch of Moscow, because in 2018 the Istanbul-based Ecumenical Patriarch of the Orthodox Church granted independent status to the Orthodox Church of Ukraine with the right to appoint its own Patriarch.

The pre-war crisis of a still low male life expectancy was greatly was greatly accentuated by wartime losses, while many Russians fled abroad to avoid military service or because, like the writer Vladimir Sorokin, they feared the Putin government. Its popularity fell, but the government benefited from the divided nature of opposition: part liberal, part more nationalist.

The government's response to failure in 2022 was to turn to more conscription and expenditure. In 2024, Russian military expenditure rose by 41.9 per cent to reach (adjusted for purchasing power parity) $461.6 billion, which was more than all of Europe. At the annual Victory Parade in Moscow in May 2023, Putin declared that Russia was in a civilisational war, with the parade, a Cold War practice revived by Putin and attended in 2015 by President Xi of China, being used by him to focus an alleged opposition to the Nazis of World War Two that in part has served as the ideology of the Russian state under Putin. The theme of civilisational war was seen in the emphasis on 'Christian values', for example by Sergey Lavrov, the Foreign Minister, in March 2025.

Aside from more conscription, there was also a reliance on private armies, notably from Chechnya and also the Wagner Group of mercenaries. Its leader, Yevgeny Prigozhin, in 2023 sought to mount a coup, and was subsequently killed on Putin's orders. His actions revealed the divisions in the coalition of forces involved in the war. Indeed, Prigozhin's forces moved upon Moscow effortlessly as the regular army could not be bothered to stand in his way.

That this conflict was waged with Ukraine, a former Soviet republic, underlined this theme of division. It was taken further by the extent to which in former republics that did not oppose Putin, for example those of Central Asia, there is no celebration of the Soviet past, not of the 'Great Patriotic War' which is so important to Russian identity. More generally, like the earlier Russian empire, the Soviet Union has splintered in consciousness and adherence. Indeed, the extension of Russian passports to the population in conquered areas of Ukraine was clearly an instance of a traditional expansionism that appealed to few in other former Soviet republics.

Russian arms innovation includes hypersonic missiles which offer range and speed; but their meaning in strategic terms is unclear. Furthermore, Russia's difficulties were seen in the growing problems of its space plans, with the attempt, announced in

2018, in the shape of Sfera, to rival Elon Musk's Starlink internet provider, hit by a failure to produce sufficient satellites. Moreover, the Luna 25 mission to the Moon, the first Russian Moon mission since 1976, failed in 2023; India's succeeded soon after.

There are multiple limitations to Russian capabilities, notably economic and demographic ones. The latter include a crisis in birth rates, and especially so among the non-Muslim population. Indeed, the annexation of Ukraine was in part intended to raise the number of non-Muslim 'Russians', or those close to being 'Russian'. In 2000-5, the annual rate of population decline, in percentage terms, was 0.6 in Russia and 0.5 for Belarus, and there were suggestions of an annual rate for 2045-50 of 0.9, and for a population decrease for the entire period 2000-50 of 30-40 per cent. The lack of support for child-rearing was an issue, as was the scarcity of housing and the need by women to work. There was also extensive emigration, notably to the rest of Europe, for example Cyprus, and to Israel.

Emigration increased as the most obvious way to avoid the issues of life in Russia, not least a lack of certainty and the fear of arbitrary policies. These affected all levels of society. In addition, social stress and governmental deficiencies have contributed to serious problems in public health, including the spread of drug-resistant tuberculosis and of venereal disease. The widespread nature of prostitution is a stark comment on the nature of society and individual relations for many.

Putin's attempt to recreate the Soviet Union, ending Ukrainian independence being a central aim in this, looked more plausible in 2025 as Donald Trump transformed American policy. Whereas Ronald Reagan had increased pressure on the Soviet Union in the 1980s, Trump eased pressure at a moment of growing danger for Russia. Aongside the resilience, adaptability and improvement shown by the army in 2023, Russia has been badly exhausted by the war: in manpower (with unknown casualties and deaths, some estimate 120,000 fatalities, other estimates are far higher), equipment and resources; and its capacity for fresh warfare is uncertain. Ukraine has maintained its position as an independent

Collection of a fraction of the rockets and ammunition fired by Russia on Kharkiv. (Courtesy Kharkiv Regional State Administration under creative commons 4.0)

state and free country that remains outside Russia's sphere of influence.

The difference between the creaky superpower of the Cold War and the weaker greater power subsequently was very apparent. By 2025, Russia had a Spain-sized economy, an inflexible regime, and a second-rate army. At the same time, the ambition of Russian policymakers and their preference for the policies of intimidation, not least with reference to their large nuclear arsenal, and the methods of disruption, remain serious factors and characteristic elements of the disruptive Russia of today.

❴ 11 ❵

CONCLUSIONS

'Britain is going full Stalin,' Elon Musk's response to the inheritance tax changes to farms in the British October 2024 budget was a testimony to the extent to which Russia, or at least an account of a key period of Russian history, gripped the imagination for many, providing for a large number a frame of reference to challenge that of Nazi Germany. Very differently, in his novel *Day of the Oprichnik* (2006), Vladimir Sorokin used the reign of Ivan the Terrible as a warning about current developments: set in 2028, a Tsardom like Ivan's has been restored and Russia is isolated from the West behind a 'Great Russian Wall' but has close links with China. Murder, torture and depravity are to the fore.

Alongside the misleading use of Russian examples elsewhere, there is the habit of simplifying Russian history, not least by pursuing a uniform context and analysis. For example, Putin exemplifies the extent to which a salient and persistent theme of Russian history is the practice and principle of *edinonachalie*, of one man in charge, whether Tsar, General Secretary of the Communist Party of the Soviet Union, or President. Attempts to democratise Russia's political institutions have consistently failed, and there is currently no sign of this being achieved in the future. The hyper-centralised system Putin has put in place over the last quarter-century, complete with a Stalin-type personality cult, seems likely to be self-perpetuating unless there is a repeat of a popular revolution to effect fundamental change, as there is no other means of doing so.

Yet, there are also pertinent differences. Putin, unlike the Assads of Syria or the Kims of Korea, has no dynastic presence or ambition. In Russian terms, this situation is very different to the Rurik and Romanov dynasties of Muscovite and Imperial Russia. Nor does Putin have an institutional backing comparable to the Communist Party. The lack of either means he has no succession strategy for long-term continuity. His situation therefore is atypical for Russian history. Furthermore, Putin is not a dictator comparable to Ivan the Terrible. Nor has he created a 'cultural revolution' of new names and titles and a comparable rebranding of civil administration. Peter the Great did so by renaming the Muscovite offices and officials, and the Bolsheviks did the same. Putin, instead, has clung to the old Imperial names for offices (ministries) that Stalin (re-)introduced in 1946 and has elevated from the past the Russian Orthodox Church with all its nomenclature.

Putin, moreover, does not have at his disposal a population largely composed of a peasantry, as was so instrumental for Ivan III, Peter and Stalin and for their ability to introduce sweeping policies of societal change. Instead, the Russian population, as a result in particular of the 1990s, but also of longer-term trends, is more educated and independent than hitherto. We can only speculate how far Putin can move with an educated populace, regardless of his dictatorial ways.

In addition, change, when it comes about, is typically at the start of a Russian ruler's reign. Too much time has passed for him to introduce anything in an all-encompassing way. Putin therefore is not the harbinger of a fourth service-class revolution following Ivan III, Peter the Great and Stalin.

As an aspect of a misunderstanding of Russian history, there has been a tendency in Western thinking to apply the argument that free competition, religious toleration, and individual independence and initiative are vital ingredients to a society's ability to adapt to changing circumstances and for a state's capacity to harness them to its grand strategic objectives. In contrast, centralisation and conformity are seen as impeding progress and ultimately leading to the downfall of a great power. As an historical explanation for the trajectory of Russian history, however, this argument has only limited exploratory powers. For example, such factors may help explain the fall of the Soviet Union in 1991, but are far less pertinent for Imperial Rusia, which fell in 1917 more due to the consequences of failure in war.

There is a misleading sense among some outside commentators that Russia could not be a great power because its economy was not liberal. For example, an emphasis on per-capita GNP, which reflects the quantity of goods brought to market and liberal economic views of the superiority of comparative advantage, is unhelpful, as per-capita GNP does not determine power. Until the 1990s, Russia's economy was not 'truly' capitalist (and even then it was to become corporatist, mediated by murder), but it still managed to produce sufficient material to underpin military strength to the degree necessary to make the Soviet Union/Russia a great power. However good militarily their opponents might be, the sheer size of the Soviet/Russian forces could induce grave strategic concern. Soviet/Russian mass had its own importance: the amount of production, rather than the means or efficiency of obtaining it, was and is significant. If it was inherently inefficient that Russia focused on the strength of the state and not the wealth or wellbeing of the individual, that was not the case in a military context.

Like Peter the Great, Stalin saw industrialization and military security as so intertwined as to be inseparable. In contrast to the capabilities of Petrine modernization, but alongside Peter's emphasis on internal surveillance, Stalin added the cultural element of ideological mobilization through Socialism backed by terror as a central feature in a new society. In both cases, it is possible to argue that the more general stimulating impact on the economy was that of a type of defence Keynesianism or stimulus through deficit spending. This stimulus was achieved in the late nineteenth- and early twentieth-century industrialization through railway building, and both then and during the Stalin Five Year Plans and after, by depressing the peasant standard of living through such tactics as raising indirect taxes (the Witte ministry under Nicholas II), or nationalizing the land, confiscating peasant grain for the collective farm administration, wiping out some of the peasantry, denying peasants the choice of finding work in towns, and keeping them immobilized by means of Stalin's collectivization, which was the second enserfment.

Thus, government policies clearly hit living conditions hard as well as limiting the investment possibilities for other sectors of the Russian and Soviet economies. In part, the 1931-3 famine can be blamed on grain stockpiling and railroad diversion in preparation for war. However, such a liberal conception about living standards meant little within the authoritarian political parameters of each period in Russian history. Furthermore, this defence Keynesianism did bring important economic benefits to Russia, notably avoiding boom and bust cycles. In addition, in some respects, authoritarian societies were (and are) partially immune from detrimental tradeoffs of expenditure on the military.

An emphasis on great power competition and the perspective of the international system would suggest that the leaders of Muscovite, Imperial and Soviet Russia – Ivan III, Peter the Great and Stalin – saw their nation as a late developer having to try harder in order to catch up. This did not entirely determine how they conceptualised their predicament (although Russians incline to the 'one-shot deal' approach in economic, social and military affairs), or what strategy rulers adopted. Nevertheless, a focus on international relations shows Russian government and domestic policy intent on catching up with rivals.

While valuable, this analysis underplays the autonomous role in setting policy of distinctive socio-political contexts and ideological drives, such as Communism. At any rate, Ivan III began the cyclical tradition of the service state, which was recast and reinvigorated under Peter the Great and Stalin who followed in his footsteps. In particular, Russian history did not begin with Peter, as in some respects, including Westernization, he copied Muscovite practice but on a grander scale.

Conclusions

The military dimension was especially important. In the case of Imperial and Soviet Russia, as with Maoist China, there were huge costs in mass-militarization. Conscripts had to be fed, clothed, housed and equipped, however poorly. There was also an opportunity cost to the individual conscripts, most of whom would have preferred to be doing something else, and an opportunity cost to society, which lost their productive labour. However, Imperial and Soviet conscripts alike were paid essentially nothing, and so represented less of a burden than they otherwise might have done. Russia and the Soviet Union, like many Eurasian societies in the nineteenth and twentieth centuries, but unlike Britain and, even more, America, were characterized by a surfeit of unskilled labour (in some key areas) and an overcrowded countryside, the latter becoming more of an issue due to the rapidly rising population. Taking unskilled eighteen-year-olds off the crowded land and out of a labour market characterized by illiterate peasants following traditional agrarian practices, was not necessarily unhelpful, nor an aspect of over-reach, while troops could be used for large-scale economic purposes, whether assisting with harvests or constructing public works. Furthermore, in Russia, the military had vital internal policing duties. These duties can be seen as a crucial aid to the economy, as they ensured a basic level of stability, including labour control. For example, the Soviet passport and residency system was a consistently significant factor in Russian history, one that linked the Imperial and Soviet periods and one that becomes even more important if the military labour represented by male conscription is included. The status quo, whether governmental or social, had to be secured by such labour control. It also served and sustained the purposes of surveillance, repression, and the subordination of the individual to the state, as seen with moving people to effect internal colonization.

As an aspect of ideologies, geopolitical strains often arising from expansionism and enforced social compacts, modernisation strategies were pursued by differing regimes in contrasting political and ideological contexts. These strategies, however, had common elements in terms of the harshness for the people of the transformations attempted, as well as the serious difficulties in implementation. Another common theme was the attempt to pursue a Russian solution separate from Western norms.

All of these elements are extant to the present day, whatever the authoritarian nature and methods of the regime. Russia remains culturally distinct and should not be viewed as some distant, enfeebled cousin of an amorphous Western European culture. The overwhelming presence of the 'government market' in most phases of Russian life for centuries is one distinct characteristic of Russian civilization; as is the dominance of government over law, and not law over government.

This subordination was also seen in the demands placed by successive governments on collectivities, law and supervisory agencies and resources, and to a degree not seen in other Eastern European countries. For the last six centuries, Russian regimes have advanced major claims to intervene and acquire land and people, and to force them into government-institutionalised survivalist strategies and moulds. As a result, the usual economic criteria of incentives have been ignored. The weakness, if not absence, of countervailing political opposition is a key cause and consequence of this phenomenon, although widespread social unrest, an expression of suppressed political aspirations, breaks out intermittently. Such unrest has been particularly acute in regions where there is ethnic/national difference and a sense of separatism. The Russian practice is that of the state creating a social contract under duress, and, in doing so, transforming the geopolitical environment.

Russia's cultural position, and also its relationship to law, offer contexts for considering her international position, not least the threat it, allegedly or really, poses to other countries. Such a threat has helped to push Russia to the fore in the Western consciousness in recent years. Earlier, in the 1990s and 2000s, Russia receded from any such position due to absolute and relative decline, Western triumphalism, and in part to the focus of many commentators on the 'War on Terror' and the rise of China. The last remained crucial even as Russian aggression against Georgia in 2008 and Ukraine in 2014 excited greater attention.

Conclusions

It was, paradoxically, the failed Russian takeover of Ukraine in 2022 that pushed Russia to the fore. Russia became unpredictable, even more so because of her resilience from 2023 in the face of failure in 2022 and of predictions of collapse of the Russian war effort and the Putin regime, as well as Russia's ability to profit from a wide-ranging international alignment. The sense that Russia might press on to attack other states was actively advanced as a reason to increase military expenditure elsewhere in Europe, and to an extent that threatened the viability of the social welfare model there. In January 2025, Kaja Kallas, the European Union foreign policy chief and former Prime Minister of Estonia, told the annual conference of the European Defence Agency: 'Russia poses an existential threat to our security today, tomorrow and for as long as we underinvest in our defence.'

In contrast, Alexei Zhuravlev, a senior member of the Russian Parliament's Defence Committee, who in February 2022 had declared 'the Russian world was and will be ours,' declared 'Europe has explained to us that in 2028-29 it will be ready to fight Russia. It is necessary to prepare the male population to defend the motherland.' The themes resonate across history, both fear of Russian expansion, with Kallas's mother, grandparents and great-grandmother deported to Siberia by the Soviets, and Russian paranoia about attack. The latter was greatly encouraged by the disintegration in the 1990s of the Soviet Union and Yugoslavia. In 2022, Zhuravlev stated that 'the Fatherland' was threatened by Ukraine.

These quotations underline the continued question of whether Russia is European, and, whatever the answer, how Russia relates to Europe, both historically and now. These questions overlap with those raised in the first chapter about the geographical spread of Russia and how best to define it. For example, to refer to Ukraine as southern Russia would be to invite fierce complaint from Ukrainians, but it might have a certain functional geographical point for some periods when there was no Ukrainian governmental entity.

This contentiousness and the related lack of fixity invites reflection on how Russia related and relates to Europe, whether

Russia is seen as outside or inside Europe, which itself is subject to very varied definitions. Despite some claims to the contrary, the Muscovite realm was certainly no heir to the Mongols: the political and administrative culture (with the exception of writing on scrolls) was not based on Mongol influence.

With the 'European space' redefined, when the Ottoman Turks were pushed back from 1683 to 1913, and notably so in 1683-1718 and 1877-1913, it became less plausible to think of Russia as excluded from Europe, not least because the Russians played a significant role in driving back the Ottomans, notably in the Balkans. Russia might seem or be presented as alien in 1500, but this was scarcely credible from the early eighteenth century. Russia related, militarily, diplomatically, economically and culturally,

Still a major force on the world stage. Putin hosts the first plenary session of the 16th BRICS Summit at Kazan, Tatarstan, October 2024. Thirteen nations were added as partner countries of BRICS: Algeria, Belarus, Bolivia, Cuba, Indonesia, Kazakhstan, Malaysia, Nigeria, Thailand, Turkey, Uganda, Uzbekistan, and Vietnam. (Courtesy Press Service of the President of the Republic of Azerbaijan under creative commons 4.0)

to Europe. The issue pertains when the 'European space' was redefined from the 2000s with the eastward expansion of NATO and the EU, and with consideration of additional expansion to include Ukraine and Georgia.

It would be wrong to see the history of Russia solely in terms of conflict, both for its external and its internal history. Yet, it is conflict, whether external aggression or internal oppression, that is the theme that resonates most strongly – and notably so at the moment. That the Russian government tells a very different story – with defence against external attack to the fore and internal oppression minimised – does not lessen the weight of the perception, which rests on both present experience and recovered history.

Scholars can explain and should contextualise. They can point to the flaws of other states. But there is an underlying reality about Russian policy at present and the official Russian account of the past, and it is not an attractive one. At the same time, within Russia, it is the stamina, persistence, and ability of Russians to put up with what would be intolerable for Westerners that is most readily apparent. These are the defining features of Russian history.